TURNING PROFESSORS
INTO TEACHERS

TURNING PROFESSORS INTO TEACHERS

A New Approach to Faculty Development and Student Learning

Joseph Katz
Mildred Henry

AMERICAN COUNCIL ON EDUCATION
MACMILLAN PUBLISHING COMPANY
New York

Collier Macmillan Publishers
London

Macmillan Publishing Company
A Division of Macmillan, Inc.
866 Third Avenue, New York, N. Y. 10022

Collier Macmillan Canada, Inc.

Library of Congress Catalog Card Number: 87-37231

Printed in the United States of America

printing number
2 3 4 5 6 7 8 9 10

Library of Congress Cataloging-in-Publication Data

Katz, Joseph, 1920–
    Turning professors into teachers: a new approach to faculty
development and student learning/Joseph Katz and Mildred Henry.
       p.   cm. — (The American Council on Education/Macmillan series
on higher education)
    Bibliography: p.
    ISBN 0-02-917221-7
    1. College teaching — United States. 2. College teachers — In
-service training — United States. 3. Learning, Psychology of.
4. College students — United States — Psychology.   I. Henry, Mildred.
II. Title.   III. Series: American Council on Education/Macmillan
series in higher education.
LB2331.K32 1988
378′.125 — dc19   87-37231
                                              CIP

Contents

Foreword

The authors of this book are no armchair strategists. They have gone into hundreds of classrooms to observe how students learn and how teachers teach. Their purpose was to find tools that would help teachers understand how their students learn and how they could further the growth of their students' intellectual powers.

Forty-five years ago, while completing a dissertation on three experimental colleges, I asked myself why I had found it difficult to appraise the role of teaching at the undergraduate level. The history of higher education in America helps tell why. Although the modern American residential college is widely said to be the hybrid product of the Oxbridge college and the German university, the latter's genes have often been more evident, at least since the United States imported the university model over one hundred years ago. The medieval tradition of the professor as guild master surrounded by his apprentices became a prestigious ideal. The application of the word *pedagogy,* with its etymological meaning of "leading the child," seemed inappropriate for anyone appointed to the realm of higher education.

But there has been another tradition that stresses teaching. One of its manifestations was the birth of the general education course, beginning as a seminar on national aims during World War I at Columbia under John Erskine's leadership. By the 1920s it had blossomed at Columbia into the required course entitled Contemporary Civilization, which endures to this day. Its influence, along with comparable courses at the University of Chicago, spread to other schools. The need for broadly educated instructors provided a curb, though not a strong curb, on growing faculty specialization. It suggested that the ability to teach undergraduates was relevant in the promotability of a rising young scholar. There are many other manifestations of a focus on nurturing student learning, among them the establishment of experimental colleges, the constantly recurring attempts in public and private institutions at curricular reform, the periodic endeavors to define freshly the principles and practices of general or liberal education.

This book is in line with the latter tradition. It throws a bright light on what we need to do and know if we want our undergraduate classrooms to be lively and effective in promoting student learning. It reveals that gems of knowledge, however burnished by the professor, are powerless to cause the growth of intellect in the student's head. Rather, it is the concepts that *the student* is moved to put together in resonance with the teacher's questions. Each student develops a pattern of meanings shaped by his or her characteristic thinking style. Having become personal, the meanings may last. To achieve effective interactions between professor and students requires a new sophistication, a subtlety of art and skill that has marked great teachers throughout history. This book offers evidence that the subtlety can be learned.

For ten years at Stony Brook, Joe Katz and I were colleagues. It is a personal pleasure to join other early readers of the book in predicting that it will have enduring influence. The book is based on what to my knowledge is the most extensive examination of the college classroom yet undertaken. It is at once practical and theoretical, a rare combination of two elements that need each other. That the authors found their experience in working with faculty so productive as to warrant the boldness of the title should stimulate readers to explore the evidence for themselves.

Louis T. Benezet

Preface

The title of this book in no way means to detract from the good work of thousands of college teachers across the land. But the book does counter the notion that teaching is a static art and the even more passive idea that good teachers are born. We think that teaching is a lifelong art, that it involves continuous learning not just for the student but for the teacher as well. We think it is an art that can be taught and that can develop through inquiry into one's own teaching. Such inquiry can deepen and enlarge the still rather rudimentary theories of student learning and student intellectual development. Through the efforts of classroom teachers and other investigators we can begin to build a cognitive science that could furnish the theoretical underpinnings of classroom practice and give the profession of teaching the intellectual base that a profession needs.

This book had its origin in two projects. The first one was funded by the Fund for the Improvement of Postsecondary Education (FIPSE Project #0029). The second one was funded by the Ford Foundation (Grant #855-0274A). Faculty in the humanities and in the social and natural sciences in fifteen institutions collaborated with us in these projects.* In working with these faculty we developed and tested the ideas and procedures that are described in the following pages. The two authors had been engaged for many years in studies of students and faculty in and out of the

---

* The institutions participating in the FIPSE Project (1978–81) were: Austin College, DePauw University, East Texas State University, Harvey Mudd College, New College of California, Ohio Wesleyan University, Siena Heights College, Simon's Rock College, Slippery Rock State University, State University of New York at Stony Brook, University of California at Berkeley, and Wichita State University. The institutions participating in the Ford Project (1985–87) were Northwestern University, the University of Chicago, the University of California at Berkeley, and Wellesley College.

classroom. But we felt that the faculty development movement that had begun in the early 1970s had not had the transforming influence upon teaching and learning that many had expected. We thought that the problem lay in the fact that the efforts at faculty development usually were too short-term and episodic. In the course of our work we developed a model that provides for long-term faculty learning — the amount of faculty time spent week by week is small but the cumulative effect of the continued effort makes the difference. Our work with faculty calls for the exploration and definition of the ways in which faculty and student think and learn. Our chief exploratory instruments are the interview, classroom observation, and the Omnibus Personality Inventory (OPI), which in Mildred Henry's interpretation has become a learning styles inventory.

In the pages that follow, the first chapter delineates the present state of our knowledge of faculty development and student learning and the need for a different approach. Chapter 2 describes the essence of our model, which consists of new and sustained procedures to discover the ways in which students learn and how teachers can base their practice on this new knowledge. Chapter 3 describes a variety of faculty and student thinking and learning styles we have discovered in our work. This chapter may be read in conjunction with chapter 6, in which the use of the OPI as a tool for learning about faculty and student thinking styles is described. Chapters 4 and 5 give examples of applications to classroom teaching and learning of the model we have presented in chapter 2. Chapter 5 reproduces reports by Professors Carton, Fry, and Miller on their work with us. Given the central role of the interview in our attempt to base teaching on enhanced knowledge of student learning and faculty ways of teaching, chapter 7 details the what, how, and why of interviewing. Chapter 8 provides two samples of interviews with faculty about their teaching. The last chapter maps out a conception of undergraduate teaching based on professors adopting an investigative approach to student learning similar to the one they adopt in pursuing their academic specialties.

Our book is addressed to faculty in all disciplines and to administrators who wish to help shape an environment in which student learning can flourish. We are very much aware of the realities of institutional life. Changes in teaching are difficult. Our book and our thinking are inspired by the belief that substantial changes are necessary if our students are to learn more and take pleasure in their learning. We realize that many teachers who really want to do better feel discouraged by institutional realities and by acceptance of and conformity with these realities on the part of some students. We believe that a judicious adoption of the methods we propose can be a transforming experience for the teacher and that these methods lead to institutional changes that can vivify the classroom.

We have recently seen a wave of national reports concerned with the undergraduate curriculum and with teaching. The reports of the National Institute of Education (1984), of the Association of American Colleges

(1985), of Frank Newman (1985), and of Ernest Boyer (1987) are particularly relevant to the topic of this book. These reports have engendered heightened awareness of the conditions of teaching and student learning. They stress the need for enhancing student motivation for learning and for engaging students in active learning. The observational and collaborative procedures we describe in this book seem to us instruments for that purpose. While this book was in progress, its coauthor chaired the Task Group on General Education of the Association of American Colleges. The report of this task group, entitled *A New Vitality in General Education* (1988), suggests that many well-conceived curricular programs have fallen short of accomplishing their objectives because too little attention was paid to the how of teaching and student learning. This book tries to put learning and teaching in the foreground where it belongs.

The book has benefited from the thoughts and ideas of many people. We want to express our appreciation to the faculty and students in the fifteen institutions who collaborated with us in our projects. We are grateful to the Fund for the Improvement of Postsecondary Education and to the Ford Foundation for giving us the means to make these projects possible. The intellectual companionship of Richard Hendrix, David Justice, and Carol Stoel of the FIPSE staff and of Alison Bernstein and Sheila Biddle, our program officers at Ford, helped us to think through our plans, ideas, and conclusions. We thank our Stony Brook colleagues Aaron Carton, Donald Fry, and Lee Miller, whose accounts of their work with us appear in chapter 5, and we thank Katherine Hope and J. L., whose interviews with us are found in chapter 8. The following have read versions of the manuscript as it was in preparation and we are grateful to them for many valuable comments: Louis Benezet, Aaron Carton, Peter Elbow, Martin Finkelstein, Mervin Freedman, Jack Rossman, Marcia Salner, and Theodore Sizer. Special thanks are due to our editors, Lloyd Chilton and James Murray, for their counsel and perspective. Louis Benezet has been a very helpful and encouraging supporter of our efforts from the beginning. Rosemarie Cusumano typed the manuscript, and her comments, counsel, and warm encouragement made the whole process of preparing this book for publication more pleasant and human.

TURNING PROFESSORS
INTO TEACHERS

1

Conditions of a New Pedagogy for Undergraduate Learning

The problem this book confronts is an old, even an ancient one. It is the eternal problem of teachers facing students who may be underprepared or undermotivated or simply not attuned or developmentally ready. Yet this book could not have been written until now. The notion that there is a pedagogy of higher education is a very recent one and even now it is an idea that would be strange to most professors. By contrast, the idea of a pedagogy for raising children is part of a longer tradition that has gathered an ever-increasing momentum since the eighteenth century. As a contributor to that tradition in the United States early in this century, John Dewey was one of the leading thinkers, working out a theory of the connection between student interest and efforts and redefining the teacher's role so that teachers would see themselves not only as transmitters of received knowledge but as professionals attuned to the learning capacities and motivations of their students. Yet, comprehensive as Dewey was in his philosophy, he did not in a systematic way apply his educational ideas to college students. This is surprising in a thinker who was as radical as he in his redefinition of the genesis and functions of knowledge.*

---

* We recently found one instance of Dewey's applying his philosophical approach to higher education. He made the following statement while chairing a curriculum conference at Rollins College in 1931 (Proceedings, curriculum conference, Vol. 1, Winter Park, Fla., Jan. 19–24, 1931): "I do not think that any thorough–going modification of the college curriculum would be possible without a modification of the methods of instruction. I doubt if the old-fashioned lecture system and recitation system do not make an almost insuperable bar to any very considerable change in the subject matter of studies." Dewey does not elaborate on this statement.

The pedagogy that is emerging and that is illustrated in the following chapters is one of tying *teaching* to *learning,* of enabling students to adopt the methods of thinking that characterize the person who generates knowledge, and of establishing the social and emotional conditions for intellectual development. The emergence of human development as a major conception and founding block for a pedagogy that can be both theoretically complex and tested and developed through practice is very recent. The idea of student development began to surface and gather momentum during the 1960s. It was prepared by Piaget's research in the 1920s (described in Gruber and Vonèche, 1977), H. A. Murray's explorations of personality in the 1930s (Murray, 1938), and the studies of Lois Murphy (Murphy and Ladd, 1944), Ruth Munroe, and others at Sarah Lawrence in the 1940s (Munroe, 1942), as well as those of Theodore Newcomb at Bennington (Newcomb, 1943). By the 1960s, there were a large variety of empirically based studies of personality development during college, each describing different aspects of student development. Among the many studies are those of Arthur Chickering (1969), Mervin Freedman (1967), Douglas Heath (1968), Joseph Katz (1968), Jane Loevinger (1976), William Perry (1970), and Nevitt Sanford (1962).

One remarkable feature of the theories of these investigators is their congruence. They all describe distinctive stages or steps in developmental progression. They differ primarily in what particular aspect of student development they focus on. Thus Perry, and similarly Piaget, feature cognitive development while Loevinger focuses on interpersonal development. But neither Perry nor Loevinger, or any of the others, make any hard and fast distinction. It is characteristic of personality theory not to segment the person into easily isolable parts — an insight that thus far has penetrated college teaching only in an elementary fashion. In the 1970s investigations of differences in male and female development gave a further impetus to developmental theory. Carol Gilligan (1982) delivered a trenchant critique and revision of Lawrence Kohlberg's scheme of moral development. Fresh theories of male – female differences in cognitive development are emerging, most notably in the work of Belenky et al (1986). They provide a fresh challenge to traditional college teaching. The new theories of student development have once again made us conscious that the mind is not an empty wax tablet. If professors want more deliberately to enable their students to think critically and investigatively, they themselves will have to learn something about the ways students can and cannot learn as a consequence of their intellectual characteristics and developmental status.

THE HISTORICAL CONTEXT

Once faculty have become aware of theories of development and the findings on which they rest, they are likely to find it impossible to teach and advise students in the traditional ways of transmitting knowledge in information-conveying ways, of zeroing in on the areas of knowledge the student is to "cover." Yet it is not likely that proponents of developmental theory would have had much impact had not historical events come to their aid. In the 1960s students protested not just the impersonality of their education, but also the contents of education; not just the relevance of their studies to their lives and to their society, but also the epistemological assumptions undergirding the pursuit of knowledge. The student movement came to a halt about the fall of 1970 but the thrust against the established curriculum and ways of teaching was continued from a new source. The sheer growth in the numbers of both colleges and students attending them and the need for attracting and holding large numbers of students brought a shift to a new orientation that viewed students as customers and consumers. During the 1960s and even more so the 1970s, universities in the industrialized countries became way stations for multitudes of students attaining conventional places in the bureaucracies and other hierarchies of society. This change has led to a new stage in the evolution of the university, namely, a break in an intellectual tradition that has been continuous since the founding of the European universities. It frequently has led to a debasement of what is expected of students and to diminished intellectual efforts by faculty and students. At the same time, these developments have frustrated many faculty and challenged them to rethink how they can reach their students. The rapid acceptance of the concept of faculty development from about 1973 onward and the many programs that exist in a majority of institutions encouraging faculty development testify to at least an implicit awareness of the historical changes.

DEVELOPING AND APPLYING
THEORIES OF STUDENT LEARNING

Faculty have found it difficult to respond to changed student attitudes and expectations. Some faculty have been looking for recipe-like formulas, the techniques that would convert their students into alert and industrious learners. That expectation seems doomed to failure. It represents the sort of thinking that Perry has found to be characteristic of the dualistic stage of cognitive development when people expect answers in ready-made, easily assimilated forms. The thrust of the approach represented in the pages of this book is to convert faculty into investigators of the learning of their students.

Any theory of student development is a mere *scaffolding* that describes in a generalized form some aspects of particular students but that leaves out much. A variety of conceptualizations are needed in order to make the picture of one's students less abstract. Moreover, beyond available theory, each teacher needs to develop specific articulations and conceptualizations of the students in his or her class; no two groups of students are ever alike. As the essence of good teaching is the greatest possible individualization of the teacher's responses to students, any reliance on general formulas is in itself antidevelopmental and antieducational.

To respond adequately to a student in front of us we must know something of the established theories. For instance, we must know something of Piaget (Gruber and Vonèche, 1977), because if students are not yet at the level of formal operational thinking any conventional attempts to present abstract theories to them may fall upon puzzled minds. We must know, with Perry (1970), whether our notion that a problem can be approached from two perspectives is disconcerting to students—because our enlightened relativism may drive them into or back to security-seeking dogmatic stances. We must know, with Loevinger (1976), what the student's emotional capacities are, because both the disposition to learn and what one learns depend heavily on one's emotional grasp; objectivity and inventiveness can be hampered by emotional rigidities or by naiveté.

But the theories thus far cited still leave out a lot when we face the students in our classes, among them students who have difficulty speaking up in class, or who want to remain passive learners, or who think that fellow students have nothing to contribute to their learning, or who have a fear of expressing themselves explicitly, or who are bored, or rebellious, or dogmatic, or who cannot brook disagreement or correction.

Moreover, there can be no adequate investigation of the classroom unless teachers spend considerable time learning about their own styles of thinking, their ways of interacting with their classes, the intricacies of the group process, the institutional surroundings, the physical nature of the classroom. These all profoundly affect what learning will or will not take place. The great fact of any classroom is the diversity of thinking, feeling, and acting exhibited by students and teachers. As every teacher has a distinctive style, the task of communicating with students whose styles are different from the teacher's is at once a problem and a source of knowledge. Teachers' awareness of the distinctiveness of their own thinking styles can lead them to become more intelligible to others. For instance more "intuitive" teachers can learn to understand their more "analytic" students' needs for structure and definitional clarity, or, conversely, more analytic teachers can learn to understand the holistic exploratory ways of their more intuitive or inductive students.

Professors need not only to know available pedagogical theories; they need also to make their own fresh educational articulations. Such articulations serve a double purpose: (1) they allow one to respond to the individualities of the ever-new students in one's classes, and (2) they make a contribution to developing more sophisticated theory about student and faculty learning. Teachers become practitioners and investigators at the same time. But how are faculty to develop the necessary skills for the changed role we envisage for them? Even though the 1970s have seen an increase of interest in faculty development and in teaching, an attitude seems to persist that to learn to teach better takes relatively little time. The notion that preparation for scholarship and science is a long process while teaching capacity is more easily acquired, if not inborn, still seems to hold in some form. Training for teaching, in graduate school and beyond, is frequently confined to events of relatively short duration. A semester's course or half-course for graduate students or brief workshops of one or several days in duration are common instruments. This hastiness is peculiar when one considers not only the enormous complexities inherent in an analysis of student behavior and of classroom process, but also the time needed for practice, experimentation, and reflection in order to build new teaching skills and philosophies. As a result, faculty development programs usually have produced few profound modifications of teaching and learning styles. (Experimental programs usually show some gain, among other reasons, because of the Hawthorne effect, according to which special attention improves performance.) It has been our experience that more substantial changes are needed that would extend over a substantial period of time — time taken to experiment and integrate, a slow ripening process that leads to the modification of ingrained habits and the establishment of new ones. After faculty members have worked at this process for a year — or better two years — something like a transformation of their teaching styles can occur and can be observed.

In the last two to three decades, methods of training for teaching, particularly on the precollege level, have often centered on the presentation of "model" ways of teaching and of objectives that the trainee is to aspire towards. For instance, teachers are shown a videotape of their own teaching and then are exposed to the tape of a "model" teacher. After an interval the trainees are videotaped again to determine to what extent their teaching now approximates the model. We consider this approach too mechanical. The force of teaching resides in its individualizing effect on the student and begins with the development of the teacher's individuality. The difference between a Picasso and a Braque is instantly recognizable and the artist's and the viewer's experience becomes more powerful because of the difference. Teachers start out with capacities and potentials that are their own, uniquely so. Mimicking somebody else is not the same as bringing one's dormant or half-finished skills of expression and communication to a level at which these skills are communicable to others. The discovery of one's teaching individuality deepens one's knowledge of oneself as a professional and as a person and can generate a fresh and enduring enthusiasm for teaching. Such discovery allows teachers to help their students to make their own discoveries.

The question of the *institutionalization* of the procedures of a new pedagogy is important. Our experience has shown that the combination of strong administrative support and the participation of imaginative, respected, and institutionally secure faculty leaders is optimal. It may be best to begin working with volunteers and at the same time try to allay the anxieties of nonparticipating colleagues. As the benefits of the procedures are perceived, more faculty are likely to want to join. Sometimes a study of the college's pedagogical situation can have a challenging effect. In one institution that we worked with, a study of student and faculty attitudes to teaching and learning uncovered wide discrepancies between faculty and student perceptions of each other, wherein a faculty image of student resistance to learning was countered by the students' desire to be educated on the condition that their needs and dispositions were more adequately taken into account. The study proved "shocking" to the college community and was an incentive for attention to pedagogy.

To go beyond tinkering and marginal attention to teaching requires an enlarged definition of the faculty member's professional role. The enlargement can best be described as being analogous to the clinical function of the medical scientist. "Clinical" means not just applying theory in practice, but the development of theory through practice. The clinical function of the physician may often consist in application rather than in the creation of fresh knowledge, but it is not so ideally. College teachers too can at once apply received theory to the evanescent moments of a particular group of students in a particular semester and contribute to the evolving theory of teaching and learning. The possibilities of this approach are exhilarating.

BASIC LEARNING PRINCIPLES

In the next chapter we will describe our methods in detail. Here we will spell out briefly some of the principles we have derived from our work with students and teachers in and around the classroom. Perhaps the most important principle is (1) *the transformation of student passivity into active learning.* This means helping students become investigators and coinquirers, approximating for themselves some of the ways in which the knowledge was originally developed. Moreover, what students learn must relate to a curiosity they already have and must build on present capacities to reach for the next step. Related to the transformation of passivity to activity is the principle of (2) *individualization.* There is uniqueness in each student's approach to the world, and this uniqueness must be tapped and fostered rather than homogenized. Teachers must have a sense of the turn of mind of the student so that what they say to the student will be in response to implicit and explicit articulations. To do this one needs to know something of the context and reference points of a student's thinking, and one needs to engage students in a series of stepwise inquiries that will draw out the potential of their understanding of the subject matter at hand. Such individuation is not easy in the large classes in which much contemporary teaching takes place. The metasessions, described in the next chapter, in which teacher and student together analyze the course, are one means whereby professors may have students articulate their varied ways of learning.

The final products of thinking are very different from the processes by which ideas and theories are arrived at. These processes are messy, intuitive, tentative, experimental, emotional. (When one looks at the published scientific conclusions, one rarely knows the person and the processes that led up to them.) Students seldom have the chance to experience the process of discovery in their college courses. This is a cardinal omission. In spite of some occasional attempts and lip service, much still needs to be done to insure that an essential ingredient in mastering the contents of a course is (3) *the process of inquiry*. This is difficult but doable even in the natural sciences, in spite of their enormously large quantity of tested ideas and the sequential, tightly logical structure of their "canonical" bodies of knowledge. To have students engage in inquiry does not blur the distinction between the ideas and techniques of a productive investigator and the steps an undergraduate must take to grasp the spirit and method of a science.

Part of learning about how to inquire is to develop (4) *the ability to inquire with other people*. Yet students often derogate other students' contributions—an implied derogation of their own thinking. Collaborative learning, using other students as a source of one's own learning, is often neglected in the classroom. Not only do students not use each other enough, teachers do not sufficiently enlist them in planning their learning and in thinking about it. Continuing reflection with students about the contents and processes of the course can be very productive. Readings need not be entirely fixed beforehand; the pace of reading can be variably adjusted; the ways in which students develop their grasp of the materials and how they are tested can be modified. This could go hand in hand with a raising of standards, but these would be appropriate standards, standards that make sense to the students. A further learning principle is (5) *participation*. When students coined the concept of participatory democracy they had their classrooms also in mind. Unfortunately this very dynamic concept has fallen into decline because it was both misunderstood and misused. Unless students are involved in reflecting why and how they are learning, they will be in danger of falling prey to cycles of memorizing and forgetting. Linked to participation is the need for (6) *support*. One of the reasons why the authors of this book have been able to influence professors to change their teaching styles has been the support available from fellow faculty members. Creating conditions that allow students to support each other, teachers to support students, and students to support teachers provides the context for the healing and stimulating power of community.

Finally, there must be (7) *the recognition that learning is an intensely emotional experience*. It requires the giving up of old and often dear assumptions. "You have learned something, you have lost something."

For the student it involves testing oneself and hence puts self-esteem in some jeopardy. This hazardous process calls for empathy and help by a knowledgeable adult. We have interviewed countless students who have told us that even in large lecture courses the empathic attitude of the professor to them could make the difference of how much they wanted to learn. It is sad to realize how the fortuitous encounter in an introductory course with a noncaring or a hostile-aggressive teacher can turn students away from a subject matter — even the choice of a major — that they might otherwise have wanted to pursue.

Considering these seven principles is a challenge to the exclusive role that contents occupy in teaching, the ever-present eagerness to "cover" materials. We stress the importance of skills. Periodically scholars and the public at large bemoan the decline of knowledge of content among students. They often omit to consider that unless we pay attention to the skills of acquiring knowledge, and to student motivation, their exhortations are at the least incomplete. Skills are important in their own right as they determine the quality of our thinking and acting *and* they are the instruments by which we acquire facts and contents. The success of a course should, therefore, be measured not only by contents attained but by skills developed.

In preparing any course teachers might ask what skills in addition to facts they wish their students to develop. Any one course might put special weight on only one or two skills. Such skills can be skills of analytical reasoning, of synthetic reasoning, of research design, of setting up apparatuses, of being able to present a narrative, of writing an intelligent summary, of learning how to put together a theory; or they can be skills of expression, skills of listening. Students at the termination of the course would know how to *do* something they did not know how to do before. Such capacity transcends the more or less incidental *accretion of facts* that often is the predominant outcome of college courses. It replaces the filling of minds with an active capacity for doing: doing thinking, increasing perception, enlarging feeling. A course becomes a cooperative enterprise of teacher and students, with both parties asking themselves deliberately what they might get out of it. At present the tendency of the student is to ask, "What will he or she hand on?" as if the teacher were in possession of a literal key to reality. Yet, except for ceremonial purposes, knowledge is not a piece of goods to be handed on. Learning is both self-transformation and the transformation of the data of immediate perception; it is only in part the transmission of the world almanac into the brain cells.

This chapter has concentrated on the cognitive aspects of learning and on the classroom, and so will the rest of the book. But we must always remain aware of the other ways in which students learn and which influence their learning in the classroom. Learning in the dormitory, learning through individual readings and through discussion with others, experiences in the outside world and on the job, activities in the arts or on the athletic field — all these shape the intellectual being of students in major ways. Our institutions continue to have an unholistic conception of learning by which other arenas for learning are considered auxiliary, reflected in often very limited budgets for out-of-classroom learning. Yet many students will readily tell us that what goes on outside the classroom is central to student learning. Future managers or politicians will describe how experiences in student businesses or in student politics are shaping their skills. Persons who plan to enter professions that involve caring for and rendering service to other people will report that dormitory and campus life provide for rich interactions with people different from themselves, give opportunity for understanding them, for mobilizing empathy — all essential experiences for their future vocations. Campus life outside the classroom provides, as studies have confirmed (Feldman and Newcomb, 1969), essential opportunities for developing students as intellectuals, artists, friends, lovers, future parents, members of civilized society. Classroom learning becomes richer when it uses and connects with what students learn on the outside.

2

An Inquiry-Oriented Approach to Faculty Development and Student Learning

In the years since the term "faculty development" has become current many efforts have been made to put it into practice. At one point or another more than a majority of universities and colleges have initiated faculty development programs, and special attention has been given to the improvement of teaching. Many approaches are available. First, there are the books describing possible curricular rearrangements, pedagogical processes, and student characteristics. As is true with students, books have only limited value as learning instruments, and they have therefore often been supplemented by workshops and seminars. These are rarely more than a few days in duration, and didactic presentation may be supplemented by films, tapes, role-playing, and the like. But even workshops have the disadvantage of being removed from the real thing. They do not take place in and around the actual classroom. From the beginning, therefore, our thinking was oriented toward finding ways in which on-the-job education of faculty members could occur. Such an approach has to be not only efficient but cost-effective. We developed and tested a new approach through prolonged work with faculty in fifteen institutions, and we took the pedagogical work right into the classroom itself.

FRAMEWORK AND TOOLS OF OUR APPROACH

Our work typically starts with bringing together a professor, teaching any course in the catalog, and a faculty colleague. The colleague visits the professor's class once a week (or more often if desirable and if time permits), meets with the professor once a week, and interviews three students individually. The interviews are designed to obtain as detailed a picture as possible of what and how students learn. These interviews provide the professor and his colleague with many data on the basis of which to chart what is happening in the classroom and what learning the students are doing.

The scheme asks the colleague to spend five hours a week and the professor four hours a week. This is not a large amount of time if one takes into consideration the educational benefits that can be derived from the work. Still, five or four hours, given faculty loads, often are too much time per week. Hence faculty we have worked with have introduced modifications of the scheme. Meeting with the professor and class observation may take place only every other week; students may be interviewed sometimes in a group of three and sometimes individually, and they may be interviewed less often than once a week. Thus at the minimum the time investment would be something like only one and a half hours per week: meeting with the colleague and observing the class every other week and meeting a group of three students every alternate week. Of course, there is less benefit if less time is spent.

Students can be selected at random, though some care might be taken to ensure variety of representation. For instance, in large lecture courses it may be desirable to take students from the front, middle, and back rows because these often yield people whose motivation and interests differ. We have often used the following selection procedure: At the beginning of the semester the professor and the class are given the Omnibus Personality Inventory (OPI), or if the class is very large, only a representative sample is given the OPI. More details about the OPI as a *learning styles inventory* will be given in chapter 6. For the moment we will concentrate on the initial uses of the OPI. The first four scales of the OPI serve as a selecting instrument. These four scales indicate degree of (1) reflectiveness, (2) analytic or scientific orientation, (3) sensitivity to literature and art, and (4) complexity of thinking. For instance, if the professor shows a profile that indicates an orientation toward reflectiveness and esthetic sensitivity, and the students in the class predominantly have a profile that indicates a high degree of logicalness but less regard for "intuition" and the esthetic domains, the difficult task must be faced of translation from the professor's perspective to that of the students. It is possible to take OPI scales beyond the first four into consideration: for instance, the three scales that measure degree of emotional openness versus emotional closedness. After we have obtained the student responses to the OPI and scored them, we sort their profiles into three piles: those most like the professor, those least like the professor, and those in the middle. We then select two students from each pile and assign one set of three students representing the three categories to the professor and the other set to his or her colleagues, but without their knowing which student falls into what category. The use of the OPI as a selection device is optional, and faculty may wish to use other selection procedures or other learning styles inventories (Claxton and Murrell, 1987).

When visiting the professor's class the colleague takes careful notes about the process of the class. The observing colleague should arrive in the room before the professor because class behavior before the session begins often provides important clues: degree of excitement or apathy, what the students talk about, whether there are references, and what kind of references, to the contents of the course or to the teacher. Observers should seat themselves where they have the best view of the class and from where they have a frontal view of the students. They should make careful observation of seating arrangements, attendance, manner of student arrival and departure, who comes late and why. Once the class is in progress, the observer should note the content the teacher presents and its organization, the how of presentation, the teacher's interactions and rapport with the students, and the pace, mood, posture, and other nonverbal behavior. The observer should watch student behavior in relation to what the professor does at any moment. Even in a straight lecture one can observe when students take notes and when they do not, when they are restless, when they look at the professor and when they do not, their various postures, moods, degrees of energy, relations with each other. Observers should pay attention to distancing, deviant, or rebellious student behavior, such as letter-writing, newspaper-reading, yawning. They should note what students say, how they say it, and who says it—for example, are the same students repeatedly speaking up? They should pay regard to the differences among students in the same class. These observations furnish data for analysis at the meetings with the professor, and they are considerably enriched by further information obtained from interviews with students.

The prime objective of these interviews is to gain as detailed a picture as is possible of student learning in the course under investigation. This includes exploration of student learning styles, the student's cognitive stage of development, and the student's interests, aspirations, personality, and social circumstances because all of these can cooperate with or defeat learning in the course. One might begin the first interviews with some general questions about the students' background: why they chose this particular college and how it is living up to their expectations, what high school they came from, what home background, what is their present residence and how is life there. Then questions may proceed to the students' actual or prospective major and why they chose it, what other courses they are taking and what these courses are like. In subsequent interviews all these areas should be explored again to gain a larger and richer picture of what may be described only superficially the first time. The questions, even during the first interview might eventually turn to the specific course under study. One can begin by asking the students why they have chosen this particular course and what their first impression is of the course (materials, modes of learning or of evaluation, and so on) and of the teacher. One then can inquire about the students' specific reactions to the class session preceding the interview, preferably a class the observer has watched. Specific parts of that class may come under special scrutiny and students may be asked to talk in detail about what went through their mind, what they thought and felt as a particularly salient event took place—the event being a teacher's presentation, other students' contributions, an interchange, a perception of their own. In chapter 7 we give a description of the rationale of the interview, how one may conduct it, and its use as a tool for developing knowledge of how students learn.

There are other data that can be used to enlarge the picture of the students' learning. For instance, inspection of the students' class notes can be very revealing about their cognitive processes. One instructor we worked with made it a practice to bring carbon paper to each of his classes, where he asked one or several students at random to put it under their note sheets so he would have a replica of what they were writing that day. Obviously students may write their notes differently when they know the teacher will read them, but people cannot write better notes than they are capable of. Such notes can be useful for letting professors see how their students understand them and the course. For instance, a professor we worked with found that his students stressed in their notes the factual aspects of the course while his aim was to enable them to make interpretations. It may be an interesting exercise to have students read and comment on each other's class notes.

The students' tests and papers furnish important data. They are particularly useful in the case of the student interviewees because one knows through the weekly or biweekly interviews and the OPI profiles so much more about their intellectual, emotional, and interpersonal functioning. The professor and his or her colleague also may devise occasional questionnaires, preferably open-ended questions, in order to have all students in the class reflect on the *what* and *how* of their learning. Teachers can learn something if they ask their students a few times during the semester to write for ten to fifteen minutes on what and how they are learning in the course. Some instructors we have worked with have set aside partial or sometimes entire class sessions to have the students reflect on the nature of the learning taking place in the course. We call these "metasessions." They turn out to be effective devices to improve both student learning and student motivation. A variant of our own metasession is the procedure developed by John Noonan at Virginia Commonwealth University, which consists in having a colleague possessing the requisite skills conduct a group interview of an entire class in the presence of their teacher. This interview can be focused on any matter of special concern to the teacher. For other efforts to enable teachers to investigate their effectiveness with students we refer to Peter Elbow's (1986) reflective reports of his interviews and observations of faculty, K. Patricia Cross's (1986) call for classroom research, and Elizabeth Rorschach and Robert Whitney's (1986) comments on use of peer observation.

EFFECTS IN THE CLASSROOM

Thus far our description has been static, focusing on the information-gathering aspects of our approach. But what happens almost immediately is a modification of the professor's behavior in the classroom, accompanied by changes in student behavior. Quite early, for instance, a possible lack of clarity in the professor's presentation is pointed out through the information that is gathered. Or a professor may have made theoretical assumptions that the students were not able to follow. Or some of the vocabulary may have been out of the reach of students. A gain in the professor's clarity immediately results in renewed and invigorated student attention.

Another instance from our work is the discovery of the importance of pacing. We found that in seventy-five-minute classes the attention sagged particularly around the fortieth minute or so. At that time it is possible to lose most students for the rest of the period. A change of focus or different manner of instruction, for example, going from lecture to discussion, can recapture or hold attention. Another instance of flawed pacing is such speed of presentation that students are not given the time or even the pauses they need in order to assimilate what they hear. Thus in one class a student remarked that it was good when the professor went to the blackboard to write something on it because that interval allowed him to review and integrate what had been said. This information was related to the professor, who could and did more deliberately build such creative pauses into his presentation.

In the longer run much more happens. Professors become aware of the variety of their students, the great differences in cognitive and emotional ways of responding to course and teacher. As they deal with a student in and out of class they relate what the student says to the intellectual and emotional contexts out of which the student speaks. This is much easier to accomplish in smaller classes. But it can be done in larger classes too, ascertaining the variety of student intellectual styles through class notes, observation of selected "samples" of students, learning style inventories. The professor gains surer knowledge of what is and is not effective in eliciting students' attention and helping their learning. Most professors soon experiment on their own with varying approaches and methods by which to help student learning. Often for the first time in their professional lives, they perceive that gaining student attention is not a function of luck or only of hard intellectual preparatory work or some special histrionic facility, but that it also stems from a growing knowledge of students through direct observation coupled with theoretical generalizations, from experimentation with differing styles of presentation and discussion, and articulation of variations in learning outcomes obtained by close attention to the students' modes of response. The cycle goes from observing the student to teaching and then back to the student for verification.

The procedures we are describing affect many teaching objectives. Professors may be led thereby to investigate, in the necessary detail, how the texts and readings they assign to their students are understood and whether other texts might not be more effective. They may initiate changes in the ways they examine students; as they begin to ask questions addressed to the learning styles and developmental stages of their students, they may, for instance, when framing examination questions give the students options so that students at different developmental levels can respond in terms of their current level of capacity. Profound shifts in the contents of courses, particularly of introductory courses, are both possible and needed. The introductory course often tends to be a miniversion of a field or subfield; it ought to be reexamined by considering its place in the intellectual development of the student for whom this course may be the only exposure to the field. For faculty members, looking at their field from the perspective of the novice can have the benefit of raising wholesome questions about the methodologies and goals of their specialty.

Interviewing one's students and meeting regularly with a colleague considerably enlarge the array of data that are available to the teacher. Professors can engage in genuine experimentation based on some working conceptualizations and can then notice effects and miseffects. They gain a more precise sense of what happens and, more importantly, how they might influence what happens. A valuable source of information comes from the fact that the students in the class pull together with their professor, reflect on their learning, and make suggestions for its enhancement. Another benefit is the relationship that develops between the teachers and their colleagues. People who may have hardly known each other before become intellectual friends and sometimes personal friends as well. The teachers may have initial anxiety about their colleagues' observing them and interviewing their students. But the anxiety diminishes and may vanish in the common task of inquiry into how students learn. Joint discovery addressed to the complexities of learning and teaching is rare in academic settings, and our model creates circumstances that make such joint learning nearly inevitable.

The procedures we have described can bring results even if used for only one semester. But it is desirable for the two colleagues to work together for at least two semesters because the effect is cumulative, and frequently it snowballs. In our experience a third semester of work has proved especially beneficial because, with the interval of a summer, thoughts and attitudes consolidate. In our experience, when we walked into the class of a colleague with whom we had worked for two previous semesters, we were struck by the feeling of good will and enthusiasm that the new group of students exuded, a consequence of the different approach that the professor had developed during the past year's work. The cycle of learning for the observed teacher is not really completed until the teacher assumes the role of the observer. Often, it is only in observing other people's classes and students that we can gain a more objective and thorough perspective on our own teaching. Having the observed faculty become observers themselves has a further benefit. It creates a chain, a fanning out by which an increasing number of faculty can be involved. Over time, an almost geometrical progression of influence can be established. A particular aspect of our method is its heuristic and clinical nature. Teachers can function analogously to other professionals whose reflections on their practice become a source both of new theoretical knowledge and of advance in their methods.

Perhaps the most important result induced by our approach is an impetus to help students to move from being *passive* to being *active*. Many students, including those who encounter an academic subject for the first time, tend to want authoritative statements, clear and sequential presentations, and little or no reference to the variety of perspectives, hypotheticalness, and interpretive multiplicity embedded in "content." Lecturers who eliminate the edges of uncertainty and tentativeness in their subject matter are welcomed by such students, who often consider discussions by fellow students a waste of time, viewing them as presentations of unauthoritative, if not false, ideas. Yet faculty can break this cycle of passivity and unexamined acceptance of content. For instance, one instructor (see the discussion of Professor Miller's course in chapter 5) began his course with the practice, continued throughout the semester, of dictating his responses to the written work of his students on a tape. (Each student provided a tape for repeated dictations.) This practice not only allowed for a more personal and relaxed communication—students commented favorably on the tape, which always started out "Dear Jim" or "Dear Jane" —but also eschewed the usually greater finality of written comments. Somewhat later in the semester the professor, who always was responsive to questions from individual students but felt that they did not sufficiently engage the other students, interrupted his lecture at certain times and asked students to turn to their neighbors to discuss among themselves the points that he had just raised. After about five to ten minutes, he again took leadership of the class. Because there was a colleague observing the class and interviewing students, it became clear that this mode, though successful with some students, did not work with many. One of the prime obstacles was the hesitation of students to talk easily with "strangers," as they called their neighbors. (This may be taken as a revealing comment on the classroom, where people sit next to each other as in a movie theater with often little sense of relatedness.) Fear of revealing oneself, often a fear of being considered stupid, inhibited the flow of talk. As a result the instructor decided to break the class into groups of about fifteen students each. When that happened talk flowed much more freely, and it could be observed that while some students almost immediately broke into a vigorous presentation of their views, others initially held back, but participated later as they gained confidence.

A remarkable by-product of this experiment with a class of largely sophomores was that students found they learned much from their fellow students. Their peers possessed data relevant to the course. Sometimes it assured them that their thinking was not so bad when compared with that of the others. The class did not, therefore, settle for a lower common denominator of interpretation. As the questions raised by the instructor for discussion were stimulating, the students discovered the vitalities of their own minds and the benefits of joint thinking. A proof of the effectiveness of this method came toward the end of the semester on a day when the instructor had given the class a question to be answered immediately on a ten-minute quiz. In the traditional manner he collected the responses and was about to stuff them into his briefcase when the students protested and said they wanted to hear what the others had said. The question had dealt with definitions of friendship, ideal and actual, and a very vigorous discussion ensued when they heard each other's views, some of them surprising and suggestive.

Another important outcome is that instructors learn in much greater detail than before to assess the *level of comprehension* of their students. The abstractive capacities of students differ considerably. Sometimes the best-laid theoretical schemes of a professor are simply misplaced. There is the ludicrous case of a philosophy professor with a German accent who found his students elaborating in the final exam on the nature of "obstruction" when he had lectured all through the semester on "abstraction." A professor we worked with organized his history course around the concept that history like other social sciences is dedicated to the method of the verification and falsification of hypotheses even though historical data are being collected and scrutinized in a different way than, say, sociological ones. While to a mature listener, he was quite clear in presenting this point of view, it simply bypassed the understanding of a large number of his students, who perceived his presentation of modern European history as being in the storytelling mode rather than in the hypothesis-confirming mode.

The problem is that some theoretical questions are not immediately of interest to some or many students. Sometimes that interest can be aroused, but one must first know what the interest is. A professor we worked with (see the presentation by Professor Aaron Carton in chapter 5) started out one of his classes by putting the words "mind," "body," and "language" on the blackboard and said he was going to talk about their interrelatedness. He assumed that the students would be fascinated to hear about these. This professor had become sensitized to his students' responsiveness and he felt that there was not much enthusiasm for the topic. He asked the students directly whether they were interested in this question and they said, "No." (The instructor asked them what they *were* interested in, and some said it was important for them to pass their courses.) Because the problem had been aired, the instructor could think of other procedures to make this topic vivid. Sometimes, of course, one may have to give up one line of inquiry in favor of another simply because there is no student readiness for it yet. Every inquiry reflects the scholar's and scientist's predilection; without personal interest they would not devote themselves to it. Similarly one must involve the interest of the students because one can then be confident that their inquisitiveness will widen their horizons and allow for a meaningful integration of facts, theories, and intuitions, even though they will ask questions different from the teacher's.

One way to stimulate student inquisitiveness is to present ideas in ways that indicate their genesis. This means for the professor not to rush into giving conclusions, but instead to ask the students to puzzle sometimes at length about what other possible answers there might be. One professor, for instance, suggested that his students guess, as they were reading the textbook, what the next paragraph or next page on their book might say and why. Understanding cannot be complete without a concrete "feel" for the methods by which ideas are arrived at and by which they are validated.

Stimulating the investigative capacities of students seems a universally desirable goal. But there is a problem. Holland (1973) has distinguished six types of students among whom the investigative student is only one. Besides the investigative he identifies the realistic, artistic, social, enterprising, and conventional student. All these are qualities of intelligence —one cannot limit intelligence to the verbal–mathematical domain. There are people whose intelligence is strongly expressed in doing (politicians and managers are examples) or in making, sensing, and feeling (artists are representatives). The classroom often is not the best arena in which such intelligence can show itself. Yet with more ingenuity we might find ways of discovering, describing, and eventually fostering these kinds of intelligence.

DIFFERENCES IN STUDENT LEARNING

A great many difficulties in teaching are due to the variety of students in our classes. Through working with the OPI, we have found that very often, if the cognitive–affective styles of the students match up fairly well with the style of the professor, there may be smooth sailing. But often in the same class there are students who are more analytic, or more intuitive, or more feeling-oriented, or more conceptual, or more empirical, or more speculative, or more narrative, or more interpretive than their professors. These modes or styles are deeply entrenched, some fixed for a lifetime. The challenge for teachers is to grasp as much as they can of the nature of styles different from their own. Usually professors conceive of teaching as getting across what they have in mind—and that not only includes content but also, though they may not quite realize it, their style. When they find inadequate responses they are likely to put it off to either inferior capacities of their students or to lack of motivation. But they might more deliberately address themselves to the differences in style. Thus professors with an intuitive-esthetic pattern on the first four scales of the OPI might spend time to reflect on the written and oral presentations of their analytic–deductive students. By attending to how these students organize the subject matter of the course, teachers can gain an appreciation of the contributions and the limits of their own approach.

Once teachers understand these differences they can provide students with some of the supports that they need to deal with the materials of the course. For certain students it might mean the provision of more outlines and more sequential structure in light of their need for clear definition and for well-defined sequences of investigation and proof. Obviously it does not mean catering to the students' initial dispositions. The students' intellectual range can be enlarged, if the professor's is enlarged too; and in our work we have seen shifts of OPI profiles in students and teachers. One of the interesting tasks in teaching is to strengthen dispositions of students in areas in which they are weak; but one cannot do so if one runs so counter to the students' initial style that their intellectual competency and self-confidence are undercut.

Earlier in this chapter we referred to the importance of pacing. A proper pace, adjusted to the students' comprehension, needs to be maintained in regard to both the individual classroom hour and the presentation of subject matter through the entire course. Some courses are overloaded. Others are overstuffed with tedious filling. "Covering" subject matter is the besetting sin of teaching. It reflects subject matter as it is in the professor's mind, acquired over many years, and often bears insufficient relationship to what aspects of the subject matter will become a vital ingredient in the students' minds. We rarely have investigated what a student retains of a course one month—not to speak of a year—after its completion. There are many indications that much of it is remembered only for examination purposes. Last-minute cramming seems to follow the principle of "easy come, easy go." Proper pacing is not only the professor's task; it needs the student's cooperation, and such cooperation is heavily dependent on the student's motivation, which is intimately related to learning styles.

Perry (1970) has given us a marvelously differentiated picture of progressive stages, or positions, as he calls them, of students' cognitive development from an original dualistic or authoritarian mode to one of flexible hypothesis-seeking and hypothesis verification. But before one can even think in Perry's terms one must take into account Piaget's distinction between concrete and formal operational thinking (Gruber and Vonèche, 1977). We have come again and again across the fact that the thinking of many students still is at some distance from formal operations, that is, it is difficult for them to adopt an interpretive scheme, particularly if interpretation involves the comparison of several points of view or different kinds of scientific theories or scientific approaches. The classroom teacher here faces a difficult problem because he or she is essentially up against the problem of maturation. Such maturation depends on many factors: experience outside of the classroom, development of relationships, confrontations with situations different, and perhaps even shockingly different, from one's own upbringing, the experience of being given responsibility, the opportunity for doing something useful or of rendering a service, and so forth. It is on the basis of such experiences that the cognitive domain can thrive and grow.

Realizing more or less implicitly that they are up against this fact of *gradual* growth, some investigators have tried desperately once more to go the intellectualist route by way of various kinds of cognitive exercises that would quickly push development forward. At times, in a typical American spirit of athletic competition, people have seen Perry's progressive nine positions of student development as so many hurdles; if they could be run through in the freshman year alone, so much greater the prize. Some reports end mournfully with the statement that either more research or more experiment is needed to accelerate people along the Perrian obstacle course. Nevertheless, things *can* be done in the classroom. If teachers set up an atmosphere of collaboration among students, if they establish caring relationships with their students, if they themselves exhibit a spirit of inquiry and respect for others and move their students to do likewise, the classroom can stimulate progress towards intellectual maturation.

Stages can not be hurried; we must work with what we have and utilize the capacities that the student shows at his or her particular stage. There is, for instance, the case of Joan, a first-year student at a liberal arts college. The students in her history course were asked to write an interpretive critique of Upton Sinclair's *The Jungle.* Joan, in contrast to some other students, only could give a narrative description of the abuse and corruption in the slaughterhouse world of Chicago evoked by Sinclair. Her teacher marked her down because he thought she had not responded to the question. Yet after talking with a colleague the teacher concluded that some considerable work had been done by Joan. She came from a very protective family in which there was a glossing over of the evil and corruption in the world. She was taught to behave nicely and it was not nice to consider that there were nasty things in this world. Given this background,

Joan had done considerable work by giving a rather detailed and almost colorful description of the slaughterhouse conditions. If one wanted to move her forward one might ask her to describe other such situations in order to strengthen her sense of the multiplicity of the world and ways of viewing it. One also might ask her to read or to imagine an account rather opposite to that of Sinclair's of the same situation. One would not expect too much integration yet, only a capacity to envisage different situations and different approaches and rely on the tension created thereby to move her eventually toward some kind of sorting out, some kinds of analytical comparisons, then some kind of synthesis. In the meantime the important thing is to give encouragement for her capacities and support her venturing out further from home.

Things get easier and harder when students proceed from more literal and authority-bound thinking, Perry's first three positions which he labels dualistic, to Perry's next set: the stages of multiplicity and pluralism. They are easier because students now recognize different points of view and their legitimacies. But things are also harder because students now tend toward a certain intellectual sloppiness. *Dualistic students* believe in the existence of absolute truth and its possession by the authorities and they will work hard to please their teachers, the authorities in the classroom. *Multiplist students,* who believe that everything is a matter of opinion and one opinion is as good as the other, challenge not only any point of view but also any method; they see their own more disorganized or more fanciful thinking as on a par with more organized critical and sophisticated methods. A good cure for this tendency is to have the students be in or imagine situations where their thinking counts for something, including making a difference to their sense of themselves or their well-being. It is hard, however, to introduce a sense of reality in the classroom; symbolic manipulations give it an air of make-believe and often the only hard reality is the final grade.

At one point in their college careers students may begin to realize, usually implicitly, that theories are conceptualizations arising from an individual's perspective, interests, and needs. This may seem narcissistic but it is not. Students now have taken a step out of an approach in which ideas are what somebody else says about the world; they now see that ideas are functions of human effort and are thus instruments, not semi-alien entities. As they proceed along this path they become able to view learning not as information transfer but as the acquisition of *ways or methods* of thinking and investigating — many faculty could do more to foster this view. There is still a further step to be taken, and that is to see theoretical paradigms as attempts to approach an understanding of things as they are in themselves. This is the acme of objectivity and difficult for traditional-age college students.

Though Perry's and others' schemes of development are presented in a linear fashion they are not intended to be strictly linear. People can exhibit different stages of development at the same time, depending on the situation or the problem at hand. As we said in chapter 1, any one scheme of student development is only a scaffold, not the building itself. We need many more categories other than those that are part of our present pedagogic equipment. The categories of the OPI cut across those of Perry and enrich our understanding of the different students before us. While Perry concentrates on development, the OPI measures "learning style" and "personality type"; the latter two undergo development, too, but they may denote the more enduring qualities of the person. *Our model encourages each investigator to be his or her own Perry or Piaget.* Teachers need to develop fresh categories if they are to be adequately responsive to the particular students in the particular class in front of them. In teaching, as in medicine, pure deductions from preestablished categories will create havoc.

Students may not themselves be as far away from concern with *how* they learn as many teachers think. In work with a colleague teaching a course primarily for sophomores, we asked the students for written statements of *what* they had learned (see discussion of Professor Miller's course in chapter 5). To our surprise much of what they said dealt with *method.* Among other things, they listed comparing ideas with each other, pluralism of perspectives — which included the self's becoming an object of study to itself — communication with peers, application to everyday situations, emotional openness. We suggested in chapter 1 that in addition to content, college courses might more deliberately focus on the acquisition of one or two specified skills. Students then can look at a course as an opportunity for learning a new skill or improving one they already possess. The outcome is similar to knowing how to dance or how to ski at the end of a series of lessons.

EMOTIONAL DEVELOPMENT

William Perry in his seminal book delineates the simultaneous development of the intellectual and ethical aspects of the person. He is very much aware of the mutual dependence and interrelatedness of emotional and intellectual development. (His term "ethical" in our view comprehends emotional development as well. We think he thus distinguishes three components of development. In addition, ethical development includes evaluation and decision making.) Any perceptive teacher is aware of the influence of the emotions on students' intellectual productivity. Teachers have encountered dogmatic students who have a need to be right, who cannot brook contradiction from either fellow students or the teacher because their self-esteem is dependent on not making a mistake, on always knowing everything. They have encountered other students who are inhibited, not just about talking up in class but about letting their minds flow more freely. These students are afraid of expression, ultimately of the forbidden things they might say. Perceptive teachers, more or less consciously, know these things; they do not try to grate the sensibilities of the aggressive, dogmatic, pugnacious, inhibited, constricted, fearful, or timid student. Instead, they try to encourage some students and set limits for others. But even perceptive teachers could acquire greater sophistication in responding to their students' emotional dispositions, which can be a spur or an obstacle to learning.

Emotional development is a major factor in determining the vitality, scope, and precision of cognitive skills. An emotionally closed person will have a pedantic view of history or an overgeneralized framework in sociology or a rule-book orientation in the lab. One must, however, be aware that impulse can push through in strange places; an otherwise restricted person may exhibit a special spontaneity once he or she puts on a white coat and is alone with test tubes. Emotional education can take place in the classroom through the relations teachers establish with their students and the relations they further among students, and above all, through their responsiveness to the student's individuality. Where a course can use the outside world, as in field trips or in observation and service projects, the opportunities for simultaneous intellectual and emotional growth are enhanced. The world outside the classroom is a powerful educational force, or counterforce, for the development of emotions.

Cognitive stages are strictly mirrored in affective ones. Cognitive dualism is mirrored in intense and one-sided emotional attachments, whether it be to friends or to heroic figures, so often characteristic of the freshman year. Multiplicity is mirrored in a promiscuous trying out of relationships, either shallow or alternatingly intense. Finding one's own intellectual orientation and putting one's concepts to the test is mirrored in the capacity for commitment to people and tasks. Relationships with peers and the storms and reconciliations in one's relationship with persons in authority, including one's parents, are experiences that shape intellectual development. There is a progression from egocentrism, where the boundaries between one's world and the outside are not very clear, where it almost seems that "I am the world," through a stage where one sees that one's beliefs and emotions are a function of the ways in which an ego structures the world, to a final stage in which the ego is no longer *distortingly* intrusive in viewing reality. Reality becomes relations among objects, and one can be objective about one's ego without losing that assertiveness of self that is a precondition for growth and a nonmasochistic way of living and thinking.

Emotional and cognitive progressions are exhibited in differing relationships to teachers. The dualist student may look to teachers as authoritarian schoolmasters, sometimes enemies and sometimes heroes. One student whom we interviewed at this stage found it very difficult to accept a teacher whom he perceived also as wanting to be his friend. In his view it was not possible to be authority and friend at the same time. To the multiplist student the teacher's view becomes one of many, perhaps not to be accorded more respect than his own; indifference, a blasé attitude can color this student's approach to thinking and to the teacher. To the committed student the teacher can be a mentor or a colleague, and the self-esteem of this student is no longer hurt by recognizing the teacher's superior competence due to training, experience, and aptitude. There are stark differences in students at different stages of their college careers. To the sophomores the teacher often is the focal reference point determining their incentives to think and to work. For seniors the teacher at times seems to be no more than a convener of classes, leaving the intellectual work to the students. This is not the utmost stage. A still more mature student recognizes the special contributions to the understanding of the problem that the professor makes. Good teachers are aware enough to recognize these differing attitudes and styles in their students. They recognize but do not rigidify the authoritarianism of their freshmen; they lead them toward tension and dissent. They recognize the at-times-defiant autonomy of students; but they help create situations in which students recognize the insistent autonomy of reality against which an uninformed autonomy is no equal match.

FACULTY INQUIRY INTO STUDENT LEARNING

Immediately at the end of a semester's work, we have made it a practice to ask the teacher and his colleague-observer to write down or dictate onto a tape what knowledge they have gained through their interviews, observations, and discussions about their students' and their own learning. The two colleagues then exchange their drafts, discussing and revising them. Their statements serve a triple purpose: They form the basis for future work. They provide a first sketch for emerging theory or conceptualizations. They are shared with colleagues in one's own institution and elsewhere to provide example and stimulus. (In chapter 5 we give several examples of such end-of-semester reflections.) One of the distinctive characteristics of the model we have presented in this chapter is its heuristic utility. It is a tool both for work with one's students in the classroom and for the continual expansion of conceptualizations and theory. The intent of our approach is to help professors become more accomplished *professionals* in teaching. The collaborative work of the observed and the observing teacher is an important means toward achieving this goal.

3

Thinking Styles in the Disciplines and in Student Learning

DESCRIPTIONS OF THINKING

Until recently, little help was available to professors who wanted to find out about their students' or their own thinking styles. There were a number of rather general descriptions of thinking such as William James's seminal differentiation between the rational and the empirical temperaments (1979a, p. 13), John Dewey's description of hypothesis formation in *How We Think* (1933), Piaget's distinction (Gruber and Vonèche, 1977) between abstract and concrete operations, Polanyi's (1966) emphasis on the personal component of knowledge, and the recent distinction between right- and left-brain functioning (Springer and Deutsch, 1985). These concepts, while useful, do not usually provide sufficient detail for the day-to-day work with students in the classroom.

It is different with William Perry's book (1970). Perry, as we have seen, describes in some detail the cognitive progress of students during the college years. In his first three stages (or positions as he calls them), truth seems to lie with the other—the teacher, the expert, the authority. Toward the end of stage three and through stage four, truth seems to belong to everyone equally. Each self has the truth. By stages five and six, the student recognizes that truth is a construction with finite possibilities in limited situations, a construction that individuals must make and test out for themselves; then choices have to be made. Teachers recognize, from their own experience, that the stages described by Perry are true to what they have found in their classrooms. They have observed freshmen to be more literal and authority-bound than upper-class students. They have encountered relativism in their sophomores, who think one opinion as good as another. They have come to envisage the possibility that differences between freshmen and juniors can be explained not only by the lesser information freshmen possess but by their stage of cognitive development. Practically no attempt has been made to apply Perry's scheme to the thinking of faculty. Our own observations suggest that some of Perry's "earlier" stages of cognitive style apply to faculty as well. Authoritarian and rule-bound thinking is by no means the prerogative of freshmen alone.

In our own work we have, as already indicated, paid particular attention to cognitive "style" in addition to developmental level. At any level of development there is wide variability in the ways in which people conceptualize the experiences they encounter and the data they gather and construct. We have developed many of our ideas about cognitive style through use of the Omnibus Personality Inventory (see chapter 6). One of us (Mildred Henry) has on the basis of over a thousand interviews of students and faculty developed an interpretation of the Omnibus Personality Inventory (OPI) that renders it a complex inventory of cognitive styles. We have often been astonished by the sameness or similarity of cognitive profiles of faculty in the same discipline. Much of the time we can predict a person's profile once we know his or her academic field. We waver between two hypotheses. The first one stipulates that different disciplines require different types of thinking patterns and that the strength of one's contribution to the field may depend on maintaining a certain consistency of approach. The other hypothesis holds that creativity in any field calls upon the exercise of a great variety of mental functioning. We favor the latter hypothesis, as we have found that creative persons in any academic discipline resemble each other and obtain high scores in a variety of thinking modes, such as analyticalness, comprehensiveness, complexity, perceptual sensitivity, intuitiveness. Our second hypothesis finds support in Paul Heist's (1968) studies of creative college students.

We have found that many faculty are surprised to discover they have a *distinctive* thinking style — as if all along they had assumed their way was *the* way to reason. Once faculty are aware of their own styles and look at the variety of cognitive patterns among their students, they begin to understand better previous problems in communication, and they can move toward enabling their students to obtain a clearer grasp of what the course offers. They have an opportunity to enlarge their repertory of thinking modes, that is, to become intellectually more creative. They are able to transcend limitations of their previous ways of thinking. These observations are in line with some recent theoretical emphases, such as those of Seymour Papert (1980), which suggest that explicit consciousness about the ways in which we reason is a prime avenue toward more deliberate and skillful learning.

In what follows we describe some characteristic thinking patterns of faculty and students we have found in our work. We do not suggest that our scheme is in any way complete. We offer it as an example of the results that are possible if one pays deliberate attention to cognitive processes. We invite our colleagues to follow our *method,* and not to rest on our results. We have used the OPI because we found it a comprehensive and congenial instrument. But other available cognitive inventories, such as the Myers-Briggs (1976) or Kolb's (1981), provide different and useful perspectives. Claxton and Murrell's monograph (1987) describes extant learning styles schemes. New possibilities of conceiving cognitive functions are suggested by Howard Gardner's (1983) theory of multiple intelligences with its distinction of seven intelligences: linguistic, logical mathematical, spatial, musical, bodily-kinesthetic, introspective, interpersonal.

A chief source of thinking is the dynamic tension and collaboration between perception and conceptualization, and the relation between the two has been well described by William James (1979b). Concepts are both derived from and ultimately tested in perception. Piaget (Gruber and Vonèche, 1977) traces the emergence of concept formation to the ability of tracking observable events and holding them in the mind apart from the actual physical events themselves. Reflection or "second order thinking" occurs as the individual moves beyond "concrete" thinking (thinking tied directly to what is perceived) into "formal" thinking. In formal thinking, the individual is able to generate all possible combinations of a given concept, both those possibilities that may have an empirical referent and those that are merely imagined conceptually. Different academic disciplines address themselves to different sorts of perceptions or "outer" and "inner" experiences, and they differ considerably in the concepts, reflected in different methods, with which they approach perception.

THINKING PATTERNS IN THE ACADEMIC DISCIPLINES

Conceptualization has many origins, embracing such diverse modes as analysis, complexity of reasoning, synthesis, esthetic sensitivity, intuition, imagination. A professor of literature, reading a poem or a novel, requires a sensitivity to its form and sensuous depth that may not be as essentially required for analysis in other academic fields. Many historical interpretations call for a capacity that we vaguely call intuition: the capacity to associate previously unrelated data and concepts, to pick from a mass of data some organizing patterns, to go beyond the frame of reference at hand, to have recourse to the imagination. In our observations of faculty and students we have found that the combinations and permutations of four cognitive scales on the OPI account for many differences among the academic disciplines. These four scales measure (1) *theoretical orientation*—analytical, abstract, categorical, logical-deductive; (2) *reflective thinking*—scanning, associative, connective; (3) *complexity*—perceiving the world as multifarious, shifting, dynamic, unfixed; (4) *es-*

thetic awareness—sensitive to form, feeling, and relationships among patterns, open to perception and to inner experience.

We have found that faculty who teach literature, drama, and poetry show a strong initial preference for the inner-experience-oriented and complex ways of thinking, with secondary emphasis on conceptual and definitional thinking. By contrast, faculty in the sciences show a strong disposition toward analyticity and complexity, with relatively lesser emphasis on either the esthetic or reflective-associative dimensions. Philosophers tend to emphasize the analytic, categorizing, and reflective-speculative dimensions, and only in lesser degree the feeling-oriented, perceptual, or intuitive ones. Social scientists, in the "softer" variants of these fields, use an observing-perceiving method in conjunction with an associative, imagining process. Professors of language and music join an intuitive-feeling with a reflective, speculative, associating process. Design engineers and architects link an esthetic, feeling-oriented to an analytic, logical process. These descriptions (which become more meaningful in conjunction with chapter 6) may sound somewhat categorical, and we would hesitate to put them forward had we not found in our work that people in different fields produce similar patterns regularly. Where we found individuals deviating from these "norms" of their discipline, they were people who were pursuing a line of investigation not typical among their colleagues or who turned out to be misfits in their specialty, such as a philosopher whose work was more like that of a literary historian and a chemist who was wholly engaged with music theory and disliked chemistry. Unusually creative individuals tend to be more catholic in the modes of thinking they employ.

Our work, as already indicated in the previous chapter, has brought us up against a difficult observation. Try as we may to separate cognitive from emotional functioning, we cannot put the two asunder. Our learning styles inventory contains three scales that describe degrees of emotional openness and closedness. A high degree of emotional openness is defined by the tendency of the imagination, impulse, and fantasy not to submit to suppressive control and by tolerance for anxiety. Emotionally open people can more freely make the daring forays and take the initiatives that overcome orthodoxy and other previously accepted formulations.

We think this a difficult observation because we have limited means, particularly in the classroom, to influence the emotional dimension of personality. Yet, as we have suggested, there are possibilities. For instance, anything teachers can do to preserve or enhance the self-esteem of their students can make a contribution toward freeing the students' emotions from self-alienating checks. Emotional openness is connected with the tendency to express ideas in action. We think of ideas and actions in two separate domains. Yet in the laboratory the two are significantly intertwined. Perhaps some lack of liveliness in the students' understanding of ideas is due to the fact that they often cannot either perceive or try out ideas in out-of-classroom situations. When they do, as in fieldwork or in service activities, the effects often are electrifying. The options for the classroom teacher are limited, but not so limited as to preclude the provision of opportunities for understanding and testing ideas in some action outside of the classroom. For teachers, this could become a more deliberate practice.

One should not talk about the process of thinking without calling attention to its collaborative nature. Thinking is collaborative from its beginning. The baby learns a language through the active sharing of meaning and exploration with parents and other people. Scientific discoveries are often the product of a vigorous exchange of ideas and of teamwork (Deutsch and others, 1971). Great cultural periods are often due to social conditions that allow for time, opportunity, and "leisure" for intellectual sharing and association of thinkers and artists. Classical Athens, Renaissance Florence, nineteenth-century Paris are historical examples. Neither faculty ways of associating as practiced today nor student relations with each other are well enough designed to make possible true intellectual collaboration—a condition likely to produce thinking that benefits from the power of joint inquiry to transcend given categories and methods. The idea of collaborative learning is receiving much attention recently and new practices are developing (Katz, 1988).

WAYS OF STUDENT THINKING

Students on entry to college exhibit the same variety of thinking patterns we have described for faculty. In the more selective colleges there are more students who enter college with fairly well articulated thinking patterns. For some of these students the main educational task seems to be one of finding the disciplinary channel in which they can find companions of similar thinking patterns and in which they can thus feel supported and productive. Some students tend to resent and to resist the first two years of exploration and general education and can hardly wait to head for the discipline in which they are most comfortable. They find support within one disciplinary home or another, but they are not necessarily helped by faculty in their discipline to become more aware of the conceptual limits of a particular mode of thinking and thus they may not be encouraged to expand their thinking repertory. Other students, with more open-ended approaches to thinking, tend to enjoy the first two years of college with its emphasis on breadth. For both kinds of students the curriculum's division between general education and the major field encourages segmentation. The capacity for range of imagination in one's specialty may be undercut together with the relegation of general intellectuality to a subsidiary level.

A group of students who have not had very productive college experiences — even though on entry into college they may have high grade point averages and high SAT scores — are those who have few traces of a complex thinking style. They may use only one thinking mode unchecked by or unintegrated with any other thinking mode. They might be observation-oriented, concentrating mainly on the here and now. What is seen is believed, though on occasion the complexity of the perceptual flux may be so overwhelming and ambiguous that they have difficulty determining what to believe. Other students might be uninhibited classifiers, catalogers, categorizers. Such students are so concerned with distinguishing and labeling every idea, observation, or action that they do not take enough time to reflect on what is categorized or to play with the relationship of one concept to another. Other students may be associative thinkers drifting from one thought, idea, or subject to another, giving little effort to check their reflections either by classification, analysis, and logical consistency, or by probing the meanings and implications of their reflections, or by examining how their ideas line up with direct observations or with knowledge gained from action. Still other students rely primarily on their intuitions or feelings. Ideas may excite them and actions may appall them, but they do not quite know how to form an idea or how to focus and express feelings through words, pictures, and other forms.

A large group of students enter college with a thinking approach that is best described as embryolike. Though they may eventually stumble into a disciplinary channel or a particular faculty mentor who will support their intellectual growth, no guarantee exists that this will happen. Consequently, they are confused and disturbed by the constant shuffling back and forth among widely different disciplinary perspectives in the first two years of college. When forced to select a major, they make their choice not out of self-knowledge and a strong sense of preference, but out of ignorance or even desperation. For instance, students caught up in absolutist thinking appear to have fused perception with conception. When asked to compare the concepts of the tragic heroine exemplified by Antigone and Cordelia, they fail to understand the term "concept" and the variability of conceptions. They write descriptive (perception-bound) comparisons of Antigone and Cordelia as observable persons. They do not comprehend the task set for them of developing ideas pertaining to the meaning of tragedy. Unable to conceptualize on their own, they depend heavily on their teachers' conceptions of tragedy and absorb these as "facts" rather than seeing them as hypothetical in nature.

We have watched students making significant shifts from one cognitive style to another, particularly under the influence of some teachers. Faculty can help students by asking questions such as: "Is there another way of formulating the problem?" "What is the information that went into the statement of the problem?" "What is a fact?" "How did the author or the

student arrive at the conclusion?" "Could there be another possible conclusion?" "How does the material or the ideas in this course relate to the
material or ideas in another course?" "How does one determine that
something is true?" By scrutinizing the answers students give to such
questions the teacher can begin to see the presence or absence of certain
thinking processes as well as the patterned usage of these processes. Out
of this comes the recognition that students using a pattern of thinking that
is distinctly different from a particular disciplinary perspective have difficulty because of the way in which they organize and use basic thinking
processes. Perhaps the course being taught is a history course where it is
important for the student to catch hold of ideas and their interrelation-
ships. If the student is closely tied to what is observed and uses an analyz-
ing-categorizing approach, he or she is unlikely to realize that reflection is
called for or to have the patience to allow for not only the emergence of an
idea, but for the relating of one idea to another as well as the contrasting of
ideas.

HELPING STUDENTS TO LEARN

Teaching must be geared to the variety of students we face. We can help
those students who have a well-defined thinking approach to sharpen and
expand this approach. We can help students with an embryolike approach
to catch hold more consciously of their emerging effort to think in a
disciplined manner. As for those students who may be moving toward
more complex, interdisciplinary, or transdisciplinary thinking, faculty can
help them cut through institutional rules and requirements that limit them
from continuing to expand and develop their ideas. In his study of Princeton students, Roy Heath (1964) provides an excellent characterization of
the rhythm and the integration of several distinctively different thinking
processes and gives this description of the "reasonable adventurer" (pp.
30–31):

> In the pursuit of a problem, A [the reasonable adventurer] appears to experi-
> ence an alternation of involvement (the action-oriented mode of thinking-
> knowing and the perceiving-observing mode of knowing) and detachment
> (the reflective, the analytical, and the inner-experiencing modes of thinking-
> knowing). The phase of involvement is an intensive and exciting period
> characterized by curiosity (perception-observation), a narrowing of attention
> toward some point of interest. It is while "on the prowl" (taking action) that
> the person takes this step toward change, makes a discovery, suddenly per-
> ceives a new relationship. This period of involvement is then followed by a
> period of detachment, an extensive phase accompanied by a reduction of
> tension and a broadening range of perception. During this period of detach-
> ment there is a greater awareness of the presence of the self (inner aware-
> ness). Here A settles back to reflect (the reflective mode of thinking-know-
> ing) on the meaning of what was discovered during the involved

state . . . then after this process of ramification (reflection, association, connection) and classification (analysis) in the extensive phase, there is an eagerness to be on the way again.

If we see liberal education not only as the transmission of knowledge from one generation to the next but also aiming at cognitive transformation, the forms and processes of education become different. Faculty know when a student is beginning to assume an active stance toward knowledge and they recognize the importance of the student's transition from passively storing to actively processing and using knowledge. But many faculty do not engage in investigating the nature and conditions of this shift. By observing individual differences among students in the ways they process and generate knowledge and by becoming more intimately familiar with the cognitive contexts within which students shape their knowledge, faculty can arrive at "maps" of cognitive functioning and cognitive change. Cognitive change may be of several kinds: (1) changes from a unidimensional to a complex mode of thinking; (2) change from a largely unconscious, mainly embryonic to a strongly articulated thinking mode; and (3) change to a creative-constructive mode of thinking that is highly flexible. The first two kinds of change are the most common and the most likely to occur with the present approach to teaching in a curricular structure which is organized around separate and well-divided disciplines. However, any changes need to be monitored and facilitated.

To ask students primarily to learn the products of thinking fails to take account of the student as one who *actively* constructs, tests, evaluates knowledge. "Intellectual structures are built by the learner rather than taught by a teacher" Papert points out (1980, p. 19). To learn how to think scientifically, for instance, students need to be given the opportunity to perceive and use at first hand, through their own active involvement, the processes of thinking that lead to the production of scientific "facts" and "theories." They need to have the experience of following up on "intuitive" hunches, of establishing, questioning, sharing, and interpreting "facts." Without such experiences students tend to weld separate thinking processes together and not to perceive the important role played by each of several different thinking processes. Leaving the students in the dark about the central role of the inquirer and the process of thinking is illustrated in the following story which we owe to John Bilorusky: The professor is working through a complicated derivation of a formula on the blackboard. A student raises his hand and says, "I don't see how you did the last step." The professor says, "It's obvious." The student persists in his questioning. The professor steps away from the board, looks somewhat puzzled himself at his own process and sequence of derivation. Without saying anything, he leaves the room and goes to his office where he spends half the class time busily writing on the board in his office to check out his thinking and his derivation. Finally, he satisfies himself that his original derivation is in fact correct. He walks back to the lecture hall and informs the class, "Yes, it's obvious."

Pressuring students to memorize and to learn by rote rather than articulating the processes and coordination of processes involved in learning how to think is accentuated when faculty persist in requiring students to cope with specific contents at a volume and pace that they cannot handle. Volume and pace of coverage can interfere with the intellectual demand of having students examine what they are reading. At some high-pressure institutions, getting an education has been compared to taking a drink from a fire hose. Regard for the student must take such difficulties into account, and it has other dimensions as well. Interest, motivation, openness to experiment are the substrata of intellectual growth. The professor's interest in students and supportive help can be crucial in sustaining them long enough so they catch hold of a disciplined mode of learning. Professorial recognition and support can be crucial for students who try to go beyond the boundaries of an existing discipline and who risk the anxiety entailed in order to become more aware and confident of their distinctive ways of thinking. Athletic coaches are able to spot the skills an athlete in training must develop to become a top player. Classroom teachers might learn something from the coaches.

The importance of professorial recognition and support is underlined by a paper emanating from the Project on the Status and Education of Women of the Association of American Colleges (1982), which describes in vivid detail the ways in which women students may be put at a significant educational disadvantage in the college classroom. The authors of the paper summarize research that describes how faculty may treat men and women students differently and the following is only a partial listing of what they say: Making eye contact more often with men than with women students; nodding and gesturing more often in response to men's questions and comments than to women's; modulating tone, that is, a patronizing or impatient tone when talking with women; being attentive when men report, but the opposite when women do; habitually moving to a location near men students; favoring men in choosing student assistants; allowing women to be physically "squeezed out" from viewing a laboratory assignment or a demonstration; ignoring women students while recognizing men students even when women clearly volunteer to participate in class; waiting longer for men than for women to answer a question before going on to another student; interrupting women students; asking women questions that require factual answers while asking men questions that require critical thinking. Women students are not the only ones who may be treated this way in the classroom. Similar reports have been made about minority students (Cones et al., 1983). Men students, too, often are not provided with sufficient opportunities and encouragement to develop their powers of thinking.

A fine illustration of nonobvious ways in which students' intellectual development can be encouraged or discouraged is furnished in the following account of two different student experiences (Belenky et al., 1986, pp. 191–193). A student, now a middle-aged woman, remembers the first meeting of an introductory science course.

> The professor marched into the lecture hall, placed upon his desk a large jar filled with dried beans, and invited the students to guess how many beans the jar contained. After listening to an enthusiastic chorus of wildly inaccurate estimates the professor smiled a thin, dry smile, revealed the correct answer, and announced, "You have just learned an important lesson about science. Never trust the evidence of your own senses."
>
> Thirty years later, the woman could guess what the professor had in mind. He saw himself, perhaps, as inviting his students to embark upon an exciting voyage into a mysterious underworld invisible to the naked eye, accessible only through scientific method and scientific instruments. But the seventeen-year-old girl could not accept or even hear the invitation. Her sense of herself as a knower was shaky, and it was based on the belief that she could use her own firsthand experiences as a source of truth. This man was saying that this belief was fallacious. He was taking away her only tool for knowing and providing her with no substitute. "I remember feeling small and scared," the woman says, "and I did the only thing I could do. I dropped the course that afternoon, and I haven't gone near science since."
>
> The second woman, in her first year at college, told a superficially similar but profoundly different story about a philosophy class she had attended just a month or two before the interview. The teacher came into class carrying a large cardboard cube. She placed it on the desk in front of her and asked the class what it was. They said it was a cube. She asked what a cube was, and they said a cube contained six equal square sides. She asked how they knew that this object contained six equal square sides. By looking at it, they said. "But how do you know?" the teacher asked again. She pointed to the side facing her and, therefore, invisible to the students; then she lifted the cube and pointed to the side that had been face down on the desk, and, therefore, also invisible. "We can't look at all six sides of a cube at once, can we? So we can't exactly *see* a cube. And yet, you're right. You know it's a cube. But you know it not just because you have eyes but because you have intelligence. You invent the sides you cannot see. You use your intelligence to create the 'truth' about cubes."
>
> The student said to the interviewer: "It blew my mind. You'll think I'm nuts, but I ran back to the dorm and I called my boyfriend and I said, 'Listen, this is just incredible,' and I told him all about it. I'm not sure he could see why I was so excited. I'm not sure I understand it myself. But I really felt, for the first time, like I was really in college, like I was—I don't know—sort of *grown* up."
>
> Both stories are about the limitations of firsthand experience as a source of knowledge—we cannot simply see the truth about either the jar of beans or the cube—but there is a difference. We can know the truth about cubes. Indeed, the students did know it. As the science professor pointed out, the students were wrong about the beans; their senses had deceived them. But, as the philosophy teacher pointed out, the students were right about the cube; their minds had served them well.
>
> The science professor was the only person in the room who knew how many beans were in that jar. Theoretically, the knowledge was available to the students; they could have counted the beans. But faced with that tedious

prospect, most would doubtless take the professor's word for it. He is authority. They had to rely upon his knowledge rather than their own. On the other hand, every member of the philosophy class knew that the cube had six sides. They were all colleagues.

The science professor exercised his authority in a benign fashion, promising the students that he would provide them with the tools they needed to excavate invisible truths. Similarly, the philosophy teacher planned to teach her students the skills of philosophical analysis, but she was at pains to assure them that they already possessed the tools to construct some powerful truths. They had built cubes on their own, using only their own powers of inference, without the aid of elaborate procedures or fancy apparatus or even a teacher. Although a teacher might have told them once that a cube contained six equal sides, they did not have to take the teacher's word for it; they could have easily verified it for themselves.

The lesson the science professor wanted to teach is that experience is a source of error. Taught in isolation, this lesson diminished the student, rendering her dumb and dependent. The philosophy teacher's lesson was that although raw experience is insufficient, by reflecting upon it the student could arrive at truth. It was a lesson that made the student feel more powerful ("sort of grown up").

Reflecting on this account of the two teachers we wonder whether we might have thought that *both* teachers had used good pedagogical techniques if we had not also been given the report of the students' reactions. The students' responses testify to the very different effects of the two teachers' approaches, at least on these two students. They reveal subtleties about the learning process we might not have suspected. In the following chapters, and again in chapter 8, we will hear from other teachers about their experiences investigating student learning and the lessons they drew from them.

4

Promoting Student Learning

For many faculty it is a new idea that they might inquire into the teaching–learning process as systematically as they inquire into the problems of their disciplines. The methods of interviewing some of their own or their colleagues' students and of making use of learning styles inventories are unfamiliar. Consequently, this unexplored territory brings to the surface entrenched beliefs about teaching, certain existing taboos, and several highly legitimate concerns. In this chapter we will list some of the questions and concerns that faculty have raised and describe some of their reactions so that others venturing to use this approach will know better what to expect. We will quote from faculty with whom we have worked.

When teachers move to the student's side of the log to observe and to reflect upon what is happening to the students seated there, impressions and reactions occur that are different from those experienced when they maintain their seat and distance. Their teaching begins to assume new directions, among them individuation of teaching approaches and designing of classes and classroom assignments in ways that encourage students to become more active in their learning. Collaborative relationships between teachers and students become important to the teacher as student feedback is solicited in and out of the classroom. Differences among students that may be etched out, for instance, at first by way of OPI profile patterns and discussions about student development theory, became part of a more habitual way of observing and thinking about students. Interviews are no longer self-consciously initiated, but are seen as an important way to solicit valuable student comments on the teaching–learning effort, comments useful in modifying teaching practice.

USE OF THE OPI AND THE INTERVIEW:
REACTIONS OF FACULTY AND STUDENTS

A common faculty fear when the OPI or other cognitive inventory is first introduced is that the use of such an instrument might lead to categorizing students too facilely. When this fear is expressed our response typically is that the first principle in the judicious use of a test is to regard it as only possibly indicating some aspect or quality of a given individual. We urge that the instrument be used heuristically as a tool for discovery, for the enlargement of perspective on the complexities of thinking, feeling, and interacting. A good way is to begin with persons for whom one has first-hand information. One can then observe and test how the abstract catego-ries suggested by the instrument do or do not fit these persons. If discrep-ancies occur, further inquiry and reflection are required concerning the relationships existing between the abstracted patterns on the instrument and the actual person's thinking modes and motivational habits. Many faculty are set back by their initial sense of the complexities of student learning styles. As one of them put it: "My first response to the OPI was that it gave me more information than I cared to know. Once I recognized that the amount of information in the OPI would be used to stimulate my thinking, rather than to diagnose or label, I was able to use it."

Faculty members' fear of falling into a too-ready use of categories or their fear of too much complexity generally lessens and disappears through the use of the interview. Interview sessions with students allow for considerable checking and rechecking of the thinking styles and theo-retically suggested patterns of development. They bring faculty into a different relationship with their students, showing them ways to individu-alize their teaching. Faculty often comment on how they learn through the interviews to become better listeners and also become more able to ask "telling" questions of their students. One professor declared: "[At first] I found it a little frustrating not being able to control the conversation as I wished; after all, *I* have an agenda! As time passed I found myself more comfortable getting data while allowing some latitude in the conversa-tion." Another faculty member reported that he came to realize that he often stops asking questions just when it could get interesting. A student would tell him *what* she or he was doing, but the faculty member had not thought to ask "how" or "why" and was stuck with his own guesses.

In our experience, student reactions to the OPI and to the interviews have been mainly positive. Students like learning more about themselves through seeing their profile patterns and learning how to interpret and use them. Many students experience a sense of exhilaration when they learn not only about their own individual thinking–learning style but about the fact of individual differences. One student (who had high scores on the autonomy and impulse and risk-taking scales of the OPI and a well-de-fined humanities pattern) said: "The OPI gave me a new perspective on learning. I can learn best in a very informal atmosphere. I have some real problems when I am forced to learn in a very formal way. . . . My instructor tells me that she learns a lot like me. She hates to write papers or do projects that are not self-initiated. Now I realize that all people cannot learn in the same environment. Students can either pass or fail a class because of the way they are taught. Some people can learn in a rigidly structured class, but there are others that need a more open, creative atmosphere."

One professor we worked with formulated four useful generalizations: (1) Students frequently seem greatly relieved when they realize the diversity of learning patterns that exist in a single class. In comparing their learning style with that of their instructor, they are able to account for both the ease and difficulty they have with learning in a particular class; (2) They develop a framework for conducting their own clarification of their educational experiences. They focus on their own unique stage of development and the capabilities they seek to develop. As a result, they see how certain kinds of educational experiences (general studies, mathematics, etc.) are necessary and more than an academic barrier created by the institution; (3) They develop a different view of the nature of intelligence and learning. Conventional wisdom among students holds to the belief that intelligence is an innate capacity represented by an IQ test score. They are delighted to discover that they are not wedded to a singular, limited capability for life; and (4) They gain a sense of the ways personality and fields of study are related—persons "fit" into an area that matches their preferred functioning and the demands of the field reinforce this particular functional mode. Students whose profiles differ from a chosen field of interest or major are able to reassess their goals and interests. More importantly, they often see the constraints imposed by the prototypical mode of thought within a field. For example, at a time when creativity and innovation are needed in science and in technology, students discover that some ways of science teaching do not promote creativity. In sum, the self-awareness and the sense of the multiplicity of thinking-learning modes that students develop make it easier for them to gain a liberal education.

Once the beginning stages of this approach to faculty development are completed and the initial fears and concerns are worked through, a second stage emerges: changes in the faculty's conceptions of their students, of themselves, and of the teaching–learning endeavor. Often the change in perspectives is initiated by a focus on student individual differences. These differences, observable in their classroom, tend to upset faculty in their efforts to develop a smooth-running course. They speak of receiving conflicting messages from their students. Some students want considerable detail and structure; others want to move beyond the details to the underlying ideas and ask for less structure from the teacher so they can engage in more independent work and projects of their own making.

Some students want interpretations, others want "facts." One faculty member said: "I learned or relearned that the students' mental processes are not mirror images of my own: many times we operate conceptually in two different universes of discourse. . . . The fact that we were once incumbents in these stages and the fact that we may have a great deal of empathy for students who are currently in these stages in no way negates the intellectual distance between us." This distance has to be understood and negotiated in ways that respect the gap between the professor as an experienced learner and the student as a beginning learner. A linguistics professor said:

> My concept of individuation has begun to change. The individualization movement in higher education has made many professors more sensitive to the need for greater diversity in course design, presentation formats, assignments for students, and the like. A famous form of large-scale programed instruction such as the Personalized System of Instruction (PSI) is a good example. But what is really individualized is merely the place and time frame for a course. All students do essentially the same things to accomplish the goal of mastering similar objectives. What a limited view of individualization! Truly individualizing the learning process means not simply providing for various speeds of learning but also providing for different types of students, different styles, interests, intellectual dispositions, needs, goals, and different positions in intellectual and emotional development. That means the instructors must have at their disposal various approaches, that they must be able to provide these approaches — in the form of assignments, tests, individual arrangements, and various emphases to each student at the right time for that student. This is a difficult but not impossible task. Above all, it means that we must focus on the individual student and know him or her as a person. That is the most difficult part of the task. Even though the faculty member cannot really know every one of thirty students in a class — each being a unique person — knowing a few in that manner, and by extension being open to and aware of the others, creates an entirely new attitude toward teaching, the classroom, and the student. These are no longer just "students," they are individual human beings with all the richly diverse needs one finds in one's own family, one's neighborhood, or the larger world.

The same professor adds that in the past he had just been paying lip service to individualization: "Yes, I had been sympathetic toward students of diverse backgrounds and tolerant of their varying views. But I had been missing some dimension in my appreciation for the differences among them and my approaches to them. The students I had 'individualized' were the ones whose eyes met mine in class and who appeared voluntarily in my office; the ones whose ambitions stood in some kind of complementary relations with my objectives and whose intellectual styles and interests resonated with mine." Another professor describes some earlier attempts to individualize students: "Previously, I, like other faculty, would tend to apply simplistic schemes to explain student behavior: he is lazy, she is not very bright, they have other things on their minds."

As faculty become more aware of the reality and shape of these cognitive differences, theories of cognitive development become more useful and hence interesting. Since some of these theories (Perry, Piaget) can be related to the OPI, the OPI becomes more useful and interesting as a tool for analysis as well as for confirmation and conjecture. For instance, there are correlations between students' scores on some of the OPI scales and Perry's major categories of dualism, multiplicity, and relativism. These correlations were found by Nancy Goldberger (1980, p. 2) who collected both OPI and Perry data. The more students become reflective, autonomous, outgoing, and the less tied to concreteness, detail, and tight means-ends relationships, the more likely they are to see the world as offering multiple views and options and eventually the more likely to recognize the need to make sense for themselves out of conflicting views through a search for context and meaning.

Faculty's growing realization of the complexity of intellectual development also raises the question for them about the relationships of cognitive to emotional and interpersonal development. As one professor put it: "Some students need very little positive reinforcement and some need very much. Some students get their reinforcement from success with the work, while others need the interpersonal reinforcement from the teacher." Some expression of faculty interest in the student is needed if students are to muster the courage to approach faculty outside of the classroom and to ask the kinds of questions they need to have answered for the advancement of their learning. Faculty frequently believe that they are highly accessible to students, but they fail to see that many students need help with the first moves required to bridge what the students see as a huge and often frightening distance between them and their teachers. One English professor said: "I asked Jane if she had been in to see any of her professors. She admitted that she hadn't. And when I asked why, she responded that she just didn't want to be a 'bother.' Why and how do we give the impression that students are a bother? She suggested that I pass around a sheet indicating the times that I was available for conferences. I mentioned to her that I always told the class before a test or a paper that I was glad to talk to any of them. She said that wasn't enough; teachers are always so busy." A philosopher reported that he found it "striking that students displayed so much anxiety about talking with a professor": "I could not help but feel their fears and anxieties had a large part to play in what they *could* do in the course and what they *could* say to me. If many or most students are anxious about themselves, contact with faculty, and their course work, I wonder just how such fears can be alleviated so that learning and growth can occur."

The importance of attending to noncognitive aspects of students if their eventual cognitive development is to be advanced is emphasized by the following comments from Nancy Goldberger (1980). She describes the problems when students are caught up in a dualistic or absolutist mode of thinking:

> Such students are often confused by contradictory information and are particularly upset when the professor's lecture diverges from the textbook. Team teaching is a problem for these students since they don't know which teacher is the true authority. In a course which emphasizes relativistic thinking, they may try to learn what the teacher wants, but are unable to formulate general rules. Their inability to succeed is often blamed on the teacher who they feel should supply answers which the students can learn. Dualistic students tend to avoid the social sciences and the humanities which they perceive as arbitrary, disorganized, and even threatening and gravitate instead to science and math where they feel right answers can be found. Too often teaching in the sciences reinforces this illusion by its overemphasis on logical proof and experimental method and not on the context for scientific thought. During an interview, one pre-med student spoke of dropping introductory sociology, saying, "I'm scared of social sciences courses. I haven't learned how to approach them. . . . Who's to say what is right and what isn't. Science is more exact." In planning a curriculum for students at the dualistic stage, educators should be responsive both to their possible intellectual limits that is, concrete, passive, and either/or thinking, and to their personal insecurity over venturing into unknown territory. As students are challenged with diversity of opinion and multiple perspectives, they must be offered concurrently structure, direction, and emotional support.

PROMOTING STUDENT PROFICIENCIES IN FOUR INTERRELATED MODES OF THINKING

In helping students to develop their thinking abilities we must take into account the differing dispositions they bring to this task. Hence in the following pages we will concentrate, in line with what we said in the preceding chapter, on four dimensions of thinking: theoretical, reflective, esthetic, and complex. Our notion is that ordered or disciplined thinking cannot or will not occur until two or more of these four modes or processes are integrated one with another in a check-and-balance manner.

Theoretical Thinking

Faculty seeking to strengthen their students' abilities to conceptualize and to find formal categories or structures for observable experiences or events, as measured by the TO (Theoretical Orientation) scale on the OPI (see Chapter 6), can experiment with varying approaches. A professor of mathematics reports her showing linkages between abstract conceptual categories and concrete examples in order to help students develop proficiency in analytical, concept-oriented thinking. She notes that when she first began teaching statistics, she stuck to the book, practiced using the formulas, hoping to get the same answers to the exercises as were in the back of the book and trying to imagine what words she could use in class between the formulae and the examples. "I remember leaving the class each day, frustrated that in spite of spewing out formulae and working problems, the connections, reasons, and applications eluded me. . . . The students wanted to know how they could apply what I was trying to teach them. By the third time I taught the course I was able to use examples of correlations, the average life of a Volvo or a statistically preposterous denial by the government that Vietnam vets exposed to Agent Orange were no more likely than the general population to contract cancer. We were taking on real issues and dealing with them statistically."

In the study *Conceptual Blockbusting*, James Adams (1974, pp. 64–65) notes that there are different "problem-solving languages": verbalization (words), visualization (pictures), and mathematics (figures, charts). Persons differ in the ease with which they use these modes. The mathematics professor just cited tried to use all three problem-solving modes in developing her class in statistics: "Some students are able to suspend their need for reality and learn mathematics perfectly well when taught theoretically or abstractly. But it has been my observation that even those students learn better when there are examples or pictures or something tangible." In looking at OPI profile patterns for students in her statistics class, she found that, in general, students with a moderately or strongly defined analytic pattern of thinking needed less exposure to verbal explanations or pictures than did students with low TO scores; but both groups of students seemed to profit from her multifaceted approach.

Reflective Thinking

Reflective thinking permits second-order thinking or thinking about thinking. It is measured by the TI (Thinking Introversion) scale of the OPI. It includes clarification, definition, the relating of things to each other, and perceiving multiplicity. A faculty member interested in stimulating reflective thinking among his students said: "Giving students an opportunity to talk frequently with one another about what they have learned and how they learned it is one of the most effective strategies for helping students to stretch intellectually." Having students keep journals and encouraging them to question and think about what they have written is an excellent way of stimulating the reflective process. Without the play of the mind that the reflecting process allows, the theories, information, data, and content that faculty like to provide to students in great abundance may be flat, devoid of some or much of their meaning, and easily forgotten. A philosophy professor was amazed at how relatively little content gets learned. He shifted to a concern with *how* the students were responding to and handling, or failing to handle, abstract ideas, definitions, concepts, and categories.

Some faculty in their efforts to stimulate reflective thinking among their students have found that unexamined and emotionally important beliefs and values that are deeply held by students often make it difficult for students to achieve the kind of distance and play required for engaging in reflective thinking. A professor of religion states: "Dealing as I do in my classes with biblical literature, I am faced with students' deep-seated piety and the need for them to 'work through' questions of the authority of the text and its critical use in the academic study of religion. I think that within the disciplines there is a need for awareness of the relationship between patterns of student development and the traditional, long-held doctrinal belief systems that students coming out of pietistical traditions bring to college." Failure to be aware of and sympathetic to the student's emotions as the student is asked to reflect on cherished beliefs and ideas may hinder the student's efforts to learn.

Esthetic Thinking

We have used an example from mathematics teaching to illustrate the analytic avenue to thinking. Mathematics, and of course other fields as well, also illustrate intuitive-esthetic thinking, measured by the Estheticism (Es) scale. A teacher of mathematics writes as follows: "Although formulae and equations are the most obvious parts of the subject to the superficial observer, mathematics shares an inner life with poetry, literature, and music. Many students perceive a mathematics course as a haphazard collection of definitions, theorems, and problems which are beyond intuitive understanding. But learning cannot occur with such a perception. The game of chess cannot be understood by knowing only the rules for moving each piece. It is similarly not satisfying to come to the end of a proof of an isolated mathematical theorem knowing only that no error was made from one step to the next. One wants a sense of the architecture of the structure that is being created as well as how it fits into the context, historically and philosophically." To involve his students in a search for the architecture of mathematics, this teacher said that it required transcending the traditional ways of classroom learning. "One facet is to emphasize questions instead of answers. My questions to my students are not *how* to solve a problem or prove a theorem, but *why* is the problem solved as it is, or what is the meaning of a theorem and its connection with other theorems in the text and why did the author place the problem of theorem where it is." To lead students to encounter the architecture of mathematics, he suggests the following:

> Almost all problems in a test are solvable because the author has contrived to match the questions with the tools and methods that can answer those questions. On the basis of such experience the uncritical reader might believe that every question has an answer. A creative exercise that gives students insight distorts a textbook problem until it is no longer solvable. Asking an unan-

swerable question that is not related to the original problem requires breaking away from the mindset of the test. Asking a question that is related to the original problem requires some understanding of the structure of the subject. Could a problem that is solvable in a rectangle still be solved in a triangle or an irregular shape? How would a change from two to three dimensions affect the solvability? What is the effect of changing some of the numerals? Could this problem have been solved in an earlier chapter, or in an earlier century? Could the problem be solved with less information?

This teacher says that the best distortions are those where the boundary between solvability and unsolvability is evident. Studying that boundary and its neighborhood takes the student to the heart of the problem. He tells his students that one of their goals will be the strengthening of their imagination and questioning ability. He informs them of the importance and marvelous flexibility of human language and the facts that new sentences can be made by men and women out of their stock of words and syntax. The attainment of a "real understanding of mathematics and science" is revealed by the students' ability to create a new sentence. He says to his students, "We shall try to make 'new sentences' out of the facts, formulas, and techniques that we learn."

An exercise that this professor sometimes uses to encourage creativity and develop the intuitive feel that experts manifest is to divide the class into two or three teams. Each team invents two problems related to the current topic. "One problem should be interesting, the other should be impossible. The teams are challenged to solve the other's problems. The discussions about the problems, the struggles to solve the impossible ones — all contribute to that 'other' (intuitive) knowledge. Sometimes special recognition or prizes are awarded for the best questions. These exercises make the student actively participate in doing and creating mathematics as opposed to passively learning facts and formulae." He focuses his students' attention on the critically important and neglected stage of incubation. This is the stage when the student must feel free to relax and allow unconscious processes to work efficiently without trying to overcontrol the situation. At intervals during the term, this teacher alerts his students to the role of beauty, that special esthetic sensibility of the creative mathematician or scientist wherein he or she searches for "good fits" and "harmony" among facts and between facts and theory. The class here referred to was a required course in calculus held to be one of the more difficult hurdles for students. (The teacher was Professor Alvin White. For a fuller account of his approach see Katz, 1985.)

Complex Thinking

Learning how to perceive freshly and spontaneously once enculturation and socialization have occurred is not easy. Preconceptions tend to hold the free play of perceiving in bondage. Consequently, a large part of the more radical function of education is to entice students to see that the categories they use for sorting what they observe into a manageable order and the conceptual frames or ideas they use for making sense of the categories are not fixed. (That tendency is measured by the Co (Complexity) scale. Typically, faculty try to get students to examine and question the categories, conceptions, and ideas they bring with them to college by exposing them to other categories and ideas they consider to be (a) better founded or researched, (b) more sophisticated, or (c) more coherent and consistent. Through such exposure the more engaged students begin to realize the multidimensionality of thinking. They may or may not readily adopt the new categories and ideas of their teachers. Students may or may not grasp the fact that the basis for a better concept or a more sophisticated or coherent idea emerges through perceiving an event or a characteristic, previously ignored, that becomes the pivotal factor either in developing a new concept or in forcing the expansion of an existing conceptualization or theory.

The importance of fresh perceptions and observations is not well enough conveyed to students. It is as important in science as in art, with the difference that in science attention is directed to events in the perceptual flux that reoccur and are in this sense stable or predictable, while in art attention is directed to the importance of really seeing and of new ways of seeing objects, events, and attributes. The freshness and durability of a work of art rests in the artist's ability to see color, space, movement, relationships, meanings in ways that are not conventionally seen or experienced. Viewers of art are thereby stimulated to reperceive their environment or culture in new and challenging ways.

One of the most successful teachers of painting and drawing we encountered was a woman with a large studio filled with an array of different kinds of paints (oil, water, acrylic) and drawing utensils (charcoal, ink, crayon), as well as large stacks of paper and canvases. Beginning students were encouraged to spend several hours exploring the different paints and drawing utensils, creating whatever images, array of colors, space-line explorations, and relationships they wished. After several hours of exploration, students were invited into a large, airy loft above the studio with white walls designed for the easy tacking up of whatever the student had created. Every student's work was displayed and the next hour or two was spent with the students and the teacher observing and noticing different aspects of what the student had created. Numerous art books were conveniently stored under window seats and wall benches encircling the loft. Frequently, during the course of the observing session in the loft, the teacher would pull out one or another of the art books, turn to the work of particular artists, and point out to one student or another how other artists had dealt with certain problems common to the problem the student was confronting.

The aim of this teacher's efforts was to get her students engaged experientially with the world of art on the basis of experimentation with an array of different art materials in the service of some kind of communication and aesthetic presentation. In the experience of many teachers, getting students to loosen up enough to become involved in the exploration and play that enable them to progress beyond the external manipulation of concepts or conventional modes of perceiving is difficult. The mathematics professor cited earlier observed in her classes that the students did not seem to know how to explore and play. This was especially true for the more anxious students: "When I gave them verbal puzzles to work with, the students tended not even to try to solve them. When I gave them Cuisenaire rods (colored rods of varying lengths) and told them to play with them as a child plays with blocks, they made unenthusiastic attempts. They wanted to know what I wanted them to do with the blocks and were frustrated when I did not respond with specific directions and assigned tasks. Yet one major road for being successful in mathematics is a willingness and ability to play with problems or ideas."

GETTING TO KNOW STUDENTS

For students to become more active participants in their learning, faculty must create opportunities for getting to know them better. They need to create a climate of trust if students are to be willing to engage in the risks learning entails. When there is anxiety, the students may turn to "learning through rote" and when they do so they are rendered dependent on the teacher as expert for knowing whether learning is occurring. To generate trust, a historian suggests that teachers must tell the students something about their relation to the subject under study. He thinks that self-disclosure is an essential activity for teachers who wish to show students that they care enough for them to risk being fully human in front of the class. "If I have decided that I need to establish some distance between me and the students, I owe it to them to say so, in as kind and diplomatic a way as possible. If I am getting bored with the material and want their help to search for a new way to make it come alive for both me and them, I should tell them so." Similarly, the students in the class need to know one another. "When people who do not know one another well (the average class), most members of the group take a wait-and-see attitude toward interacting with each other." A psychologist commented that "student learning would be greatly enhanced if students were just *noticed* by faculty members."

A teacher of biology writes:

> I have discovered that students are frequently rather remote from the learning process. Students seem to come to lectures as if they were turning on a television. They don't realize that they need to engage actively in the learning process. I am concerned about the lack of curiosity and of concern for knowledge that I find in many students. As a result I have begun gearing all my courses to trying to awaken curiosity and to awaken a concern for knowledge,

perhaps also to awaken a realization in students that I also am in the process of learning even as I teach, that I require feedback from the students in the courses I teach. . . . Students who are at low levels of Perry's developmental schema tend to dichotomize and don't understand that there is much interaction between disciplines. I have tried consciously to structure my course so that pigeonholing becomes increasingly difficult. . . . I have also become conscious of the ways in which I engage the class during the presentation. Even with a very large class, such as Zoology 10, I have been able to develop a more conversational interactive style of presentation. I have learned from my interviews with students that this sort of conversational presentation is apt to engage the students more actively and carry them into the subject better than a straight lecture format. The chance to interact with students and discuss the course has in a sense been institutionalized in my ornithology course through breakfasts. I go to breakfast with students and thus can interact with a number of them just before the laboratory section of the course; I get to them informally and have a chance to discuss the course with them, its content and its presentation. I have instituted discussion sections in Zoology 10 for the same purpose, to give students a chance to do the talking, and me to do the listening, and then both of us do a certain amount of interacting.

Learning to react to the variety of students' cognitive levels led a professor of religion to experiment with "meeting each student's ability with assignments [that would] best benefit a given student": "It brought to my attention the failure of monolithic assignments and opened up some possibilities for group work, various tracks in which students may work differently. . . . In the design of a new course I will have the students working on two tracks, each with different material, one working more descriptively, the other more analytically." The eye must be on the students. A philosophy professor writes: "It is important to ask when I prepare any class just what the students will be *doing* to learn the materials. My suspicion is that the more I answer that question with 'they will be listening to me,' or 'answering *my* questions' the less I am preparing a context for *their* struggling with the ideas and *their* questions about them."

A group of faculty at a state college instituting a freshman studies program have aimed at empowering college freshmen to become more effective in their cognitive development. The core of the course is epistemology: learning how to learn in various academic disciplines. Since students have preferred ways of learning, each topic is designed to be taught for different cognitive modes. Thus, a unit identifying chemical unknowns begins with weights, formulas, and descriptions of interactions (concepts); then the reagents are distributed to the students with test tubes and solvents, and they proceed to mix, observe, code by color, and describe the precipitates (experience, observation). Then they organize the data to create some results in a chart and other pattern (meaning). Students typically prefer one approach over the other. But with discussion of their preferences they are often willing to become competent in additional modes of treating materials. The students become aware of the mixture of intuition, concept formation, observation, calculation, and active organization needed to generate data, create patterns, and solve problems. The students are allowed to use modes of thinking natural to them and then are challenged to integrate their usual modes with other less usual ones.

OBSTACLES TO STUDENT LEARNING

We face many obstacles when we seriously consider how we might enable our students to learn. A professor who has wrestled with this problem describes how she addressed her students. On the first day of a new class, she asks them to think why they are there together. She then says that the present system of teaching dates from a time when books were not available and continues: "Not only is everything I'm going to say probably written down somewhere, but it has probably been said in a much more profound and interesting way than I am going to say it. So what I should do is hand you the syllabus and a list of books on the topic and say, 'Blessings on you. Go to the library and I will meet you at the end of the semester. You will write a couple of papers and I will read and comment on them and return them to you. If you would like, maybe every fourth week we could schedule a discussion.'" When she says that, her students look more bewildered than ever, but it opens up questions about learning and the role of the teacher. What does this professor herself consider the best way to learn? She responds:

> I don't know what the best way to learn is. I don't think it is the lecture, though I love a good lecture. I don't think it is discussion. I think learning in the classroom is the most inefficient way of learning. You could say to me, "Do you think that the best way to learn is to go to the library and read a lot of books?" No, I do not, is the answer to that. The material you are apt to master and understand is the material that for one reason or another *you want to know.* I would assign students the task of finding out what they really want to know at this particular moment in their lives and say, "OK, you're going to have to teach this to a group of very intelligent but ignorant twelve-year-olds, fourteen-year-olds, sixteen-year-olds, or college freshmen. If you really want to know something, teach them. When they ask you some questions about things you thought you knew and you realize you cannot answer their questions, you will start to begin to understand." We can't do that. Logistically it wouldn't work to have every student teach. But it is by teaching something that we begin to understand it. You have to come to grips with it. You appropriate it in a way that you never have before.

A major point in this professor's response is that students need to want to know. A turning point in teaching comes when beyond the question of *what* we should teach we intently explore the question of how we can bring our students to "want to know." The professor talks about the learning we do when we teach. An old Latin saying *docendo discimus* (we learn by teaching) gives support to her statement from teaching a long time ago. Means are available to allow undergraduates to have this experience, such as their analyzing the presentations, papers, and exams of fellow students or their serving as teaching assistants. When the professor says "go to the library" she focuses on another aspect of learning: self-learning, learning without teachers.

The classroom is in many other ways constricted by institutional and student norms, practices, and attitudes. Work load in other courses, jobs to help finance college, social lives and relationships on campus or at home, problems and pains of growing up, all these exert their shaping and constraining influence. In *Making the Grade,* Howard Becker and his associates (1968, pp. 130–131) observe:

> College faculty typically see their interactions with students as an individual matter. The teacher presents material and attempts to interest students in it so that they will devote their effort to learning what he wants them to know. If they do not learn, it is because they do not have the ability to do so or because the teacher has insufficiently interested them. But the faculty view is faulty. It assumes that student performance depends solely on ability and interest and ignores the complicated network of social relations, group definitions, and obligations in which students find themselves. It sees student performance as a simple response to the professor's offerings rather than as a construction of a complex line of action in a complicated and demanding social setting. It underestimates students' rationality in attempting to meet and satisfy the many demands made on them. It fails, in short, to give full weight to the socially constructed conditions of student performance.

When faculty begin to see the psychological and the sociological complexity of the teaching–learning endeavor as revealed in talks with students and can survive a sense of being overwhelmed, they typically see a great need to rethink what they are doing in the classroom and how they might affect the institutional environment to help their students to benefit more from the classroom.

The grading system is a familiar obstacle to student learning and development (Milton et al., 1986). Becker and his associates have described the disruption of learning because of the students' preoccupation with grades. A student leader who had very high grades made the following statement (Becker et al., 1968, p. 60): "The grading systems are so cockeyed around here you can't tell what's going on. One guy does it this way and another guy does it that way and, as I say, in a lot of these courses the only thing you can do is get in there and memorize a lot of facts. I've done that myself. I've gone into classes where that's all you could do is memorize . . . memorize and memorize. And then you go in to take the final and you put it all down on the paper, everything you've memorized, and then you forget it. You walk out of the class and your mind is purged. Perfectly clean. There's nothing in it. Someone asks you the next week what you learned in the class and you couldn't tell them anything because you didn't learn anything."

A good description of how a student terrorized by a learning task can still manage a satisfactory external performance likely to elicit good grades is given by Carl Gustav Jung (1965, pp. 27–29):

> The teacher pretended that algebra was a perfectly natural affair, to be taken for granted, whereas I didn't even know what numbers really were. They were not flowers, not animals, not fossils; they were nothing that could be imagined, mere quantities that resulted from counting. . . . Oddly enough, my classmates could handle these things and found them self-evident. No one could tell me what numbers were and I was unable even to formulate the question. To my horror I found that no one understood my difficulty. . . . Equations I could understand only by inserting specific numerical values in place of the letters and verifying the meaning of the operation by actual calculation. As we went on in mathematics I was able to get along, more or less, by copying out algebraic formulas whose meaning I did not understand, and by memorizing where a particular combination of letters had stood on a blackboard. I could no longer make headway by substituting numbers, for from time to time, the teacher would say, 'Here we put the expression so-and-so,' and then he would scribble a few letters on the blackboard. I had no idea where he got them and why he did it. . . . I was so intimidated by my incomprehension that I did not dare to ask any questions. Mathematics classes became sheer terror and torture to me. Other subjects I found easy; and as, thanks to my good visual memory, I contrived for a long while to swindle my way through mathematics, I usually had good marks. But my fear of failure and my sense of smallness in face of the vast world around me created in me not only a dislike but a kind of silent despair which completely ruined school for me.

Jung's expressive statement indicates clearly the fear and anxiety students experience when confronted by a task that is too difficult for them to master. In such circumstances, when they intuitively know that they are up against an impossible learning demand, they may develop ingenious ways of coping and may even be able to earn grades higher than students who have learned and understood more about a given discipline.

A faculty member we worked with was struck by how the OPI, which indicates degree of interest and intrinsic motivation, bore little relationship to academic ability as measured by grades. "I observed students ranging from those with only modest ability excitedly discussing a wide variety of topics to presumably extremely bright students locked into rigid thinking and interests." Another professor working with honors students was intrigued by the fact that so few of them exhibited much genuine interest in learning and ideas or an ability to learn in an independent manner. After administering the OPI and looking at the cognitive profiles of these students, he found that only a few had well-defined intellectual or aesthetic interests, although all had high grade point averages. A third professor wrote: "Grading is always a special problem. One student said that she was fed up with school, but it turned out that what bothered her was getting poor grades for something she had put effort into and thought she had done well with. Objectivity is a problem: the same paper may be graded quite differently at different times or by different instructors. More important is the fact that the grade does measure neither involvement nor progress. Worst of all, it gives a bad mark to something that the students may deeply feel at this point and hence may imply a devaluation of their reasoning or feeling that can only lead to seeking a way out through safe superficiality, for example, definitional thinking."

DEVELOPMENT OF THE TEACHER

Throughout this chapter we have tried to show how faculty have developed their skills as teachers. First, the interviews with students and the use of the OPI (or other inventories) confront faculty with the array of differences among their students and between them and their students. These differences excite interest and inquiry. Acquaintance with various developmental and other theories helps faculty to develop conceptually sophisticated and useful ways of looking at and understanding the differences they are finding. At first, faculty tend to concentrate on the cognitive differences they are discovering, but as their work with students continues, they become aware of the importance of the emotional and motivational aspects of teaching and learning. They see the importance of building relations of trust with and providing social and emotional support to their students in order to further their intellectual growth. The roles of anxiety and risk-taking in learning become critical concerns. Faculty begin to rethink what and how they are teaching. They make diagnoses and test hypotheses. Finally, some faculty begin thinking beyond their classrooms. They have gained a rich and complex sense of their students as members of groups lying beyond the classroom and beyond the boundaries of the educational institution. They see the need for helping their students attain the understanding and competencies which will give them some genuine leverage and enlarged perspective as they engage with people, forces, and pressures in their lives beyond academia. Distance decreases between faculty and the student when professors see their students as implicated in problems connected to the human condition as they themselves are. The students too come to see the faculty as complex, involved human beings. The faculty member as "professor" becomes more fully the faculty member as "teacher."

5

Three Professors Report about Observing Their Teaching and Their Students' Learning

In this chapter three faculty report on their work with us. In chapter 2 we have described our method of affiliating two faculty members with each other: one observes and the other is observed; both interview students, and the OPI is administered to a sample or all students in the class and the two faculty members. At the end of each semester the teacher and the observer write a statement of what they have learned during the semester about student learning and teaching. The following statements are such end-semester reports. We begin with Professor Aaron Carton writing about his experience in teaching a course in linguistics. He introduces his report with an account of his own evolution as a teacher. His statement is followed by a report from Professor Donald Fry, accompanied by the reflections of his observer, Joseph Katz, the coauthor of this book. Finally, there are statements by Professors Lee Miller and Joseph Katz reporting on their work in a philosophy course. These statements have been somewhat edited but largely are rendered here in the way in which they were originally written. The reason for writing these statements was not only to have teacher and observer reflect and articulate what they had learned but also to provide a basis for future classroom activities and to share what was learned with colleagues on campus and at other institutions.

The statements show that the impact on faculty of the procedures we have described in earlier chapters has been a strong and lasting one. Our approach is to engage the faculty member intellectually and to engender an ongoing inquiry of faculty with one another about fundamental and subtle issues of teaching. Our ultimate aim is to have an impact on the institution. To do so, we enlist a large enough number of faculty who we hope will come to adopt the view that teaching is a practice in need of continuing attention and who through reflecting on and studying student learning will contribute to the development of theories about learning and teaching that will give the profession of teaching a conceptual base and lead to continually refreshed practice. If one starts with even a small group of observed faculty in one year and if these in the following year turn into observers of their colleagues, one can soon affect a substantial portion of faculty. An institution may wish to pay special attention to selected groups, such as teachers in their first years of teaching or graduate students. Our method may also lend itself to reclaiming "burned out" faculty though we have not yet tried it ourselves.

The methods we have described in this book are particularly apt instruments for assessing not just individual courses, but curricular programs as well. The teachers themselves and not just outsiders engage in the assessment. It is "formative" assessment, aimed at improving courses and programs while they are in progress. Observations of student learning quickly lead to questions about the curriculum, and these may stimulate collaborative inquiry with colleagues and with students.

What is the impact of our methods upon the students? We held out to the students we interviewed the prospect that not only we would learn from their reports and reflections but that they too would find out many useful things about their own ways of learning, knowledge that was transferable to other courses and other situations. We found that we had not held out false prospects; students sometimes achieved important changes in their ways of learning, such as increased theoretical grasp, active learning rather than more passive ingestion, a more autonomous intellectuality. We found that students' motivation was greatly increased through their collaborative effort with faculty to articulate their ways of learning; this experience at time modified their attitudes to school, their sense of themselves and their future plans. Much work needs to be done and we agree with the external evaluator of our FIPSE project, John Bilorusky, who wrote: "Most of us who have been involved with this project are only beginning to become aware of the depth and extent of its contribution to student learning."

LINGUISTICS 111
*Aaron S. Carton**

My Evolution as a Teacher. Should I not have been involved in something like this some twenty years ago, I asked myself many times during the

* Professor of Linguistics, State University of New York at Stony Brook.

semester. Certainly the thousands of undergraduates who have passed my way would have benefited from the insights and development of new skills that the project stimulated. My warrant to teach had been justified by training and credentials that attested only to my ability to conduct and lead formal empirical research on specific problems in as dispassionate and objective a manner as possible. The jobs I was given involved me with young people, who, at a most critical moment in their lives, wanted and needed guidance and understanding of how the range of human knowledge and art pertained to their lives and their growth.

In my early years as a professor I had encountered fiascos in my teaching. But I might have encountered more had I not had other experiences that did not appear in my credentials. I had worked as a camp counselor and been interested in clinical psychology and even entertained the possibility of becoming a movie director or working in the theatre. A large part of my graduate training was in educational research. While there is little evidence that people with formal training in educational research are more effective teachers than others, I was at least formally prepared for college teaching. In addition, my discipline, the psychology of language, is itself concerned with the basic questions of teaching: communication processes. It was, however, the students in my classes who over the years molded and remolded me into someone who is, I believe, considerably more qualified to teach than was the person who first taught equipped only with a prestigious doctorate. The development did not occur without its faux pas. And it occurred despite the fact that peers and seniors frequently approved of what they heard I was doing in my classes. Eventually I learned to allow recollections of my own youth to resonate with the quandaries of the youth who found themselves in my classes. What use, then, after those years of lonely learning, could the invitation to reconsider my teaching serve? Might not the project do better to involve younger colleagues earlier in their careers? What has a project in college classroom teaching to say to a tenured full professor who had survived the sixties with their emphasis on connecting university knowledge to public and private life, who was surviving retrenchments, and who was, seemingly, proceeding with a modicum of success?

To me the project was the balm of Gilead; nothing less. For, if I read Erik Erikson correctly, the crisis that a full tenured professor of fifty might face originates in the internal conflict between impulses to remain generative, productive, or creative and impulses to stagnate, wither, and dissolve. And however self-determined and private one might wish to be, there is little doubt that external forces can decisively determine the outcome of an internal conflict.

Externally, there is no dearth of forces acting upon today's university that favor stagnation and demoralization. In the semesters of my participation in the project on college teaching, my campus was threatened with retrenchments that, if carried out, would have been the second wave in a space of five years. Locally and nationally, institutes of higher education were suggesting to their personnel that they doubted the value of their work. Much of the nation seemed to be suggesting that it doubted the value of the university. The value and structure of knowledge faced, and will continue to face, a crisis of criticism and restructuring even from within academia itself. Many have doubts about the value of some aspects of knowledge and there are even a few who have doubts about the value of most aspects of knowledge.

So to a professor in his fifties, a personal invitation seriously to reconsider his teaching is an invitation to his internal forces of generativity to take heart. Implied in the invitation was the suggestion that what had been learned in my private experience in years of classroom teaching was worthy of public examination. The invitation suggested that work in one's classroom and one's thoughts about it deserved the attention of the uppermost echelons of the campus; that as an individual the professor in the classroom was worth training and retraining; that there was a belief in the possibility of training him and in the value of what he had already learned. Most importantly the project implied that the students we work with require our serious attention, that there is much that we have to learn about them, and that we have to discover them if we are to teach them. What could be more heartening? What could resonate with one's personal commitments more? To understand even more fully why I should have been enthusiastic about the project we should also consider that a tenured full professor has nothing to lose. His position in the university is secure. By honing his skills in teaching the senior full professor adds to the areas in which he can exercise leadership.

Participating in the Project on Learning and Teaching. Toward the end of the fall semester Joe Katz and I got our project under way by Joe's coming to visit in my classes and by beginning some planning. I remember experiencing some of the same kind of excitement I experienced when I first began to teach. But because it is my habit to spread my commitments widely and because my participation was not an official part of my "load," I found little time for making the running notes and keeping the kind of log and diary I would have wished to keep. I was glad that Joe did take frequent notes during our conversations. The ideas we exchanged always seemed interesting and valuable. And the process most assuredly gratified some of my (forgivable, I hope) narcissistic needs. The effect of our conversations and of the process of notetaking is worth some consideration. In teaching we frequently call attention to ourselves as one of the ways by which we make the process work. But teachers must be wary lest attention to oneself become an end in itself and the degree of attention one obtains become a measure of one's effectiveness. The ultimate measure of teaching effectiveness is the amount of attention paid to that which is to be learned. Thus in teaching we must learn also to surrender the adulation of students as we work — and the presence of a wise companion taking notes about what I had to say about my teaching became an excellent compensation for the surrender in the teaching process.

Joe discussed aspects of teaching that I might be interested in looking at. I bubbled with ideas and questions that I thought might be researchable but we never made plans for systematic observations. Instead, I suppose, those sessions provided Joe with something of my sense of my orientations and objectives. It was reasonable to expect that I would name questions that would index the issues my teaching was concerned with. As I reconsider the themes I proposed I note that my educational objectives were concerned largely with (a) what kinds of habits of thought my course might involve, (b) what significance my course might have in contemporary life, and (c) what kind of personal development I might effect in my students. The fact that I relegated the subject matter per se of the course to an instrumental rather than central status may at least in part be attributable to the degree to which I am imbued with a Deweyan educational philosophy, the degree to which I have been influenced by arguments that universal cognitive processes may be applied to any area, and the degree to which I am seeing the academic disciplines as representative modes of the various possible human approaches to reality. Certain personal factors also affected me. I sit on faculty committees wherein competitors justify the value of their respective academic pursuits to each other. While discussions in such settings may often enough consider the specific value of specific knowledge for specific individuals — and I could make an excellent case for introductory linguistics in such terms — the very fact of our differences and our competition reminds us that education and the university participate in achieving certain general and essential goals and that we are under a collective obligation to identify them. More personally still, I had been awakened to the possible transience of the value of branches of knowledge by my need, some years earlier, to scamper from a retrenched department to a new departmental setting. My interdisciplinary wanderings, both as a student and a professional, had helped me to develop understanding of concepts and, in my research and published scholarship, to apply methods from one branch of study to another. But as those interdisciplinary wanderings enabled me to save my professional career where others found themselves ousted from the academic community, they also reminded me of the fatuousness of excessive disciplinary loyalty. Of course the fact that the study of language is in itself in a state of theoretical turmoil adds to the self-consciousness students of language have about their discipline. The status of my course also led me to justify my educational objectives. For a course in introductory linguistics rarely has been a required course for undergraduates and not typically offered to undergraduates.

An interesting question to raise is about the degree to which there are educational objectives that lie beyond the manifest and purported subject matter that is taught, objectives concerned with the kind of mind, methods of inquiry, and creativity students develop and with the social and ethical characteristic of students. These objectives are a function of the *methods* of instruction that we employ and the character and organization of the institutions in which we conduct education. As far as I can perceive, this question has been "in the air" but not explicitly stated since education began to abandon notions more prevalent earlier in the century that held that there were associations between the nature of mind and the subject matter studied (for example, mathematics develops precision, Latin leads to rigor, etc.). If the notion is correct that "hidden agenda" of education lie in the methods of instruction and the organization of schools, we will have to acknowledge that American colleges and universities have been proceeding largely unconscious of the effects they produce. A professoriate trained almost exclusively to consider subject matter almost necessarily knows little about the educational consequences of selecting one or another method and mode for communicating subject matter.

Once underway, the probe into my teaching was comprised of the following specific activities that were not typical of my teaching routine: (a) Joe Katz visited my classes in Linguistics 111 in the spring semester on a regular basis and observed students there as they responded. After most of these visits we engaged in discussions and reflections concerning what we had observed and what we believed to be the educational implications of the events; (b) at Joe's behest, I conducted some "metasessions" with my class, which concerned themselves with the students' understandings and reactions to my objectives and methods; (c) two instruments were administered in my spring class: the OPI and a one-page homemade scale attempting to ascertain the student's development position as defined by Perry; (d) five students were selected for frequent interviewing on the basis of their responses to the Perry scale — Joe interviewed three and I two; (e) other students were, when some special occasion arose, asked to come for interviews; (f) I provided Joe with xerox copies of the written work of several of my students.

I was surprised by what Joe enabled me to discover both about what I did not know about my management of my classes and about what I did know. Joe proceeded from the positive. He showed me that attentiveness in my classroom was comparatively high. Students seemed interested in most of my lectures and when I evoked their responsiveness, they revealed a certain degree of relatedness to the subject matter and efforts to assimilate the materials both in personal ways as well as in the abstract, formal, and intellectual ways the course ostensibly called for. We attributed this responsiveness to my approach. Often enough my lectures were formal and abstract. Often enough they were built upon anecdotes, personal reactions, and those specific facts and events that exercise students personally and emotionally. Linguistics lends itself to such approaches. The relevant data for study are ubiquitous and readily obtainable. The issues to which linguistic data are brought to bear include the most pressing issues of community, affiliation, rejection and prejudice, the expression of feelings, the expression of personality, the nature of thought and mind. It is a relatively simple matter to begin a class with a question such as the social or public "impression" an individual makes — one can select a teacher, a classmate or a public figure as an example — and turn the discussion into an examination and analysis of the specific elements of linguistic style that seem to be related to such an impression. I find linguistics an arena in which one can examine and contribute to understanding almost any important intellectual issue and I wonder at what we must be doing wrong to keep courses from being much more popular with undergraduates than they are.

The examination of my classroom allowed me to reflect upon the degree of virtuosity and range of skills in classroom management I had acquired over the years. Whether my skills are, from a public point of view, praiseworthy is a question I had received little information about during those years in which I had hammered out some skills in almost total isolation from peers who should perhaps have been more interested. Nor have I had the opportunity to watch enough classes of others to be able to develop some yardsticks by which to make judgments about the quality of my own classroom skills. At last, Joe had led me to identify my skills and begin to make an inventory of the techniques I had at my disposal. I found that I can lecture fairly systematically and organize my lectures with consideration for the structure of my message. I can also establish certain rhythms in my delivery by which I can manage to keep the attention of my students for the better part of a seventy-five-minute class session. I can lead and conduct discussions in an impersonal style and I even seem to be detached and pedantic or I can be extremely, perhaps even invasively, personal. I hope I strike a balance. I can be serious or playful and humorous. I can proceed inductively from examples to principles or deductively from principles to their manifestations as examples. I can use what Ausubel (1968) calls "advance organizers" presenting first a technical term or name or an "empty category" (Roger Brown's term, 1958) and turn it into a concept with meaning. I can develop a concept first and give it a name after I perceive that students understand it. When Joe suggested that I conduct a "metasession" to ascertain how students were receiving the course, I was able to plan a procedure for stimulating a lively and open discussion in the time it took me to walk from my office to the classroom.

I wonder whether Joe noticed how savvy I was in the physical arrangement of my room. That room was long and narrow and had originally been laid out with a podium in front of short rows with the last rows very distant from the front. I changed positions so that the teacher faced wide rows of students and the windows thus providing students with nearness to the teacher and light from their backs. While my first session in that room, in its original arrangement, had been a disaster, the rearrangement provided me with a chance for fairly good eye contact with a large part of the class and made me audible to all. In the original arrangement neither I nor those in front could hear a comment from students in the rear. In the new arrangement I could, if necessary, relay the comments from students on my left to those on my right.

College teachers rarely comment on the physical characteristics of rooms. They seem largely unaware of the mechanics of the communicative process or reticent about making use of them. More generally, outside of faculties of education, it is not usual to hear college teachers speak about their teaching or methods of instruction. I myself had devoted a portion of my career to educational psychology and had analyzed the teaching in many classrooms at precollege levels. As a student of linguistics and communication I knew about kinesics, proxemics, eye contact and a variety of subtle analyses of the mechanics of interpersonal processes. I had once been interested in the dramatic arts and retained an esthetic sensitivity to communicative processes. Yet, given my background, I was selling myself short. I was mobilizing only a fraction of the technical skills I had at my disposal.

A Fresh Look at Student Learning. As Joe shared with me his perceptions of what he observed in my classroom, he touched off streams of free associations and lists of considerations for improvement in an atmosphere that was psychologically undefensive and open. But with all his encouraging and generative positiveness, Joe did not hesitate to stump and perturb me. Thus while I would give myself good marks for my general success with the class and with those students who resonated with my intellectual rhythms and harmonies, Joe would trouble me with puzzlers about individual students. Why did Anne behave so outrageously, leaving and returning, giggling and purposely seeking to distract her companions from paying attention to my stimulating lecture on the history of black English and Yiddish that so well illustrated some general principles of linguistic development and reactions to minority status? Why did Bill so frequently show a surly face, express disgust, nod off in his corner of the room and silently seem to express both a sense of distaste for the class and a sense of shame for himself? When I engaged Anne in individual conversation her friendliness and cheerfulness exceeded my expectations. There was a touch of seductiveness, of eroticism in her manner that led me quickly to realize that Anne wanted from me or the boy next to her a kind of attention I never deemed appropriate to a classroom but which is indeed an integral part of the growth and life of a healthy sophomore. Perhaps my allusions in class to sexual matters — mating rituals among birds and courtship conventions among humans — played a part in touching off Anne's behavior. Yet a short seemingly irrelevant conversation about her plans helped me understand her and sufficed to make Anne to become a participative member of the class.

Joe asked Bill for an interview of an hour's duration. Bill came from a high school in a lower-class neighborhood that had prepared him badly and in college he felt isolated and inferior to the talkative, "aggressive," and successful middle-class students, including female students, such as the one who so frequently received my attention when she spoke in class. Bill thought that what I taught was important, that he could handle the material, and that he was reasonably satisfied with me as a teacher. Bill's difficulty was with the pace of my teaching. I took many twists and turns too frequently and too quickly for him to follow. I went rapidly from one issue to the next and Bill would get lost and nod off into daydreams. Of course I know about the need for pacing and the need to provide moments for incubation of concepts and the need to provide interruptions and respites as one learns. But my pace was typically determined by two other considerations. One was the kind of feedback I got from those students with whom I did maintain eye contact and the second was that I was worried about covering the material. I had lost eye contact with Bill perhaps because our eyes had never met and I certainly had not caught his pace. Joe's report of his interview with Bill alerted me to many other glassy stares that would occur just about fifty minutes after class began. I began to plan to change activities, methods, and topics that would provide for respites but would also make the final twenty-five minutes more productive for a larger proportion of students than I had hitherto been reaching.

I had always felt that as far as possible within the constraints of classroom instruction, I did an excellent job of thinking of my students as individuals and treating them in ways suited to their intellectual and personal needs. My responses to their written work were always addressed specifically to the paper before me. My responses to class comments were always tempered by my perceptions of the student who made them. I suggested topics for research to students based on what I knew of their interests. Often a sentence in a lecture was directed toward a particular student and a particular question he had earlier asked me. Students came to my office frequently, individually or in small groups. I gave students special tutoring help and tips on reading and on study skills. I was frequently asked by students to supervise their independent study courses. After all this, Joe confronted me with Anne and with Bill and subsequently with Marian and John, and it seemed to me that I had been paying just so much lip service to individualization. Yes, I had been sympathetic toward students of diverse backgrounds and tolerant of their varying views. But I had been missing some dimensions in my appreciation of the differences among them and my approaches to them.

It seemed to me on reflection that the students I had "individualized" were the ones whose eyes met mine in class and who appeared voluntarily in my office, the ones whose ambitions stood in some kind of complementary relation to my objectives and whose intellectual styles and interests resonated with mine. With Joe's prodding I found myself doing blind predictions of the OPI profiles of students after I had had a single conversation with them. I amazed myself with the possibilities that lay before me.

The OPI was an instrument that was new to me but once I took it myself and read the manual I found its dimensions coherent with categories that were familiar to me. I was able to predict my own profile with remarkable accuracy and I found I could characterize students in the terms of the instrument as readily as in any other terms and with considerable coherence with their actual test profiles. Over the years, and without formal training, I seem to have acquired a substantial store of accurate intuitions. But I had never used those intuitions to teach better, to predict what individual students would do with specific assignments, to recruit the diverse intelligences of the Bills and Annes before relations deteriorated, to avoid behaving as though students shared my particular brand of political liberalism and pantheistic agnosticism, to avoid behaving as though I assumed their personal ambitions and modes of enjoying life were similar to mine. Despite my commitment to individualization and my rather advanced sensitivity, perceptiveness and appreciation for personal differences, my experience in the project suggests to me that I have but scratched the surface of the possibilities for conducting education in ways that recruit and relate the special characteristics of my students.

The concept of the "metasession," at which students are encouraged, over the period of a class hour or less, to ventilate their perceptions of the objectives and directions of the course, proved so illuminating that I very quickly developed a new habit of consulting with students about their perceptions of specific class sessions. At the first metasession many students seemed to be aware of my objectives, knew where I was going, and appeared interested, while others proved to be bewildered, uninterested, and annoyed. A request to write a short paragraph elicited the same pattern. There were students who expressed pleasure and satisfaction with my teaching style and there were those who were dismayed and annoyed by it. The fact that I use a diversity of methods and styles hindered neither me nor my students from attempting to characterize my teaching as consisting of a single style. It was logical enough to expect that a single teaching style cannot satisfy an entire class because a class is filled with too many and too various minds at different levels of development. Nor can the use of a diversity of styles satisfy everyone all the time. The problem remaining to be solved is how to aim specific methods and styles at those students who would benefit most from each method and style.

Most students during the metasession were candid and did not hesitate to criticize. Such criticism, voiced bluntly and harshly without the observing colleague's supportiveness, may be painful, but a teacher must be ready to set an example of openness if he is to require students to be receptive to *his* evaluations. And without such openness we do not learn. I had comparatively little control over the criticisms students voiced. Some students expressed their displeasure with the "disrespectfulness" some of their classmates had shown in the metasession. So I learned that my campus was not a completely free society and that many students had much to learn about how to be open, about whether to be open, and about the nature of mutual responsibility up and down the echelons of a free social hierarchy.

At one class hour I had placed on the board the words *language, thought, brain,* and *mind* as advanced organizers and a prelude to analyzing Whorf's and Chomsky's views of language and thought and Chomsky's argument for a dualistic approach to the psychology of language. Met by glassy stares, I turned the class into a brief metasession and asked in simple terms who in the class had ever been exercised by the question of the mind as a vehicle for experience against the brain as a location for the physiochemical processes related to that experience. Who had been exercised by the question of the relation of language and thought? It turned out that a question that had burned holes in my mind when I was a student were matters of indifference for my students on that day. But by starting with concrete questions and examples, by developing the theory of linguistic relativity with rather vivid demonstrations and in small, illustrated steps, I was eventually able to engage their interest. But I was not, in the main, addressing them with thoughts about questions they brought with them to college. So the gulf between most of them and me is wider than I had thought. But we do have the resources for teaching them and that's what we will have to do next year and the year after.

Some Years Later

The impetus from the work just described has continued to affect my teaching and has led to continual revisions of how I approach my classes. What follows is about a recent course on language acquisition devoted to three issues: How an infant acquires a native language; how subsequent languages are acquired; and what research has to say about foreign language education. I have developed something of an internalized "metateacher" with which I observe myself and keep track of what I am learning. My teaching still has its rough edges. The feeling that I am teaching as I ought to be teaching occurs only occasionally. The sensation that I am making progress toward improving my teaching is persistently present and most welcome. Here are two episodes from my recent course.

Correcting the Misuse of a Film. It was a film in which leading researchers on child language acquisition who were (or would be) mentioned in class or the readings illustrated their research on children in their laboratories. The dimmed illumination in the classroom and the opening titles became immediately a cue to the students for chatting among neighbors or glassy stares at the screen. I should have known better than to expect a warm interest in a prepackaged audio visual aid because I could have recalled how, in the army, we greeted films with a sense of anguished boredom mixed with a pleasant welcome for the opportunity for a snooze. I sought to salvage the fiasco by going to a chalkboard and writing the name of each new researcher mentioned or a phase for each new concept as it was alluded to. I imagined that I was highlighting the significant content elements of the program, providing students with correct spellings, and hinting that the contents of the film consisted of academically valid materials for which they "might be held responsible" at some future juncture.

Before the next class session, I reflected about my students' inattention and upon what might distinguish film materials from other modes of teaching. Are there, for example, possible differences in our attention and recollection mechanisms as we encounter stimuli that we can examine and scan voluntarily as opposed to those, like flying objects or movies which we must "track" because they pass us by at their own rates? Although I was only partially informed by some of the research on such issues, I undertook a metasession with my class to enhance my understanding and theirs of what was at stake. They, after all, are of the television generation, which needs to understand what cannot be learned from visual communication. When I asked the students to write down some of the names and concepts they had encountered or to jot down anything they remembered, I got sheepish shrugs for responses. Only a few were able to remember anything but a few of the names and "facts," and these were names and concepts that had already been treated in the course. They had not paid attention. They did not know or understand exactly what the tape dealt with. They were totally unaware that the depicted researchers did not all agree among themselves. They did not remember anything they could put down on paper. Had they unconsciously and inexorably evoked a mechanism for ignoring what was on the screen, a mechanism that they may have developed in their years of doing schoolwork in the presence of turned-on television sets in their homes? Possibly. As far as having stimulated them to learn anything goes, the film seemed a total fiasco. Yet they had "enjoyed it" and agreed readily to view it again and to look at it more attentively.

In the week or so before my getting around to showing the film again, many students got started on their assignment to prepare a report on their own observations of an infant in the process of language acquisition, and at least some of them read their texts. I started by showing a small segment of the film and interrupted it to comment and ask for reactions. I went on to another segment and noted a disagreement between two researchers. Which one took the more plausible position? The question not only elicited a modicum of debate but also reports from observations made in the context of their assignments. Soon the film assumed the status of a text for our analysis and criticism. Partly on my initiative and partly in response to students' requests and observations, we switched the film back and forth, compared statements, noticed new elements in the behavior of the depicted infants, ferreted out contradictions, proposed counterexperiments, and agreed to study further in this manner by asking some students to bring to class the audiotapes of infants they were observing for their reports. This analysis of the film continued for over four sessions. In the process some of these undergraduates began to behave as though they were colleagues and competitors of the noted authorities of their texts and film. They began to evaluate the appropriateness of data, dispute the validity of observations, and explore alternate formulations. The names of researchers and the catchwords for the theoretical concepts of the area became second nature to them.

However satisfactory as an experience in the evolution of a college teacher and as an educational experience for my students, the episode leaves many unanswered questions about the nature of teaching and about the use of ancillary devices and materials. What would have occurred had I been more savvy about the limitations of prepackaged videotapes? There is a considerable body of research literature on the use of films, programmed instruction, and computers. There also is some lore about the use of such materials that university faculty sometimes share if they consult with each other, but few of us in higher education have been required to give the matter any systematic thought. Had it not been my custom to arrange for film viewings on days when I had to miss classes, I might have learned about the nature and limits of the effectiveness of films considerably earlier.

The very existence of films raises questions of what constitutes the knowledge encompassed by a college course. What of demonstrations and images that are not readily coded into words? Might not some of the reluctance of my students to attend to the film be attributed to their anticipation that they would have difficulties in turning the experiences of what they saw into the kinds of sentences which count as academic knowledge? By stopping the film at different points and conversing about the segments, I may have opened for them the possibility for overcoming such difficulties. Before this experience I had relied directly on the evidential nature of the visual medium. Now I had found out something about how to make the medium, through appropriate intervention, more useful for student learning. I had helped them to "see" and to become articulate in translating from one medium to the other. Beyond that some intriguing questions about the epistemological peculiarities of verbal and nonverbal experience have opened up for me. One cannot reflect upon one's classroom very long without being stimulated to a fresh intellectual endeavor, often of great theoretical impact, as in the present case.

Daily Concepts and Formal Concepts. The news of the day was about the scandal-dashed chances of the front-running presidential hopeful. Even my otherwise politically apathetic students were exercised enough to be chatting about the story when I arrived in class. So I listened and eventually made an observation about how the television camera had focused upon the hands of the candidate's wife as she spoke during an interview. What did those tense hand gestures betray? What did they communicate? What perceptions and messages were intentionally or in-advertently communicated by the person who prepared that tape? Soon my class discussion was about nonverbal communication; how kinesics differs from and resembles speech; instances in which manual gestures support speech and in which they belie spoken messages and how they proceed with a lawfulness or grammar that resembles the grammar of speech; how the absence of conscious control in kinesics runs parallel to the nature of speech and how it can be brought under conscious control by professional orators, actors, or scholars of kinesics; how the research on kinesics has alerted students of child language to what might be going on when infants produce "telegraphic utterances" or one-word sentences.

Like a kid who has discovered he's just taken candy-coated medicine, a student named Tom chided me with the friendly banter that indexes the easy rapport I had been able to establish with this class. "We thought you would get around to something like that." (Had they been doing an analysis of the teacher? Students usually do.) But now they had opened my way to yet another one of my objectives and I launched into a metasession. What happens when I start with what you are thinking about and coax it into something I want you to consider? Can you help yourself to become more interested in an assignment you find no motivation for by exploring and analyzing how it may be dealing with something in the world of your experience? Then I went on to some harder issues and tried to make the case for scholarship: What are the differences between the casual observa-tion of the commonplace — noticing how a woman wrings her hands — and a systematic analysis that defines a category of events and establishes a set of relationships? What do we gain when we learn to look at the animals of the world as elements in an evolutionary scheme, the objects before us as manifestations of molecular structures, the words we utter as elements in syntactic chains — and what do we lose?

"But," Nancy all but whined, "why does it always have to be made to seem so unreal, so unrelated in books, journals, and lectures?" That pinched a bit and an internal voice — my metateacher — told me that the cliché says that if a shoe fits, you should wear it. My credibility with the class requires me to acknowledge that there are occasions on which pro-fessorial language may be as obfuscating as systematic scholarship can be informative; that I know how hard it is to find the middle ground between the informativeness of disinterested systematic thinking and the decep-tiveness of uninteresting formalities. Sometimes, in our efforts to estab-lish and keep to the rules of scientific communication, we get lost in those rules and lose the essence of our inquiries. Thus those who listen to or read scientific communications sometimes face the task of separating essence from formalities. None of these concerns, however, outweighs the advantages of appropriately applied scientific conceptualization.

My metateacher remembers that L. S. Vygotsky (1987) establishes a clear distinction between "everyday concepts" and "scientific concepts."

In his studies with schoolchildren he found that concepts that were learned were usually established as formal or scientific concepts and could be handled as such even by pupils in the second grade, but that on tests requiring them to deal with causality or other kinds of relations, the pupils resisted treating everyday concepts with the logicality associated with scientific ones. Now at the college level I was trying to sharpen the distinction between everyday, intuitive, "folk" thinking and systematic scientific thinking by bringing the latter type of thinking to bear upon concepts that are typical of everyday talk. Certainly my students were not struggling with the problem of logicality that the second-graders encountered, but it occurred to me that possibly in my effort to breathe life into the scientific conceptualization by bringing it to bear upon commonplace events I might also be bringing some of the aridity and emotional neutrality associated with objectivity and formal science to events that were otherwise emotionally charged. Emotional sterilization and complexity can be off-putting, and that reaction may have lain at the basis of Nancy's complaint. As this is an issue I may expect to encounter again and again, I need to be prepared with teaching strategies that will clarify the trade-offs, intellectual advantages, and potentials to be gained in evolving scientific concepts. It would be helpful to be able to find ways for minimizing the unattractiveness that may accompany the occasional surrender of certain treasured everyday concepts. We should expect that such considerations are related to the specific intellectual and emotional predilections of each student (as these might be reflected by their OPI profiles), and sensitive tailoring of strategies to individual needs may be called for.

Structuring Thinking for and by Students. Reflections such as these have led me to change my ways of conducting courses. These days I do not work very much from the conventional kind of course schedule, which contains week-by-week outlines, assignments, and lecture topics. I acknowledge that the requirement of my university to provide students with an outline and a statement of requirements and objectives is appropriate to establishing a fair and somewhat stable and "appeal-proof" arrangement, but I regard these documents more as proposals and bases for renegotiation than as the kind of legal documents they seem to be becoming in our ever more bureaucratized and legalistic institutions. If a teacher hopes to be a contributor to the student's maturation, that teacher must be prepared to renegotiate objectives as the course progresses.

My course outlines, therefore, assume a somewhat general aspect. The texts that describe or comprise the subject matter of the course are listed with instructions saying that students may be expected to be knowledgeable about their contents before the end of the semester or before the end of a segment of the course devoted to a specific issue. Nothing is said about when to read which pages and I am not at all troubled to learn that some students use some of these texts only for reference. (Not many texts available to the college market can survive the requirement of adequacy as reference works.) I may, depending on the course, also provide lists of concepts, technical terms, and catchphrases for major ideas, urging students to check them off as they come to understand them from readings, lectures, or exercises as I also check them off after dealing with them in class and again after discerning from exams, discussions, and papers that students seem to have grasped those concepts. Proceeding thus from an inventory of concepts, I find that I can manage to meet my obligations to students and colleagues in the programs I participate in. I can provide the technical information the students will need in other courses or are believed to need as part of their education and training, while I can also proceed opportunely following students' interests and inclinations or seizing upon occasions that might stimulate interest in one or another issue. I have provided an example of the use of that kind of strategy in the preceding section.

What of the systematically organized, carefully sculptured and organized lecture? Have I given up on this as a method of teaching? Not at all. I reserve those lectures for occasions when the subject matter calls for them and students seem ready to benefit from them. It is the case, after all, that I ask and hope to receive from students papers, essays, and presentations that are well organized, that bespeak an understanding of which concepts are subsumed under which superordinate concepts and what the relations among the elements of a system might be. I urge them to use forms of presentation that are clear, rhetorically persuasive, and appropriate to their subject matter. Such work must be the product of rather protracted efforts, of trials and errors in identifying component elements and repeated efforts at assigning them to their proper places in a system. If I require such work, I am obligated to provide examples. They are to be found in assigned readings and in my presenting a systematic lecture. Such lectures may be appropriate, for example, early in the course or at the beginning of a segment when a general overview is called for, when a "top-down" mapping of the domain is in order and students need a definition of the domain they are about to enter. After a period of examining disconnected concepts, there may be a need for organizing them into a systematic structure. But in such instances, it is probably preferable to require students themselves to attempt the systematic formulation.

Sometimes there is material in the literature I assign that has not been systematically organized, and, if I should be able to perceive and formulate a structure, I do not hesitate to share it with my students. The formulation of courses nowadays may be motivated by the emergence of new bodies of literature in which concepts are but vaguely interrelated or by considerations for vocational objectives that put certain concepts together because they are associated with certain activities and not because there are any intrinsic intellectually motivated relations among them. Thus one encounters many residual concepts that call for treatment in class or through texts or through experiences but which may best be left, at least temporarily, in the minds of both students and teachers, unconnected and unrelated. While students may ask for clearly delineated structures, it seems to me appropriate first to acknowledge honestly the instances when we cannot supply such formulations. Even when we can, it seems to me to be most important to return to my students some of the responsibility for formulating the structures they ask for, to educate them by challenging them to do as much structuring as they can be challenged to do.

ENGLISH 238
Donald Fry*

The Nature of the Course. I was very pleased to take part in the teaching project because I had been an administrator for three years and was in transition back toward full-time teaching and scholarship. I was still acting provost for Humanities and Fine Arts, and against my better judgment I was also teaching full-time, including a graduate *Beowulf* course. I was badly overloaded, and I do not think that I taught either course very well. I simply did not have the time necessary to teach either one.

English 238 at Stony Brook is the introduction to English literature, beginning with *Caedmon's Hymn,* which is dated in the seventh century, and ending with some of the prose writers of the seventeenth century. It is a very fast survey, covering a lot of ground; about half the students in it are English majors, for whom it is a required course, and about half are majors in something else; some of these are trying to fulfill the humanities requirement. I had never taught this course in my whole career of eleven years. I had always wanted to teach it, but somehow as a graduate medievalist I never got around to it. I had asked the chairman this year if I could teach it, even though it would be an overload. He advised against it, but I taught it nevertheless.

I spent most of the semester just scrambling to get that course prepared. I had not read any of the material *after* the medieval period, that is, after Malory, since studying for orals in graduate school in 1964. One of the reasons I wanted to teach the course was to refresh my own knowledge of the first half of English literature. During the medieval period, I could coast. But the latter two-thirds of the course required material I had not read in a long time and secondary material that I had not read at all. I saw it as catching up, getting up to date on some of the latest thinking on some of the texts I was teaching. The mechanics of the course were fairly simple. Students read short assignments but a lot of them, and I made them short because I wanted the students to read them carefully. Some students, we

---

* Associate director, the Poynter Institute for Media Studies, Saint Petersburg, Florida. Formerly professor of English and Comparative Literature, State University of New York at Stony Brook. (The present report was written at the latter institution.)

discovered, read them two and three times in preparation for class, and immediately after class. The course required three papers.

Project Activities. The team project with Professor Katz consisted of meeting with six students whom we chose on the basis of Omnibus Personality Inventory (OPI) profiles. We were trying to select students who showed extremes on several categories. In particular, we chose two students each who were high, intermediate, and low in the "Humanities" dimension. (This humanities profile consists of high scores on scales measuring reflectiveness, estheticism, complexity of thinking, and tolerance of ambiguity, against somewhat lower scores on a scale measuring theoretical orientation or scientific thinking.) We began with the list of students we could choose who would show extremes on the scales. I don't think the list really worked out to give us the extreme students, although I haven't checked that idea against their OPIs. Professor Katz took three of the students, and I took three. He met with his one hour a week, and I met with mine a half hour to forty-five minutes every week or every two weeks. I was quite overwhelmed by all this; I really didn't have time to do it. But I met with them when I could. My talks with the students were generally tied to the events of the week's classes. In some cases I met with them the afternoon after a class. Some issues carried over into series of discussions. But mostly I was introducing a new topic each time.

Professor Katz and I would meet for lunch every two weeks and discuss what we had found out. And we also discussed in some detail the nature of the field of English, the nature of literary studies, the nature of literary scholars and scholarship. We discussed problems I was having in teaching the course, and we also discussed Professor Katz's own reactions. He attended classes about once a week, and sat in the front row and pretended to himself that he was a student. He made an effort to observe the class and to observe me and also to gauge his own reactions. We had one very amusing moment which he spoke of during lunch, in which he confessed that he was afraid in class, quite apprehensive in fact, that I would call on him and that he would not know the answer, and that this possibility brought up all his old fears from his days of being a student. I then pointed out to him that I didn't call on any student who did not raise his or her hand for recognition, and he had to confess that he had never noticed that procedure in his anxiety. I don't know whether he relaxed after that or not.

What I Learned. I learned a great deal from this experience, and I learned it in several ways. I learned it from talking to the students. I had never really sat down with students and asked them close questions about what was going on. Secondly, I learned a great deal from Joe Katz's observations. He was a very expert observer, in my opinion, not very experienced in the way the minds of literary professors work, but very acute in observing teaching technique and classroom dynamics. And the third thing I learned was from observing myself. Having a group of students who are observing you closely and who are being questioned about their observations, and having an expert psychologist sitting in your class tends to make one very self-conscious about technique, impact, and so forth. And as a result, I have never been so self-conscious in front of a class. I might add that I would have been self-conscious anyway because I was teaching a course I had never taught before. I was teaching a large undergraduate lecture course of about seventy students, which I had not done in three or four years, and I was also teaching outside of my field. So I would have been very self-conscious even if Joe had not been there, but probably more self-conscious about the material than about my delivery. It was a very rewarding experience in terms of raising my own awareness, and I think once those antennas have been tuned up they're going to stay that way.

One interesting side reaction was that the awareness of teaching lapped over into my other course, the graduate *Beowulf* course. And it made me extremely self-conscious in teaching that one too. Although it was the least talented, worst prepared, and most poorly motivated group I've ever had in that *Beowulf* course, which I've taught a number of times, I think I learned more about my teaching of it than I had before, simply because of this raised consciousness.

Let me talk a little bit about the interaction with the three undergraduate students I interviewed. None of them had particularly high abilities. They were B and C students. One of them proved to have extraordinary memory. But I don't think that they had any particular excellence in academic ways, or even in literary interest. They were just ordinary students. And that is an advantage. Stony Brook students don't as a rule come to office hours, but generally the people who do come are either having trouble or they are extremely bright and interested and motivated students who come and talk about the material and about academic careers, particularly literary careers. The poor students have a tendency to come before the papers are due; and before midterms and finals or afterwards, they come in to complain about grades and weep about them, and so forth. But here we had an unusual situation. We had students who would come and sit for a specified length of time, and none of them was having any problems. Some of Joe's students had personal problems, but mine I think were pretty bland.

It is a valuable experience to sit and talk about teaching to ordinary students. I would ask them questions such as "How do you take notes?" and they would tell me, and I would have them read me their notes. Then I would ask them questions about what the notes are for, what the notes record, and what they think they're going to do with them. I noticed that after the midterm, all three students decided that their notetaking was not gaining the results they expected, and therefore they turned to a different style of notetaking. Most of them had been taking pretty factual notes for the first half of the course, and then they decided that the midterm wasn't a factual midterm, that I was really interested in judgment. And that was not recordable; it was something that went on in their heads. So they all changed their notetaking style.

One woman among my three interviewees was directing herself toward a career in high school teaching, and she tended to ask me questions about teaching for her own interest, not just from my point of view. I always ended the sessions by asking the students if they had any questions that they wanted to ask me, and one of them was struck by the technique I used for analyzing poetry in which I would zoom in on a very small passage, analyze it in great detail, and then make general statements from it. He wanted to know why I did it that way, and I told him (in a rather long and pompous answer) that there are different styles of mind and different styles of approaching text, and there are different styles of thinking and teaching among literary professors. Some come at things from very large questions and stay at that level, and some come from very large questions and go down to details. But my own way of thinking in literature, and indeed in everything else, is to start with detail, to find the really telling passage, the really telling part of something, which I can then use to generalize up to larger issues, and so on. And that is largely the technique that I use both in class and in my scholarship.

The students I interviewed were very honest in the things they told me. We made an effort to see that they were relaxed. I had my three interviewees meet as a group the first couple of times so they wouldn't be frightened by this little one-to-one conversation with a professor, which is such a rare thing at Stony Brook. I managed to convince them that the grading in the course would have absolutely nothing to do with their participation in this project, either for good or for ill. And I think they believed that. And as a result I think they were simply less guarded than they might have been, and I did not fish for compliments, as I might have. I tried to keep things on a fairly objective level.

In my luncheon meetings with Joe Katz I had some very interesting reactions. I was very self-conscious, and I was watching myself. One of the things that struck me was how deeply involved my ego was with my teaching, and to a certain extent how much I wanted him to think well of my teaching and of me. I was very worried in class about this particular aspect. Joe of course doesn't know the subject of English literature, and I must say I was gratified by some of his reactions to things. He said at one point that I had made him very aware of words individually, and that in reading the *New York Times* he had been struck, as a result of the kind of heightened awareness in my class, by how much the news stories are actually wielding of slogans and tags. I was very gratified by that. But I was worried throughout the course about his reactions, and I was worried that I was not putting on a good course for the students. I'm very touchy about criticism. I welcome it, I ask for it all the time, I tend to put out questionnaires for my classes asking for their help, I ask my graduate students to report errors they find in my books, and that sort of thing, and I generally act on criticism. But of course I don't want anybody to have any. I want everybody to think that my teaching is just terrific and that I am the best, a perfectly natural reaction. But I must say that I have this need to an extreme degree, that I want to be the very best at whatever I do, particularly at teaching and scholarship. But I want to do it without any effort showing.

This led to some very interesting conversations at lunch. For instance, very early in the course I wrote an Anglo-Saxon word on the board, and as I started to talk about it, I realized I had misspelled it. Now none of the 60 people in that room could read Anglo-Saxon. Not a single one of them could know that I had misspelled that word. Even if they wrote it down, none of them would ever check it later to see. But *I* knew it was misspelled. Now the question was: was I going to admit that I had misspelled the word in front of the class and correct it on the spot? What would have been their reaction? Well, one reaction might have been, this being very early in the course, that this guy doesn't know what he's talking about. The students knew I was a specialist in Anglo-Saxon, and here I am misspelling words on the board. So I felt it might undercut my authority with the group if I were to admit to such a mistake very early in the course. On the other hand, it has always been part of my teaching technique to admit the things I don't know, and if I make a mistake in interpretation or something like that, to admit it and say, "Well nobody's perfect." All professors use little devices to cover up their gaps in knowledge. A student asks a question you can't answer, and you say, "Well, why don't you write a paper on that?" or "Why don't you go over to the library and look that up and give us a report on it?" or something like that. It's an old trick. But there I was with a misspelled word on the board, and only I knew it was misspelled, and only I would *ever* know it was misspelled. Well, my relation with Joe was such that after class I could admit it to him, but in class I didn't correct it. I decided I really didn't have my personality well established for the group, that I should not undermine my authority by correcting the word. [N. B. Rereading this passage in 1987, I regret that decision. Professors, like journalists, are in the truth business.]

The image I portrayed to this class was very important to me and indeed to the students we talked to. I tend to be a very formal dresser, not because I'm an administrator, but because I just tend to be a formal, put-together person. And a number of the students remarked that they were put off by my mode of dress. They found it a little too elegant, and they didn't expect friendly demeanor from such a person. They expected me to be fairly stiff, which I think I'm not. Most of them changed their opinions as they went on through the course, but in the rag-and-tatter faculty at Stony Brook, a person who wears three-piece suits to teach a sophomore class is going to stand out as an oddity. Nevertheless I think by my humor and later by admitting errors and so forth, I was able to come across with fairly good rapport with students in the group even though the group was quite large. Sometimes I had the feeling that Joe was not in this project to study the class at all. Sometimes I thought he was doing this project with me to study *me*. I know that sounds egocentric, but Joe did ask a lot of questions about the way literary minds work and the way literary scholars work and so forth. And I just had the suspicion now and then that the project was to study me as much as it was to study the students.

Teaching Style. We developed a number of issues that I found important. Joe was very good on one issue that was bothering me quite a bit: the relation of discussion to lecturing. This was a very quiet class, partly because it was a very large class, and partly because of the cast of characters. There were about five or six people you could count on to talk, and toward the end of the course, there were about ten of them. But the fact that the class wouldn't pipe up and talk really bothered me a lot. Generally my courses, even the larger ones, are conducted strictly as discussion. I don't like to lecture. I can do it and do it quite well, but by and large I prefer the discussion mode. I would ask questions, and I don't think they were bad ones. I would ask questions designed to elicit answers and discussion, and hope then to play one student's answer off against another. "What do you think of that," and so forth. But we never really got to that stage. Another factor that complicated all of this was the pressure of time. It is much easier in a course like this to lecture, simply as a matter of retaining complete control over the rhythm of the thing that's going to be discussed and what's going to be asked and so forth. And as a result a lecture takes much, much less time to prepare. So occasionally when I was somewhat pressed for time in preparing a particular section (and I'm sorry to confess that that was a great deal of the time), I would just lecture in the interest of time. At the very beginning of the course I had a great deal of terminology and certain notions to get across, and I tended to lecture to get through those. Perhaps the early sessions of the class set the tone that this was to be a lecture course, and the students subsided into that mode. It was something that bothered me considerably.

To me teaching is not a matter of conveying information so much as it is a matter of teaching modes of judgment. My way of teaching students a mode of thought is to think aloud in front of them. I can then examine for them the limitations of such thinking and spell them out, and I can spell out the advantages of it, and to a certain extent in discussion I can test the things I'm saying. Mainly what I'm trying to teach is a way of asking questions about a text and a way of formulating answers about a text. Asking questions about literary texts is also very good training for asking questions about everyday life, why the characters do what they do, what are their motives, and what could this teach us about how to understand our own lives. We understand a great deal of what we understand about other people from what they say, and I've always felt that literature is excellent training for dealing with everyday life. Literary training is basically a matter of teaching people to think and write and talk, and those are the basic skills of organizations and executives and leaders everywhere. So I tend to teach from my own experience; I tend to teach what I'm interested in. The characters are not marks on a page. They are real people, in real situations, even though they are imaginary. And there's a great deal to be learned by generalizing from their experience, their reactions, and their motives. *Beowulf* is just as relevant as anything written today and perhaps even more so, in terms of understanding why human organizations do not work. I am intensely interested in organization. It's part of why I'm a university administrator. I like to look at things from the inside, and I like to fiddle with organizations, try to make them work better. I spent part of a class on *King Lear* talking about administrative errors made by the characters.

I want always to teach extremely well, and when I try to lead a discussion class and it doesn't come off, I find myself battering my own personality, trying to figure out what's wrong, and it never really occurs to me to blame it on the students. When I tried these questions on Joe and on my students and indeed on the students he interviewed, they all said that the students had their part in it. It was just that they tended to prefer to listen to me talk, rather than to talk themselves. We had a few characters who did like to talk. One student, for instance, was a very good and frequent contributor. I found her an interesting case in her style of contributing in class. She would start off with a challenging and aggressive but somewhat vague statement. I would either play somebody off against her, or I would give her an answer to it. Her reaction would be to restate what she said the first time but in a sharper form, a clearer form, sometimes in a little more detail. I could then play somebody else off against her or even digress onto another subject or answer it myself, and she would usually come back a third time. She would always say the same thing, but she tended to sharpen her answers up. She got a little better at this as the term went on. She became a little more confident with her answers. But all through the semester, even at the very end, when I should have known better, I was still suffering from this thing: What was I doing wrong that was preventing discussion in this class? It nagged me and made me even more self-conscious than I was, and I found myself muttering to myself as I walked the dog in the morning about what I was doing wrong, should I try this, should I try that, and so forth. And this problem proved to be a main topic Joe and I discussed in our lunches.

Uses of the OPI. I'd like to comment on the use of the OPI. The OPI, I think, is a very believable instrument. I don't find it believable just because Joe says it is, but also because I took it myself, and it told me pretty much my own self-image. I remember that Joe questioned one item on it and said that it did not reflect his picture of me, and I explained that in fact that was the way I was. So I found it very accurate. And I don't know what predictive value it has, but it certainly squared with my observations of the three students I worked closely with. It is interesting to use the OPI in a literary course, getting some sense of what the students are like, what their tastes and styles are. We discovered that my class was on the average pretty much like me in terms of personality profile. So we were fairly well suited for each other. I could imagine a class where that's not true at all. And I could imagine an instructor changing his teaching style in order to fit what the OPI says about the students. Being a literary person I think particularly about the scale that indicates tolerance of ambiguity. The students I had were shown to be very tolerant of ambiguity, and it just happens that irony and ambiguity are very much part and parcel of my style. I don't give the students answers. I tend to pose questions, and then I'll spin out about three or four answers, and I'll tell them the bases for forming an answer and also for forming a question, and then let them make up their own minds. This process proves exasperating to beginning graduate students who want to be told what to think, but this particular group of undergraduates, and indeed all the undergraduates I've had at Stony Brook, reacted very well to this open-ended, there-is-no-proof sort of approach.

The difficulty with the OPI as a teaching device is that so few people can possibly be equipped to interpret it properly, and even if they had it interpreted for them, I'm not so sure that they would be able to trim their teaching styles and demands in any sophisticated way toward what it would reveal about the students. I think *I* could do it, but I'm not so sure that others could do it. In the case of the ambiguity index, for instance, it would be possible in a class that did not have a tolerance for ambiguity to devote yourself to lecturing, largely on a factual basis, and you could weigh out different answers to a question and then tell them what the best one was. I think the students would accept that mode. But wouldn't it be better to think of ways that would allow the students to understand and accept ambiguity? [Joseph Katz: "I agree that it would be better."]

Another problem with the OPI has to do with the way literary professors tend to react to social science instruments. They regard them as an invention of the devil, an invasion of privacy, and a reduction of very complex human reactions and attitudes to numbers, to marks on a scale — which is very much foreign to humanistic thinking, at least we would tell ourselves so. I must admit that I was a little bit worried about the tone that might be set by administering a social science instrument at the very beginning of the course. The problem would turn around the students' feelings toward the instructor and toward the observer. They would perhaps feel that they were being examined, and I was afraid that that feeling would distract their attention somewhat. In practice I don't think that happened. The students were very good about it. They were told that the OPI was voluntary, and I don't think anybody refused to do it. When we gave a retake, I don't think any of those students refused to do it. At the end of the course when we had one session of the class devoted to a report by Joe and me on what we had discovered, the attendance was high, about 80 percent of normal attendance, and the students asked very intelligent questions. All this leads me to think that my worries about the OPI's effect on the students probably did not come true.

Assessing the Course and the Project. In the end I didn't have time to make up my own questionnaire about the course. I had wanted to ask them what they liked best and why and so forth. I think these students like literature and understand it better as a result of this particular class. I do not think that I taught it nearly as well as I could have taught it, but I taught it at a level at which I would say I got to at least 80 percent of the students, and in general it was a success. If I had not been so badly overloaded, I could have prepared those texts better and given much more coherent classes, and I think ultimately I could have converted the students over to largely a discussion group despite the size of the class. I've had a lot of remorse about this failure, even though I know I was overloaded. There were classes that I reviewed with Joe that he felt went very well, and everything in them was very put together. I would have to say to him later that in fact 40 percent or 60 percent of it had been done extemporaneously. One of the ironies of our discussion was that the parts the students liked best and the parts Joe liked best tended to be the same, and they tended to be the parts I extemporized. I remember well one session in which I gave about a twenty-minute digression on the necessity for authors to find their own voice, the particular voice in which they are going to address their audiences. And since voice is part of meaning, it's really a matter of discovering one's own meaning, one's own style of writing. This is done to a certain extent by imitation of other authors, and it's done to a certain extent by rejection of other authors' styles—and it's done to a certain extent by experimentation. This digression proved to be a very influential part for the students. Several of them talked to me about it later in terms of their own writing careers. Joe talked about it on several occasions. It was completely extemporized.

At no point in the course did I, because of pressures of time, not prepare a complete class before coming in so that I had to depend entirely on extemporizing. And at no point in any class did I find myself without enough material for the fifty-minute session. In fact it was the other way around. I usually had seventy-five minutes worth of material for the fifty-minute class. But I've always tried to keep an eye on the clock and to have each class end with a real sense of an ending, a real sense of heading toward something, a kind of summing up, maybe a little upbeat touch at the end. About two minutes from the end, I usually asked if the students had any questions. And some did, but most of the time they didn't. But even that is a kind of closure. Joe said (and I was very pleased about this) that he didn't notice the stitches in putting together parts of classes. He also said that everything seemed to have a beginning, a middle, and an end, and he said he could not really tell when I was extemporizing. I tend to extemporize in classes that I have had *more* time to prepare, and some of my very best things in my own scholarship and writing in fact have come about as a result of extemporized parts of classes. I have been talking to our dean of Continuing Education about the possibility of videotaping courses for TV, and in the light of that discussion I have been thinking about the problem of interacting with the group. For a videotaped class you would want a script. You would want to write out everything you are going to say, and even though you might deliver it with an audience present just for reaction, you would not want to extemporize. I fear that that script would take away my spontaneity, and some of the best stuff just simply would not get in there.

I think the work that Joe and I have done would be helpful to every *good* teacher, to have this sort of exposure to everyday students in discussing what they're doing and to have a peer observer with whom to compare reactions. I also think it might have impact on people who are having trouble with teaching. I would like to summarize some notions about what makes it work. First, the students must be made to feel comfortable and not threatened by the process, and this includes the class as a whole. They must not have the idea that they are under constant scrutiny. The students who are selected to be individually talked to must understand clearly that what they do or say in private sessions has nothing to do with the grading, that it is a service to the instructor and likely to be useful to them. I would suggest that there should be some earlier recording of reactions. I find as I record this tape that I have forgotten a great deal of what Joe and I talked about and I have forgotten a great deal of what I thought about the interactions with my three students. I think it would be very useful to do exactly what I'm doing right now, to debrief into a tape recorder and have it typed later. That way we would have some fresh reactions, and we could put them together later. I have learned a great deal from this project, and I don't think it is over yet.

ENGLISH 238

Joseph Katz

I began my collaboration with Professor Fry intending to concentrate on the cognitive aspects of student learning. As it turned out, the emotional components loomed equally large. But my own ways of looking at things may have been a factor. It is clear that English 238 presented the students with learning tasks that, at least for two of my three interviewees, went beyond what had been asked of them in the past. They were asked to look at poems and other literary works with finer attention to detail and with greater accuracy of determining what is actually there. In addition they were asked to consider the historical contexts of the writings and to interpret each work in the light of its context. My three student interviewees, whom I saw once a week, were able to meet these challenges. The steps to their success included thorough reading and rereading of the texts, as well as exercises in interpretation of their own and rereading and reworking of their class notes. They said at the end of the course that their greater accuracy in reading was one of the achievements of the semester.

In considering the achievements of the students, it must be borne in mind that Don Fry's manner was elicitive and supportive. Students' comments in class were treated for their positive worth and used as a basis for further exploration. Never in my presence was a student put down and told in one fashion or another that he or she was "wrong." This means to me that implicitly the student's level of cognitive achievement was recognized, not demeaned, and was used as a base from which the student could go forward. The students' base, however, seemed to me a limited one. Their thinking seemed to be still caught up in a relatively literal concreteness. For instance, they saw such concepts as that of "Satan" as persons or forces rather than as symbolic representations of aspects of human reality or fantasy. This literalness expressed itself in more or less plodding descriptions of the contents of a poem and often rather thin interpretations. I was also struck by the moralism that characterized many of the students' interpretations. Far from conveying insights into human beings or their feelings, they seemed to offer derivatives of personal fears or judgmental pronouncements. Here is one area where the cognitive and the affective join. It is hard to see how students could arrive at better interpretations without a psychological "loosening." I also wonder what sort of literary interpretations students would make in a less supportive classroom. It is less of a surprise to me now that students panic when their own psychological rigidities meet with a dogmatic or demanding and unsympathetic teacher.

One of the themes that seemed to characterize English 238 was that of "finding one's own voice." It came up in the context of interpreting one of John Donne's poems. But it also shone through in the teacher's manner of interpretation. Poems were not academic objects to him, but rather of the stuff of life, in which he took an obvious delight. Occasionally he referred to the place that writing, reading, and reflection had in his own personal and creative life. The feel of the class was as little as possible one of fulfilling some set requirements. Yet such is the force of many years of schooling that none of my three students could free themselves from being constantly on the alert to find out what the teacher wanted. Never mind that the teacher "wanted" them not to be concerned with what he wanted. The effect of that seems to have been that the students did not succeed sufficiently at going in the direction that the teacher himself had gone: making the poetry more their own, cultivating their own esthetic and cognitive responsiveness, and raising their active rather than their passive energies. Some illustrations from my three student interviewees follow:

One student's career in English 238 began with the instructor's comment on his first paper that he needed help with his writing because of his "rather unsophisticated ways of expressing simple notions"; he ended up with a respectable grade and the instructor's assessment on one of his last papers of "some good thoughts and some vague expression." This student conscientiously worked his way through the course, rereading his assignments and rewriting his notes on the basis of a fresh look at the poems. But he seems to have used the readings in the course in such a way as to make them fit into his somewhat literal religiosity, which seems to have been the basic ideological structure of his life for some years. By contrast it emerged in more casual conversation that this same student had a special love for the guitar and during the semester had put on a review of songs from the 1950s for high school students. He had acquired a fair amount of knowledge about the fifties, and when I asked him why he thought the fifties held such fascination for people, he made some shrewd guesses, such as one might expect from a social historian. I was impressed by the wider intellectual range, imaginativeness, and zest that he could display once he could move outside of the confinement of either his ideological structure or of the school.

My second student probably was the freest and most imaginative of the three. Nevertheless, she did not participate in class discussion. Earlier in the semester she had mildly criticized the instructor for not encouraging class discussion. But toward the end, in a singular burst of insight, she said to me that she felt that this criticism had been a rationalization for her own reluctance to express herself—about which she was unhappy. We briefly pursued that reluctance into other areas of her life, and she indicated that she had a fear of writing short stories because of the lack of control over what she might express. So in the classroom, this young woman preferred to sit back and to listen pleasantly—and perhaps in other parts of her life to keep herself from fuller discovery of her own individuality and to submit needlessly to others.

My third student described her instructor in a concurrent English course as a "Harvard" type, which to her meant among other things the use of big and complicated words. When she wrote papers for him, she had her thesaurus next to her, and she would translate her shorter words into big and more circumstantial ones. I remarked that I had always thought that the words had to fit the occasion, and that what she was doing was more than translation but changing what she was saying. Even though I repeated my comment once or twice, she ignored it. It did not seem to fit with her sense of having found one way of giving the instructor what he wanted.

I have pointed to two restrictions upon student learning: students' tendency both toward literal concreteness and toward conformity to the demands of the organization and the authorities. A third component, the student's emotional disposition, is particularly well illustrated by my third student. She could not hear my questions because they interfered with her need to be right. I found her to express this need in other contexts. Whenever she was confronted with a question, a comment, or a discussion that she interpreted as challenging her "rightness," her thinking would freeze and become rigid and difficult to permeate by further argument. The interviews afforded glimpses into the possible genesis of her need to be right. It may have had an origin in the desire she talked about to win her father's respect. It also was an instrument of control. Luckily for her, the need to be right was not equally strong in all of her thinking. But her cognitive capacities were such as to suggest that she would be a much more effective thinker if she could proceed from a less restricted psychological base. It seems equally clear that in the case of my other woman student, her fears and inhibitions of "expression" may be a primary factor in the casual attitude she seems to be taking to school, keeping it at a distance, not letting it touch her, as she may not let other things and people touch her.

The experience of talking to these three students has led me to think that we will not be able to do much about these emotional resistances and the implications they have for cognitive learning as long as teachers confront students in semester segments. Whatever one instructor may learn about a student is not transmitted to the next. Hence whatever one teacher discerns about a student and whatever work he or she may have done is largely lost. (We will, similarly, not get better writing from students until difficulties are tackled in a sequential way over several years.) What I say implies a need for competent analysis of emotional disposition early in the college years. The fact that it would be difficult to have enough people with the requisite competence does not mitigate the desirability.

During my work in English 238, I once more observed the impersonality of the classroom. In the time before the instructor arrives, students do not easily talk to each other, not even to students sitting next to them. It so happened that two of the students I worked with had early in the semester found themselves together in the lunchroom of the Humanities Building and had together with a third student formed a small group that met regularly to discuss questions aroused by the class. For many people, perhaps for most, ideas can become vivid only through such exchange. Facilitating such exchange might in the future become a more direct task for any professor giving a course.

Having spoken about student passivity and fear of expression, I want to mention the discovery of such fear in myself. Don Fry in his account has told about my fear that he might call upon me, and my ignorance would thus be exposed. John Holt has written extensively about elementary school children's fear of being considered stupid. That fear seems to reappear at many other stages of life. Professors might be doing more to see to it that this fear does not unduly interfere with their students' learning.

PHILOSOPHY 285
*Lee Miller**

My Own and My Students' Development. I begin by describing something of the personal context in which my teaching this ethics course took place. Fall semester was not a very productive semester for me outside of my teaching. My own research and writing were not going as well as I wanted. I was undergoing some rather trying times personally. The slowdown in writing and my personal upset had to affect my work in the classroom, though I am not sure of any direct way in which my teaching was affected. I know that I often wished that I were better prepared. I also did not have the opportunity to read very much of the many materials on the topic of my course that I had hoped to sample.

Nevertheless, I enjoyed the course very much. I always looked forward to the class and always wanted to come and teach even when I was less than well prepared. Having the chance to work with Joe Katz as my faculty associate and have him come to observe my class was also a positive aspect of the course for me. Working with him helped me understand and shape the course so that it better fitted what I had come to see as my goals as a teacher, formulated in light of my experience in the Federated Learning Community (FLC) program on world hunger at Stony Brook. As the result of my experience in FLC I came to understand that I am interested in student development as part of a broader interest in development generally. One elegant parallel proposed by Patrick Hill, the originator of the FLC program, was that faculty are to students in educational matters what the developed countries are to the underdeveloped countries in economic and political development. This parallel has helped me realize how often a university's organization imposes itself on teaching and learning (what is learned and how it is taught, not to mention how fast and in what context) in ways that may have little or nothing to do with the trajectory of personal intellectual development most appropriate for students.

What finally had become clear to me was that I could profitably focus my own commitment as a teacher on student development and my own growth in relation to that goal. Just as underdeveloped countries have much to tell the developed countries about how both can best participate in the contemporary world, so my students have much to tell me about how they can best develop and how I can best aid that process, if only I know how to listen and respond. This does not mean that I sacrifice any loyalty to my professional work or research or to the exigencies of my subject area, philosophy. To work with Joe Katz enabled me to focus on student development and to get constant feedback from him and the

---

* Associate professor of Philosophy, State University of New York at Stony Brook.

students about it. Such help enabled me to attend to and extend my own commitment as a teacher.

My Faculty Associate. Let me speak about my work with Joe, my faculty associate, with whom I met weekly. First, Joe — both through his presence in my class and our weekly conversations — was a concrete expression of constant support, interest, and acceptance. I found that he interpreted even rather questionable things I did or tried in a positive and encouraging light. I appreciated his presence in class and felt that he saw me on good and bad days — yet some that I thought good he felt were not so great, and some that I thought bad he saw as very productive, if not for the students, at least for me. One ironic outcome of his attending half or so of the classes was that his experience of the course was much like that of many students, who came about 60 percent of the time, if that often. (The total number of registered students was about seventy.) I would expect that such sporadic attendance should make a difference in the intellectual continuity and coherence of the course, but I don't think it did for my faculty associate, so I wonder if it does for students.

I am convinced that I did not get as much from our weekly conversations as I could have if I had been less pressured by so many other things. I found each session very encouraging to me and I particularly valued the suggestions my faculty associate made regarding what to ask students in class and in interviews, as well as his use of the questionnaire at the end of the course to get some qualitative comments from students. What is significant about the questionnaire is that it asks students what *they* did in the course and whether the teacher helped *their* learning. So many course evaluations focus only on the teacher, yet I believe the teacher's focus even in the classroom time should be on *student activity.* I have come to see that it is important to ask when I prepare my class just what the students will be *doing* during it to learn the materials. My suspicion is that the more I answer that question with the thought that "they will be listening to me," or "answering *my* questions," the less I am preparing a context for *their* struggling with the ideas and *their* questions about them than just preparing a stage for *my* performance.

I also have found myself reflecting about my faculty associate's ways as an interviewer in comparison to my own. I realize that I often stop asking the students questions just where it could get interesting. This is usually a response to signals from the student, often nonverbal, such as a change in bodily position or attitude or facial expression, which leads me to think he or she doesn't want to be questioned further or finds my line of queries uncomfortable. I noticed in a joint session we held with a student at the end of the course that my faculty associate kept pressing when the student figured she had given her last word. She recognized it, too, in saying with a chuckle, "You always do that." She had just definitively (and defiantly) remarked how it is unfair to let English usage, grammar, spelling, and punctuation count against a student in a course outside the English department. And he asked calmly why she thought so. Often I would report that a student had told me in an interview what she was doing or feeling or how she was studying in a certain way. Joe would then ask me if I had asked her why and I would realize that I was stuck with my own guesses instead of the student's.

Clearly there are skills in interviewing students in one's class that I need to acquire. My faculty associate has the advantage of more experience and training along these lines, not to mention the advantage of not teaching the students he interviews and not evaluating or grading them. Some of the discomfort I perceived in them might be due to the fear of looking bad to their professor. What is interesting is that the students came to realize that they would not be penalized for talking with me frankly. Yet I may well have hesitated to press further both because there are formalities in the teacher-student relationship that I instinctively observe ("be interested, but not *too* interested") and because I have a certain kind of power over them that they do not feel they have over me. I also wonder whose perception this really is and whether it makes as much difference as I feel.

Interviewing My Students — Feedback and Redirections. Another important activity was speaking with the three students I chose at random from my class and whom I interviewed almost every week. Especially valuable was the happenstance that no one of the three was a particularly able or especially slow student. Their differences as individuals were quite striking once I got to know them. Two of them, a male and a female student, came together to these sessions. The third student, a woman, usually saw me alone. I enjoyed speaking with the three very much and found them quite likeable, though they were not the three I might have chosen out of the class just by looking it over. One thing they all shared was anxiety about our conversations. Each was noticeably nervous and insecure about talking with me since this had never happened to them before at the university. Two of them chose to come together as a way of being more comfortable; the third came alone although she often seemed more obviously upset and anxious about other things in her life than the two.

Since all three fell in the range of B students I found it striking that they displayed so much anxiety about talking with a professor. The male student, for instance, often tried to assume my viewpoint and to comment on the course and what was happening as favorably as he could in terms of *my* performance; clearly he figured that was most interesting to me and he may well have been correct. But this also left him free not to talk about himself except about his appreciation of the class. (He *was* positively appreciative.) The woman student who came with him made the most forthright criticisms. She did not like Plato; she did like the discussions. I was surprised to notice that her Omnibus Personality Inventory (OPI) put her anxiety level rather high — perhaps she dealt with her fears by putting on a bold front. I also believe she enjoyed putting on that front and watching my cautious reactions to it. The woman student who came by herself expressed the most need of help and most anxiety about her work in a direct form. On one of the assignments she tried to get special help from my teaching assistant, from a former philosophy teacher, and finally from me. She found herself in that certainty of failure that prevents any success.

All three students were quite different in style, but I could not help but feel that their fears and anxieties had a large part to play in what they could do in the course and what they could say to me. If many or most students are that anxious about themselves and about their contact with faculty, their other problems, and their coursework, I wonder just how such fears could be alleviated so that learning and growth can occur. One possible answer is to consult the fearful about what will alleviate anxiety, at least in my own courses. And these three rather average students helped me immensely by making suggestions about the use of class time, about the pace of the class, and about the usefulness of the readings as they did them. All of them preferred more discussion and the chance to hear other students; this seemed not only to reassure them but also to enable them to formulate their own ideas better in an area where they felt others were as unsure and struggling as they were. They all found the assignments useful though I think they were puzzled about what one had to do to get better grades on assignments where there was no correct answer. All three found Plato's *Symposium* foreign and difficult to grasp and wished we had spent less time on it. Even where I disagreed or decided to override their judgments on such matters, I always found their comments a reliable index of where a good number of students in the class were at a given time.

I found that when I followed their suggestions and occasionally divided the class into smaller discussion groups, the class was almost always successful. A perceptible difference in student activity and interest was the result. The interviews convinced me that breaking the class into two-person teams was not successful unless students had already completed some kind of worksheet and were comparing their answers. Breaking the class into three discussion groups of about fifteen students apiece was more successful. The students also let me know that they enjoyed discussions of the class as a whole, especially those wherein I canvassed large numbers of students and put their opinions on the board. For instance, once I asked what insight each had gained into heterosexual relationships from reading *Rubyfruit Jungle,* a novel about a young gay woman. From interviewing these three I got some notion each week of how the students in the class were finding the readings and where they might be confused or have trouble understanding it.

No one has a stake in personal growth the way a student has. No one sees some parts of student learning quite as clearly as the student, just as these three students helped me and the others in the course more than they could know. I believe I can now assume that more student behavior is motivated by pressure and even fear than by desire or interest. I should be interviewing a few students from my classes regularly. This practice may prevent a lot of professorial illusion and self-satisfaction and, more importantly, it will benefit the students once I learn the right things to ask and how better to listen. Many teachers I have known do this informally in chance encounters with students, but by doing it regularly with the same students it is possible to build some mutual trust and affection that makes the feedback from those interviewed quite credible, even when one cannot act upon it.

Another conclusion forced upon me by my interviews with the students is that undergraduates cannot do justice to five courses of three credits each in one semester. It is like expecting a third world country to industrialize in six months. The work load is too heavy, given the fact that most students work to pay their expenses and have activities besides their classes as well as relationships and social life on campus or at home. Sometimes I feel the worst time to be in college is the years from eighteen to twenty-three — one's personal agenda, except for a minority of students, simply cannot put academics first; too many other developmental issues intervene. All three students I interviewed had to cope with difficulties in their families. Just living on campus, but not that far from home as is the case for many in my institution, is making the break into adult life, but not quite. One of my women interviewees had a relationship with a male friend break up and spent a hysterical weekend. The other woman interviewee lost a weekend and had to skip an exam because she was working on a dance marathon to benefit retarded children. The man I interviewed lived at home and found himself constantly questioned by his father about what and how he was doing. A clear side benefit of such regular interviewing for me was that it forced me to be more sympathetic to the problems my students had in learning anything, given the pressure from other courses and the rest of their lives.

So much else besides my course occupies each student's attention that I am forced to reconsider class time very carefully. If I use it solely to perform myself instead of structuring it so students actively learn, I am preventing them from doing as well and learning as much as they might. I am also undercutting their confidence in their own abilities and reinforcing the class-time passivity that seems to be standard student behavior. By knowing the particularities in just three lives I was forced to recall the whole rich and varied experience that my students have outside of class. This puts their course work in a new light and lets it have a different and fuller meaning to me. Even when students do not reach my standards of clarity or explanation or questioning or careful thinking, I have to acknowledge that they may be developing in their own ways through the course of a semester and that some of these ways will be intellectual, too.

Teaching the Ideas of the Course. When I look back to the subject matter and content of the course in more intellectual terms, I fear I am struck by how relatively little content gets taught. We explored only a few of the descriptions and definitions furnished by the authors we read and these ideas were not plumbed to any great depth or worked out systematically enough for their implications and assumptions. Nor did I feel that I stressed how these different views could shed fresh light on the areas of human experience we were discussing. More discussion with the students of the differences in emphasis of the various thinkers should occur in the future. Another question I have is how much rigor to expect from students or from the teacher. I did stress careful reading of the texts for the *authors'* ideas and gave some outlines of materials to summarize main points from the reading. This could be done still more carefully. Even more significant is the timing of spelling out meanings and connections so that at the appropriate moments it can become clear how helpful such skills as analyzing and making connections can be for our understanding of pressing, yet complex, issues.

Nonetheless, I am convinced, due in part to my conversations with Joe Katz and the students, that a course such as mine may not be for ingesting or being exposed to huge amounts of information about many different authors. Part of the function of my ethics course should be to open the students' eyes to new possibilities and alternatives in their lives and to engender or enlarge their capacity to articulate the issues. It could enable them to see their own attitudes and behavior as neither odd nor particularly unique, while it may lead them to become more reflective and explicit about their own whys and wherefores. If philosophy should teach us to focus on ideas and their relationships and systematic connections, it should also get people to be more questioning and reflective about their own opinions and practices when the ideas bear directly on important life issues. I hope that what this course may have lacked in the former dimension was made up in the latter, as student responses to our questionnaire in fact suggested.

Some people in the course came hoping for some formula or do-it-yourself idea kit that would help them shape up their lives. Others came to have pet ideas confirmed. Some seem to have left the course as they entered, convinced that they knew the right answers. What I hope the papers, discussions, and classroom exercises accomplished was to help us realize that there might be other ways to see, think, and talk about the same experiences that do not deny but rather extend our own favorite views. I believe many of the students taking the course have immensely naive and incredible expectations, fostered by their upbringing and the media images, not to mention deeper psychic forces that work out of infantile fantasies. While the idealism present in these unrealistic expectations is heartening, the naiveté of such hopes is also a source of suffering. What I take from these reflections is the conviction that next time I teach the course I will have to spend more time on this tension between reality and fantasy.

Many other things will have to be changed in the course. I want to keep the readings from Plato and Aristotle, but I hope to use the *Symposium* more selectively to suggest parallels with contemporary ideas. I especially need to find some readings written by women about the difficulties in relationships. And I would not mind using some proper short stories instead of *Love Story,* though I think *Rubyfruit Jungle* should be kept. It is a wonderful eye-opener about homosexuals having problems and being human just as much as heterosexuals. And the overall structure of the course should include more than just reading and discussing various concepts. I will want to emphasize the point that personal relationships have a process dimension as well as an ideal or normative aspect. Noting that relationships have a course or history, as well as an ideal that they more or less approach, should make it easier to see where discussion of the various difficulties in relationships connect with the readings.

I am not certain how much more intellectual content can be crammed into this course so long as I assume that my students are in different places developmentally. Especially if more than fifty students continue to take this course, there are limits to what such a range of students are intellectually and emotionally ready to tackle on this topic. My experience with the material on homosexuality and *Rubyfruit Jungle* suggests that many students are rather conventional and resistant to or threatened by certain views. The course draws students from the sophomore through senior years, so they bring a wide diversity of experiences regarding relationships and no little divergence in personal maturity. Moreover, if a good part of class time is devoted to discussion and workshop exercises that draw from student experience and apply ideas from the readings, there is not enough intellectual time or space for much more material.

It would hardly be honest to pretend that everything about the course pleased me. I have some regrets and resentments beyond the doubts just expressed about the extent to which the course pushed students intellectually. I am certain that many students pushed themselves emotionally and personally, using the course and its ideas as both occasion and prod. I resent two things that are in part due to the fact mentioned earlier, that students take too many courses per semester. One of these is that many students came to class so infrequently; there was a group of regular attenders who seldom missed unless ill or terribly anxious about other courses, but a second group came on and off as convenient, and a third group seldom came at all, even letting others turn in and pick up their papers. About forty to fifty students out of seventy would typically be present at any class. This means that either I have to insist on attendance and take valuable class time to check who is absent, or else I have to plan that each session is somewhat self-contained as well as continuous with the others. Many times my summaries and transitional points were useless, since a good number of students had no experience of the ideas I was talking about.

I also resent the fact that a good number of students were forced by other courses that cram information and skills, often at the expense of student learning, to treat my course as their easy one. Yet really mastering any of the readings or ideas in my course can be just as intellectually demanding. Sometimes I felt that the requirements of their majors and future professional schools forced students to put the materials of the course aside whether they wanted to or not. I perceive this as a problem with the way earning a degree gets organized in a university where the focus is not on undergraduate development, including intellectual or academic development. The requirements of certification and academic advancement undercut intellectual issues that may be important for students as intelligent persons in their own right. I suspect that no student found the materials of the course or the way the class worked so threatening that he or she cut class for that reason. (Some may have been bored or distracted.) The threat students talk about is that of not maintaining their grades; for this they feel forced to sacrifice even their own learning.

I felt upset that many students found Plato's *Symposium* so difficult and foreign. I was gratified that a smaller group of students enjoyed both Plato and Aristotle and remarked that this was the only course in which they had a chance to read them. Alas. I was distressed at the hostility of the class to the final exam even though it was announced at the first day of class. Many seemed to feel it was inappropriate to this type of course. Yet all questions were given out in advance and students were allowed to bring notes and books to the exam. Clearly I should have prepared them for the kind of rethinking and reconsidering that the exam required by giving a midterm of the same sort.

The written assignments will have to be reformulated as well. Although the general approach is one I favor — asking students to explain and make application of something we have discussed and then give their own opinions about it — it might work better if I could come up with familiar situations where the fit between the situation and the theoretical point they were asked to explore was better. Only the *Rubyfruit Jungle* paper did this well, in my opinion. The purpose of each assignment is to make students rethink what they have read, apply ideas discussed in class to the reading, or ideas from the reading to something else, and then take some personal stand or express some personal opinion and give reasons for it. The papers I assigned seldom tagged all three of these bases. Interesting to me was how many students liked best the assignment where they could play "Dear Abby" and give advice. But these papers were universally boring to correct and seldom gave any reasons for the advice proffered. Correcting four short papers for some thirty students (my teaching assistant did the rest) is only bearable if I am learning from the tedious work either where the students are coming from or what they understood or failed to understand from the reading and classwork. A poorly constructed assignment penalizes me as well as them.

Concluding Remarks. All in all I have to count Philosophy 285 as a great blessing to me in a trying time. Talking with the students outside of class and conferring with Joe Katz and working through the course for the first time kept me more alert and more sensitive to what I was or was not doing and its impact on students. I think I found myself consciously trying to be more patient and sensitive to student viewpoints in and out of class. In class I have the bad habit of cutting students' comments short by interrupting when I think I see their point. Even if I am correct, this in effect means there is no space for student comment. Part of this is impatience; part of it is irritations from other sectors of my life erupting as impatience in the one arena where I have "authority." When I reflect on how I felt when I did this, I believe that I heard the students objecting or being stubborn or obtuse about something I felt was utterly clear. But my "hearing" surely had less to do with where the student was coming from and more with my own internal pressures. I also have the bad habit of thinking I must answer *all* student questions, even the silliest. I now find that turning student questions that I hear as captious or irritating over to other students to answer works much better. I simply ask if anyone else would like to respond and if no one does I try to say gently that perhaps the questioner and I should discuss it after class since I would prefer to go on to another point.

My experience in this course has helped me question the whole expert syndrome and handle it better in other courses. It has helped me see that playing the expert is a game that leaves students passive and does not correspond to my commitment to *their* learning. In this course, interactions, insights, and new realizations kept happening all fall even though I was much pressed by other affairs at work and at home. The course was a stimulus and curb, a lab for learning, teaching and trying out things for the first time. It kept me doing what I see myself as committed to as a college teacher. I feel fortunate for the experience and grateful for the chance to work with my associates as part of a larger project about student learning. It is seldom that a course one teaches in college also comes into one's life as a gift. Philosophy 285 did just that for me. I am confounded by this fact, and very grateful.

Philosophy 285
Joseph Katz

The Students and the Teacher. In this ethics course the students found themselves confronted with a teacher who would present his ideas forcefully, "with flashing blue eyes" as one student remarked. But at the same time the professor would allow for interchanges with students, for challenges of his position and for frequent reconsideration, in the light of student remarks, of what he had said. He treated their remarks with respect, they felt, and even though he was vigorous in asserting his ideas he made it very clear that he considered them tentative and was from his perspective challenging the students to develop their own ideas. He would engage in such practices as interrupting his lectures and having students turn to their neighbors for five to ten minutes of discussion. When, through our joint work, we determined that many students did not like to engage in discussion with a person who was completely strange to them—as the person sitting next to them often is—he modified this practice and divided the entire class into three groups. This arrangement [as discussed in chapter 2] turned out to be much more productive, and students commented on the enrichment they experienced by listening to the variety of student points of view and the information they brought forth. In spite of the great openness of this course, many students felt there still should have been more opportunity for hearing other students. It is interesting that once students are engaged in *inquiry,* their fellows' views are much desired by them. We tend to underestimate the variety and richness of students' contributions once they speak about things of which they have experience.

The students also encountered a teacher who would give his comments on their papers on a tape rather than writing them in the margins of their essays. Hearing a teacher's voice made it more personal and, I assume, allowed for more detailed and perhaps less seemingly judgmental comments. The teacher almost invariably distributed at the beginning of each session a written outline of what he was going to talk about during the hour. He often provided for some surprise, stimulating class thinking. For instance, one day he would bring in a very challenging excerpt from an essay by a psychiatrist writing on jealousy. Another day he would give a brief quiz on Aristotle's conception of friendship and then would have students turn to each other for critiquing what they had written down. These stimuli made for lively class hours. Students said that they liked to come to class and enjoyed their classes. One of the special rewards was that problems with which the students were currently struggling became the focus of detailed and lively discussion, such problems as the breakup of friendships, friends borrowing money from each other, male dominance, and sexual relations.

Cognitive Impact. The course had undoubted appeal because of the salience of its topics for the students' lives. Its objective was to show how reason can illuminate these problems and to teach some basic philosophical reasoning skills. Whatever the students might have intended by taking the course, they found themselves in a situation where they were learning about reasoning. The basic injunction of the teacher was: "*Support* what you are saying." He showed them ways in which they could ferret out assumptions they were making and then had them look for the kind of evidence that might support their opinions. The course began easily enough with the novel *Love Story.* But even here the teacher introduced a different slant, stressing the parent–child relation rather than the relation between the two lovers, thus showing the familiar in the light of a new principle. By stages the course included such difficult readings as Plato's *Symposium.* Here only a meticulous analysis could yield an understanding of what the people in the dialogue were saying and of how one might critically evaluate their views. Characteristically, one of the students I interviewed told me that she had tried her first reading of *Symposium* with the television on. She soon realized that this would not allow her to open up the text to herself. This is only one of many instances where students try in a very sloppy and casual way to amass some basic ideas that will see them through exams and this method must be often successful enough. Even in this course some students complained at the end that the final examination demanded too much work. But it is not "too much" if some of the basic ideas of the course are to be grasped in a more definitive and firm fashion.

The professor's asking for support of opinion by argument made reasoning inescapable because for almost all students it was too embarrassing to be without reasons when matters of obvious vital concern for them were in focus—for example, whether one should continue in a relationship or not. In this course, as in so many others, many students would have liked to have the subject matter rolled out for them in a univocal, sequential, and perhaps simplified fashion. To some extent the teacher accommodated them. He himself thinks clearly and he provided them with many definitions. This reflected his own work of articulating matters that are usually left to more allusive and elusive formulations. Such articulation required sustained work by him; for the students the definition may become a prepackaged reality of its own. But the teacher did not leave them there because he often demonstrated the tentativeness of his definitions and his willingness to modify them or give them up under challenge. To some students this was confusing. As one of my interviewees told me, they are used to being given the outline of a theory that in their minds assumes almost narrative dimensions. In this course theory did not seem "clearcut." For students still struggling out of the dualistic state described by Perry, the definiteness of the world was called into question.

One student struggling with the open-endedness of the definitions resorted to evasion, saying that she did not care about failing the course and that she was not willing to seek help. (Yet in the course of the semester she did seek help with her math. Perhaps the challenge of her philosophy course helped overturn some previous thinking rigidities.) Other students had fewer problems with the pluralistic perspectives of the course. One interviewee described herself as being convinced by each argument in turn. The challenge of the course for her was to recognize the need for making some kind of a choice. This student was stirred up very much by a class discussion about the breakup of friendships, and in her interviews with me she talked about the double loss of her father, the first time through divorce and the second time through his death. She was planning to seek psychotherapy. It is hard to know what share the course itself may have had in her making this decision. But the course was putting some emphasis upon sorting out conflicting views and coming to a decision.

The teacher's method was to provide structure through his outlines and definitions, more so for those who still strongly needed them, and at the same time — through his reconsiderations, his challenges to the students, his embodying student objections and redefinitions — to break into rigidity of structure and suggest that productive thinking is a continual restructuring. The instructor tried to develop his students' thinking skills by asking them to determine what an author says rather than just express their own opinions. He meant them to get outside of themselves to understand what somebody else is thinking or doing. Students found that difficult. One interviewee told me that he found his thinking inhibited because he thought he could not use his own experience. Another interviewee said that to be fluent in her papers she needed to use her experiences. In fact, the instructor did not want to undercut such use, but he wanted the students to go one step further. This, from what we know about developmental stages, is hard at certain phrases of late adolescence which can be characterized by cognitive and emotional self-centeredness.

One student who had complained about not being allowed to refer to his own experience suggested in a later interview with me that he may have been avoiding a challenge that he already felt, to see the world through somebody else's eyes. The instructor's insistence that students look at ideas from the author's point of view helped to encourage their implicit readiness to go beyond themselves. This tendency probably got a strong boost in the reading of *Rubyfruit Jungle.* In that novel the main character, a lesbian, presented for most students such a dissentient and originally antagonistic point of view, yet presented it so persuasively, that she forcefully encouraged the view that quite divergent ideas can have their own integrity. Good thinking is looking at the same thing from many different perspectives; the capacity of going beyond one's own egocentric system is a major condition of objective thinking.

Emotional Impact. One understands another's point of view, but one also *feels* it. One listens. The relationship with the other person becomes different. Another person becomes really present; he or she is not a projection of one's own wishes or just an instrument for the fulfillment of one's own desires. One of the students I interviewed told me that one of the great lessons of the course was that he learned that one had to work at relationships as one had to work at one's baseball. Up until that point in the course he had somehow taken it for granted that one might "fall in love" and then stay there. Recognizing the intellectual and emotional effort that is required if relationships are to work strikes me as a major insight and accomplishment for any course. Particularly a number of males were stunned by one of the readings that suggested that men may be rather closed up emotionally and sensually and that hence their erotic-sexual sensitivity was below that of women.

The course raised the specter of authoritarianism. Some of the students showed more or less strong authoritarian inclinations; one male student went as far as to say that sexual excitement depended upon a male's dominating the sexual act. The teacher, by his manner itself, challenged authoritarianism. His pluralistic approach to ideas was unsettling. The more authoritarian students were provoked by finding themselves in conflict with a liked authority, a conflict between their own authoritarian views and the different views pronounced by the authority of the teacher. One male interviewee described his conflict between his allegiance to a somewhat strict father and his respect for a teacher and authority whom he could please by not being authoritarian. This student was beginning to work his way out of this dilemma with some good humor. (The interview, in his case as in others, revealed the usually hidden sources of students' grasping or not grasping what the course was about.)

The sympathetic presentation of homosexuality in one of the readings caused a moderate shock to many of the students. It was a strong challenge to deeply held beliefs. While students in the short span of a semester did not greatly modify prior feelings of strangeness about homosexuality, they began to think that other people could have this sexual orientation with integrity and with pleasure. It made homosexuals seem no longer monstrous and even seemed to make friendship possible while maintaining one's own orientation. Students showed an increase in understanding and tolerance. The root causes of the fear of homosexuality did not come into view. But it may be that the students' ways of feeling about both heterosexuality and homosexuality were changed.

Methods of Learning. How did the students learn in this course? First of all they learned because the teacher set an atmosphere of trust in which it was possible to speak up, to try one's ideas without fear of being considered stupid or being ridiculed. At least three characteristics of the teacher were very helpful. He was forceful in his own ideas, and such forcefulness set the example that even in difficult-to-articulate and uncertain intellectual territory one can arrive at one's views with some firmness. The teacher's forcefulness could have been discouraging had it not been coupled, second, with respect for the students. Their views counted. Some were encouraged by the teacher's forcefulness to be assertive themselves. Third, the teacher by constantly trying fresh educational devices not only showed caring for the student's learning but also demonstrated that there was a multiplicity of ways in which one could go about mastering the ideas of the course. The teacher might have paid more attention to the emotions, resistances, and fears that some of the ideas of the course aroused. At times by focusing on the rational he may not have given all the signals he could, such as giving respect not only to the student's reasons but also to their anxieties. Such recognition could help students take courage to move on to new and, to them, dangerous territory.

The teacher encouraged discussion not only between himself and the students but also *among* the students. The readings provided a balance between challenge, nearness to the student's experience, and sober analysis, with different kinds of analyses requiring different levels of conceptual sophistication. In the future the teacher might further investigate what kind of readings are the most apt, at what point introduced into the course, and in what sequence. The papers he assigned were always such that students could respond to them only by going beyond narrating what they had read and by formulating new points of view. Rewriting the papers was part of this endeavor. It did more than encourage better expression. It loosened the student's previously held system by encouraging viewing the matter at hand from other perspectives. One interviewee, still in a more dualistic state, strongly objected to rewriting. She felt there was nothing that she could say differently in a second attempt. I read this as her saying that she did not see her way out of her present system. This problem is not confined to undergraduates; much older people as well can be such first-draft thinkers. Some of the students were still, in Piaget's terms, at the level of concrete operations. "Happiness" to them meant a concrete feeling (for example: "I am happy when my boyfriend calls"). Plato's definition of happiness as creation in beauty—with its complex theoretical ramifications—was beyond their grasp. Yet the course, by showing that apparently simple relationships have hidden ramifications and can be talked about from many different perspectives, was an experience helping to break through the level of concreteness.

At the end of one class hour the teacher turned to me with great excitement saying how nice a class it had been. Indeed it had been a very nice presentation; the teacher had freshly and creatively developed some ideas of his own. The students had been carried along by his effort and enjoyed what he was doing. But probably the best learning in that hour was done by the teacher. We must think of more ways in which students too can have such productive experiences. At the same time we should not forget the teacher's needs. To be able to develop ideas is indeed one of the incentives why teachers chose academic life.

Students' Report of What They Learned. What conceptual map can we draw of the students' learning in the course? First, there are some familiar features. Students showed the varying Piaget levels of concreteness and abstractness. They showed Perry's dualistic, multiplistic, and pluralistic stages. Their thinking was advanced by the teacher's insistence on support for argument and by the consideration of many different points of views, including those of their fellow students. Emotionally, their thinking was advanced by their opening themselves up to other points of view; listening to others is one of the conditions of arriving at more complex ideas.

Close to the end of the course I asked the students to write down what they had learned in the course. One might have expected that they would have listed content primarily; the question was what they had learned. To my surprise, much of what they said dealt with *method.* It probably shows greater student readiness to improve method than I had realized. Students expressed surprise that so many different views could be held about one and the same thing. But this discovery became for them an opportunity to realize the hypothesis-building nature of investigative thinking and the special ways in which thoughts and objects interact. One student remarked that things look different when we think about them. The students commented on the significance that thinking had taken on for them when they found it applicable to everyday situations. They articulated the virtues of comparing ideas and different books with each other, of organizing one's thinking, of learning to look at emotions in objective ways. An analysis of the students' description of what they had learned yielded at least nine dimensions: (1) pluralism of perspectives; (2) organizing thought as a condition of understanding; (3) giving reasons instead of relying on assumptions; (4) transforming reality through thinking about it; (5) learning through listening and talking to other students; (6) applying thinking to everyday situations; (7) learning about the distinction of self from others, an antidote to wishes distorting thinking; (8) looking at emotions in objective ways; (9) learning about feelings.

The students felt they had improved their thinking skills. They also had done emotional learning, which in turn influenced their cognitive progress. Some students said that they took the course because they expected to obtain formulae, perhaps magic, to guide their behavior. Some were disappointed that it had not happened. The course weaved back and forth between theory and emotion, with the emotional impact probably depending much on the student's current stage of development.

Late in the semester the instructor asked the students to respond to the question of how they would behave in an ideal relationship with a member of the opposite sex. A look at thirty usable responses indicates a gradation in line with Jane Loevinger's work (1976): Students were in varying stages of moving from self-centeredness to altruism. Four of the thirty stressed identity, maintaining and fostering the boundaries of self and others in a relationship. By far the largest group, seventeen, saw a relationship as sharing, doing things together, and understanding, with strong suggestion of the quid pro quo, beyond the level of Aristotle's utilitarian friendship but not too far removed from it. Nine of the students (mostly women) thought of relationship as caring, giving. These are considerable differences, and one may assume that the same course was quite differently heard by the different groups in the class.

My work with Lee Miller showed me once more the value of collaboration for encouraging learning. Support comes from the relationship between the observed and the observing faculty members, their relations with their student interviewees, and the cooperation of the whole class as they participate in the inquiry. This liberates energies of all parties concerned, is a stimulus to fresh ideas and actions, and creates a group, collegiality, and even friendship where before there was the lonely teacher uncertain of cause and effect and bereft of opportunity for communication and community.

6

Tools for Understanding Students: The Omnibus Personality Inventory

We have used the Omnibus Personality Inventory (OPI) as an instrument to describe to professors their students' and their own thinking and learning styles. This chapter gives a detailed description of the OPI and can serve as a guide for the interpretation of its scales and their configurations. These interpretations are based on many years of work by Mildred Henry, which has involved detailed data gathering and observations of over one thousand individuals, both students and faculty. Readers may find it profitable to read Heist and Yonge's manual *Omnibus Personality Inventory* (1968).

We think of the OPI first as an instrument that can contribute to advancing knowledge about the ways in which students and faculty think and learn. In our work with faculty we have also used the OPI as an instrument for having faculty and students become aware of and explicit about the *distinctive* ways in which different people think and learn. Faculty from all disciplines have responded very positively to the OPI and have found it very useful. Students with whom faculty discussed the students' OPI profiles found the OPI equally useful. We suggested to faculty we worked with that they frame their interpretations of the OPI profiles in the form of questions or in very open-ended ways so that the students could decide whether they thought a particular description applied to them or not. We wanted to avoid labeling that is either false (any instrument is fallible) or premature (in the case of a person not yet ready to accept the description).

The faculty we worked with did so under our supervision and counsel. We think it is essential that other faculty who would plan to interpret student OPI profiles do so on the basis of consulting with colleauges who are knowledgeable about personality measures and their interpretations and who are thoroughly competent in the practice and the ethics of interpreting psychological instruments to other people. One might, with such guidance, begin by giving the OPI first to people whom one knows fairly well in order to gain an idea of what it can or cannot do. But whether or not faculty use the OPI in working with students, we see the OPI as a tool for discovery (and one that can be administered to groups of students without being interpreted to them). This chapter can be read as an attempt to arrive at fuller definitions and descriptions of learning styles.

BRIEF HISTORY OF THE OPI

In the late 1950s, several researchers at the Center for Research and Development in Higher Education at the University of California at Berkeley developed the OPI as an instrument for measuring the intellectual, interpersonal, and social–emotional development of college students. One of the principal creators of the OPI, Paul Heist, began using the OPI in a series of longitudinal studies of college students in a diverse array of institutions. Attempts to relate the OPI to anything meaningful with regard to students and their development proved to be difficult in the center's first two longitudinal studies (1958–1966) mainly because there was no firsthand observational or interview data to which to tie the OPI measures. Hence mean or average OPI scores were generally used, and these scores obscured individual differences. Toward the end of the second longitudinal study Heist (1968) asked the faculty at three of the schools in the study (Antioch, Reed, and Swarthmore) to name students majoring in their department who had demonstrated unusual creativity. He also asked students to nominate those among their peers in their major who had shown unusual creativity in their discipline. With these two sets of nominations in hand, he examined the OPI profiles of these students and found a similar pattern appearing for all of them. After the identification of the "creative" pattern on the OPI, it was only a matter of time before it became possible to identify other patterns by observing actual students and their learning behavior.

THE FIRST FOUR OPI SCALES

The OPI consists of fourteen different scales. They measure different modes of thinking, of handling affect and impulse, of relating to self, others, and society. The OPI is capable of indicating change over time.

Our description begins with the four scales that attempt to measure basic cognitive processes.

The *Complexity (Co)* scale seeks to measure how open individuals are to William James's "perceptual flux." It indicates how much ambiguity a person will tolerate. Persons scoring high on the Co scale typically exhibit a high tolerance for openness to the varied, multidimensional character of life around them. They may even exhibit or proclaim a liking for chaos. Persons scoring low tend to search for structure and order in the world about them. They find lack of structure to be upsetting and find multiple perspectives confusing. They resist the change that comes from seeing events and persons in different ways.

The Theoretical Orientation (TO) scale reveals the degree to which an individual tends to use concepts, symbols, and categories to organize and systematize the fluctuating worlds of feelings, intuitions, perceptions, and observations. This is an analytical and generalizable word- or symbol-oriented process. It permits the pinpointing, isolating, and abstracting of aspects of events, things, or persons. In mathematics, this process is used to invent or construct abstractions that do not refer to *actual* events, things, or persons. Persons scoring high on this scale tend to be very "word–thing" or "symbol–definition" oriented. They arc interested in what a word, term, concept, or symbol stands for and then enjoy using this "fixity" of the word or symbol as a basis for reasoning about the world in a linear, logical–deductive manner. Much "formal" education is built around developing this dimension of thinking. Persons scoring low have little interest in or awareness of how to use words or symbols as a means for ordering the outer world of complex, varied perceptions or the inner world of reflections, feelings, or imagined possibilities. Hence, they do not see how language can serve as a tool for thinking and reasoning in certain areas of human existence or human imagination.

The Thinking Introversion (TI) scale suggests the extent to which an individual engages in reflective thinking or "lateral thinking" as DeBono (1973) terms it. It is a contemplative, associating, connecting-up, pattern-forming mode of thinking. It is sensitive to an individual's inclination to wonder at the world and to ask questions of it. High scorers tend to be curious and speculative and enjoy making linkages. Low scorers tend to cut off reflection and associations and are not interested in speculating or wondering.

The *Estheticism (Es)* scale reflects the degree to which an individual makes use of an intuitive, feeling-oriented, immediate experiential mode of thinking as contrasted with a concept-oriented mode. High scorers tend to be open to their emotions, feelings, and intuitions and to use them in their thinking. They are high in their appreciation of art, drama, literature, or music or they engage in creative endeavor in these areas — or both. They tend to be aware of and open to the "felt" dimension of knowing that Michael Polanyi (1966) has labeled the "tacit" dimension of knowledge.

Low scorers tend to be disinterested in emotions, feelings, intuitions, and the arts.

Thinking in the Frame of the Disciplines

Each of the processes of knowing just described are only partial and highly limited ways of knowing if used in isolation one from another; however, when one or more process of knowing is used integratively with one or several other processes of knowing in a check-and-balance manner, a style of thinking becomes discernible. Through our extensive work with students in longitudinal studies, following them through four years of college and giving them the OPI nearly every year and through our later work with faculty, we have been able to identify nine distinctive thinking–learning patterns. The majority of these patterns are tied to existing disciplinary perspectives. We will describe these nine patterns as they appear in various configurations of OPI scales.

(1). *Scientific Thinking.* Mode 1 (figure 6.1) depicts this pattern. It takes the shape of a "Z" and we call it the "Science Z" pattern. Persons producing this pattern indicate a preference for using a definitional, word-oriented, analytical, logical–deductive mode of thinking (TO) integrated with perception (Co). They tend to focus on perceptions that are recurring and stable in nature. They are searching for order and fixity in the perceptual flux and holding it through conceptions. The two modes of thinking not strongly preferred or used by individuals who show this pattern are the TI and Es scales. Persons who exhibit flatter "Z" patterns, however, that are also above the mean are likely to be closer to making use of reflective-speculative thinking processes (TI) and attending to intuitions and feelings (Es) — particularly the "feeling out" of the larger significance and multiple meanings of their conceptions — than are persons who exhibit sharply defined "Z" patterns, with TI and Es receiving low emphasis and tending, therefore, to be below the mean. Typically, faculty who teach in physics, chemistry, empirically oriented biology, experimental psychology, and to a large extent in mathematics as well, tend to produce a "Science Z" pattern. People who like to establish principles for ordering their lives and the lives of others tend to exhibit this pattern; hence, this pattern turns up among such professionals as administrators, lawyers, political scientists, behavioral psychologists.

In interpreting OPI scales it is useful to bear the following in mind: The degree of lag before an individual utilizes one or another mode of thinking is suggested by the distance between thinking modes and by their position above or below the mean or threshold line, the latter suggesting the strength of the mode. For instance, mode 1 suggests that a large lapse of time is likely to occur before an individual strongly immersed in the conceptual–analytical (TO) and perceptual modes of knowing (Co) will reflect speculatively upon the existing analysis in

Mode 1
Scientific Thinking: Logical-Deductive,
Concept-bound, Concept-ordering

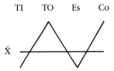

Mode 2
Literary Thinking: Perception-oriented,
Intuitive-Esthetic, Reflective-Imaginative

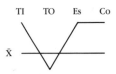

Mode 3
Historical/Philosophic Thinking: Rational-
Categorical, Scanning-Synthesizing

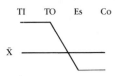

Mode 4
Social Science Thinking: Reflective-
Associative, Speculative, Pattern-perceiving

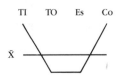

Mode 5
Artistic Thinking: Intuitive, Holistic, Feeling,
Perception-oriented, Qualitative

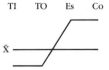

Mode 6
Language and Music Thinking: Reflective-
Connecting up, Feeling-based, Intuitive

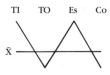

Mode 7
Engineering/Architectural Thinking: Analytical,
Logical-Deductive, Esthetic-Intuitive

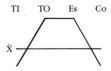

Mode 8
Generative Thinking: Conception- or Idea-
generating, Reflective-Speculative,
Perception-oriented

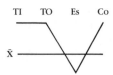

Mode 9
Creative Thinking: Reflective-Speculative,
Intuitive, Perception-oriented,
Inductive-Deductive

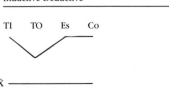

Figure 6.1. The Nine Major Thinking Modes

terms of a larger context or intuitively assess its implications. If the distance were smaller between TI and Es and TO and Co and if all four modes were well articulated (TI and Es above the mean instead of below the mean), it would take less time or effort before the individual either reflected upon or tried to intuit the implications of what he or she had abstracted from the perceptual flux.

2. *Literary Thinking.* This pattern is produced by persons who emphasize three of the major cognitive modes of the OPI in an integrated, coordinated manner (mode 2). These modes comprehend openness to perception, liking for the changing, dynamic nature of the perceptual flux (Co), attentiveness to feelings, emotions, and intuitions as guides for actions and thoughts (Es), and liking for reflection, association, and inquiry (TI). This pattern assumes a "J" shape and we call it, therefore, the "Humanities J" pattern. The mode of thinking *not* strongly accentuated in this pattern is the analytical, categorical, logical–deductive, sequentially ordered mode of thinking (TO) that is prominent in the "Science Z" pattern. It is typically found in faculty and students interested in literature, poetry, drama, existential philosophy, humanistic psychology, or religious beliefs and values. The order that emerges from this mode of thinking, though accessible to others following the same path, tends to be unique and more personal in nature than is the order that emerges in a scientific mode of thinking, which is expected to be common to all, publicly testable and verifiable. A comparison of the "J" and the "Z" patterns shows that where an individual using one of these patterns zigs, an individual using the other zags; so the overlap between the two patterns is minimal. These two distinctively different modes of thinking and constructing reality reflect the two "cultures" described by C. P. Snow in his essay *The Two Cultures* (1964).

3. *Historical and Philosophical Thinking.* Persons exhibiting this mode on the OPI (mode 3) show a preference for the reflective, questioning, connecting, scanning, speculating, lateral thinking process (TI). The second highly preferred mode of thinking exhibited in this pattern that checks and balances TI is the analytical, logical–deductive, categorizing, ordering-classifying, organizing, concept-oriented mode (TO). Of the two modes of thinking less prominent in this pattern, one is the esthetic–intuitive mode (Es) of openness to influence from inner experience, feelings, emotions. The other less prominent mode is that of openness to perception of the changing, dynamic multidimensionality of the observed world and its orderings (CO). Faculty who teach philosophy or history tend to produce this pattern, and sometimes so do faculty in mathematics. These individuals tend to be highly conceptual or rational in their approach to the world. Though neither unfeeling nor unperceptive, they are more likely to dominate their feelings through analysis and intellectualizing them than through allowing feelings and emotions to develop into intuition as a touchstone for truth. They tend to handle the perceptual flux

through ordering and organizing it. Their relative lack of emphasis on the intuitive (Es) and the complex, perception-generated (Co) dimensions of thinking may show up in a lack of attention to the jumbled, ambiguous *felt* and *lived* meaning of events, people, words, and ideas. They may sometimes show a tendency to "jump the gun" conceptually, thereby failing to allow time for a richer and more complex perceptual or experiential picture to emerge.

4. *Thinking in the Social Sciences.* Persons producing this pattern (mode 4) indicate a liking for a reflective–associative, speculative-questioning mode of thinking (TI), along with a tolerance for and enjoyment of the complex multiplicity of the perceptual flux (Co). Such persons tend to deemphasize a sharply descriptive, analytical–categorical, logical–deductive mode of thinking (TO). They do not immediately focus on feelings and intuitions (Es). This "U"-shaped pattern tends to show up for many faculty and students in the social sciences — anthropology, political science, social psychology, and sociology. These fields are highly complex and can be theoretically messy; no abstraction of a single variable or set of single variables is likely to bring an easy conceptual order to the intricate, complicated interpersonal, social, cultural, or political events. Speculation, questioning, trial-and-error linking up of attributes (high TI), together with a high tolerance for ambiguity and the multiplicity of social–cultural–political events (high CO) can take place before strong, reliable, conceptually delineated patterns (TO) that are grounded in perceptions can emerge.

5. *Thinking among Artists.* Individuals producing this pattern show a preference for the Es and Co scales (mode 5). They focus on their feelings, emotions, and intuitions (Es) as well as on the multivaried, complex nature of the perceptual flux (Co). Their creations are calculated to affect or transform experiences and feelings. The two modes of thinking not emphasized in this pattern are Thinking Introversion (TI) and Theoretical Orientation (TO). Typically, most creative, arts-oriented faculty show patterns in which all four scores (TI, TO, Co, Es) are above the mean. Such persons, with also fairly high scores on TI and TO, can reflect on their art, discuss it, critique it, and put it into some kind of verbal order.

6. *Thinking in Language and Music.* Individuals who enjoy the *expressive* qualities of language and music produce a pattern like the one in mode 6. They emphasize the speculative, inquiring, imaginative, connecting-up mode (TI) and the feeling, emotionally open, intuitive mode (Es). They deemphasize the TO and Co modes. This pattern is the direct opposite of the "Science Z" pattern. It indicates a strongly open-ended approach to thinking. Persons interested in language, music, and nursing tend to create patterns of this kind. When words or language are not used as tools for ordering the world of events and constraining the perceptual flux, words can be appreciated for their expressive and evocative qualities.

In music, the search is for varying patterns of sound and meaning. In nursing or in psychotherapy, the focus in on the varying elements of social exchange that will create a caring, nurturing, supportive relationship with another individual who is in need of help. This sort of relationship with an individual is necessarily singular in character and unique, and the creation of such a relationship is highly dependent upon a concentration on aesthetic appreciation and intuitive hunches.

7. *Thinking among Design Engineers and Architects.* This pattern (mode 7) is produced by persons who think about the world in an analytical, ordered, logical–deductive manner (TO) in coordination with an emphasis on feeling, intuition, and esthetic sensing (Es). Modes of construing reality that are not emphasized are the TI and Co modes. This pattern is the opposite of that produced by social scientists. Persons interested in design engineering, architecture, the pragmatics of esthetics, the blending of forms with functions which are logically related and can be tested in action and intuitive evaluation are among those who produce this pattern. Such persons are not immediately interested in philosophical speculation nor are they interested in the changing flux of events themselves. They appear to be searching for ways to order and to manifest their interior, intuited sense of beauty through the outer medium of structured form and spatial organization.

8. *Generative Thinking.* Persons exhibiting this mode use *three* major cognitive modes (TI, TO, Co) in an integrated, coordinated manner (mode 8). The mode of thinking not emphasized in this pattern is the esthetic–intuitive, feeling-oriented mode (Es). This pattern is very much like the "Science Z" pattern with the important difference of a strong emphasis on speculative-reflective thinking (TI). Individuals exhibiting this pattern are devoted to developing ever more comprehensive and complex conceptual and logically coherent explanations for the perceptual flux. They are strongly idea-oriented, enjoying ideas for both their comprehensiveness and their organizing power. They are very much interested in comparing ideas critically one with another, in questioning basic assumptions, and in developing complex understandings of multiple events. Persons using this mode of thinking are capable of what Piaget calls "second-order thinking," thinking about thinking. Occasionally, however, idea-generating, reflective–speculative thinkers may become so interested in building an integrated, logically sound, conceptual order that they substitute this order for the ongoing flow and complexity of events. They then tend to substitute a conceptual order for existing reality and this can lead to encapsulation within an ideology or a set of ideas.

9. *Creative Thinking.* The complex way, exhibited in mode 9, involves a coordination among all four of the different thinking modes that constitute the first four OPI scales. Attentiveness to feelings and intuition (Es) and to the perceptual flux (Co) is accompanied by an interest in specula-

tive inquiry and reflective-associative thinking (TI), all three of which modes just slightly precede the fourth mode (TO), the analytical, logical–deductive mode. This pattern tends to be exhibited by individuals who are open to using both external perception (Co) and inward experience (Es). Using knowledge from these many sources, weaving back and forth among them, reflecting, perceiving, feeling, experiencing, and intuiting, they creatively construct an order (TO) that fits best with what they have perceived, experienced, and imagined. The order constructed may be a theory (a conceptual order), a spatial–relational order (a design), a symbolic order (a painting, a dance, a musical composition). Creative individuals in *any* field tend to show the pattern of mode 9, transcending the particularities of their science, art, or profession.

STUDENT–FACULTY DIFFERENCES

The thinking of students often differs from that of faculty in certain notable respects. The OPI is capable of catching these differences. Two major differences lie in (1) the degree of complexity and (2) the developmental status of the student's thinking (to be discussed in more detail in the context of figure 6.3). Most faculty members tend to show distinctive, well-articulated thinking patterns, the patterns that lie at the base of their disciplines. A fairly large number of students tend, on the other hand, either to emphasize unidimensional thinking (making predominant use of only one process of thinking) or to produce embryonic thinking mode patterns. Embryonic patterns are indicated by scores *below* the mean or threshold line of the OPI; they are largely unconscious and can be raised through practice and use. Other students exhibit "threshold" patterns of thinking. These are patterns that show up around the mean on the OPI and are on the verge of becoming consciously used and practiced. Finally, a few students arrive at college with patterns of thinking just as distinctive and well articulated as those of the faculty. Their scores are well above the mean or threshold line of the OPI.

We take this opportunity to reiterate that when interpreting the OPI to students it is wise to avoid statements that may label students or even box them into set categories. It is best to indicate that the profiles are only suggestive. As we have said earlier, we often translate what the OPI says into question form, asking students whether a particular mode of thinking or feeling characterizes their ways of learning or knowing. This gives the student the chance to accept or reject a proffered characterization and prevents the possibly injurious effect of seemingly fixed categorizations. Even when the OPI is accurate, what counts is the student's arriving at the awareness himself or herself. We also must recognize that the OPI can be fallible with any particular individual. The caution in interpretation here suggested applies as well to the use of the OPI with faculty.

THREE FURTHER OPI SCALES

The emotional and experiential dimensions of thinking are indicated by three scales on the OPI: the *Impulse Expression (IE)* scale, the *Personal Integration (PI)* scale, and the *Anxiety Level (AL)* scale. The IE scale indicates the extent to which individuals are aware of and free to express their feelings and impulses. High scorers tend to involve themselves actively in events and the life around them. They take risks and garner experience. Very high scorers may be highly aggressive and more compulsive and explosive than spontaneous and open. The PI scale provides a measure of the individual's sense of self or identity. Very high scorers may have sharp and rigid self-definitions. The AL scale is scored in the reverse direction; persons who score above the mean are indicating *less* anxiety than persons scoring below. Exceptionally high scorers, however, may be denying anxiety, refusing to recognize their feeling of anxiety and tension.

Individuals tend to produce different configurations of IE, PI, AL, indicating the extent to which they are open or closed emotionally and experientially. In the first pattern (figure 6.2, mode 10) the Impulse Expression (IE) score is higher than the scores expressing preference for Personal Integration (PI). Additionally, a willingness to endure the anxiety that often comes with the expression of impulse and the risks attend-

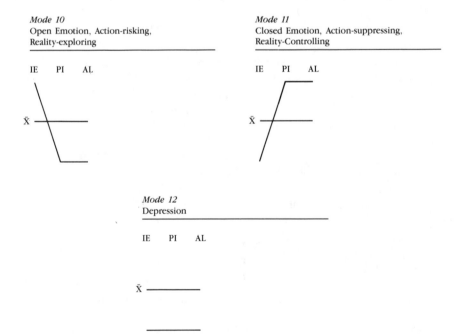

Mode 10
Open Emotion, Action-risking,
Reality-exploring

IE   PI   AL

X̄

Mode 11
Closed Emotion, Action-suppressing,
Reality-Controlling

IE   PI   AL

X̄

Mode 12
Depression

IE   PI   AL

X̄

Figure 6.2. Emotional Modes

ing it is exhibited by the relatively high Anxiety Level (AL) score. This pattern is exemplified by individuals who allow their impulses to action, feeling, and experience to take precedence over self-definition and more rigid limits. These individuals tend to be aware of and open to their feelings, inner experience, tensions, and anxiety.

In the second pattern (mode 11) Personal Integration (PI) is higher than Impulse Expression (IE); awareness of feelings of anxiety and tension (AL) is low. Individuals showing this closed emotional pattern have a tendency to use criteria or rules, which may or may not be based on prior experience and action, to preenvision, precontrol, and suppress impulse and urges to act spontaneously and on the basis of experience. Their lack of awareness of anxiety may be due either to the possibility that the individual rarely takes risks, hence incurs little anxiety, or to the possibility that the individual is anxious, but tends to deny the anxiety.

When individuals do not produce either of the strongly defined patterns exhibited in modes 10 and 11, that is, when the distances between IE and PI or IE and AL are not as great as in modes 10 and 11, we can expect more moderate versions of emotional openness or closedness. Occasionally individuals produce a pattern in which they indicate little or no inclination to engage in impulse expression (IE), no sense of personal integration or self-definition (PI), and considerable anxiety and tension (AL). Individuals producing such a pattern (mode 12) may be depressed and may need counseling help.

Cognitive-Emotional Relations. When the cognitive modes of thinking (TI, TO, Es, Co) are brought into juxtaposition with the emotional and experience-generating modes (IE, PI, AL), it is possible to visualize more clearly how the various modes intersect with and influence one another; characteristic cognitive and emotional patterns are shown in figure 6.3. Openness to inner experience and to the consequences of involved action is often a precondition for intellectual imagination and conceptual and perceptual flexibility. Emotionally open and experience-gathering persons will allow themselves the freedom to develop and express thoughts, whereas others may remain fixed in an obedient and more fearful or less aware stance. Closely tied to emotional openness is the readiness to express ideas in action, including the action of thinking. As ideas are developed through and tested in exploration and action, a thinking–acting split can be inhibitive. A thinking–acting split is shown in the individual producing the pattern shown in mode 15 under figure 6.3, a highly impulsive (IE) individual who is very likely to plunge into new experiences and to take action, but at the same time likely to feel very disoriented, unintegrated (PI), and, not surprisingly, considerably anxious (AL). The individual is not as yet reflecting on or trying to make sense of the experiences generated through his or her impulsiveness and action-orientation. This individual's scores on the first four thinking scales of the OPI are quite low and embryo like in character. The individual cannot intellectually (TI,

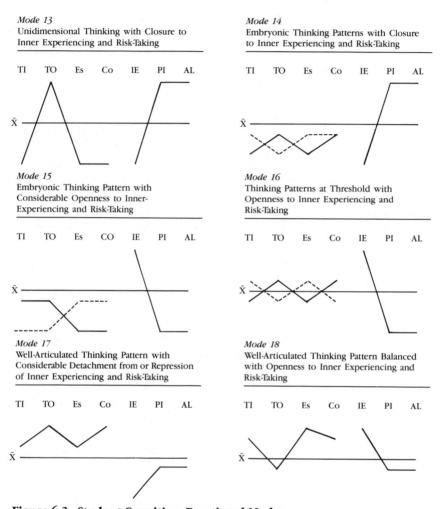

Figure 6.3. Student Cognitive–Emotional Modes

TO) or intuitively–perceptively (Es, Co) process the experiences and the outcomes of action that he or she is busy producing. The reverse situation is that of the individual whose intellectual or intuitive–perceptive modes strongly predominate over the emotional–impulsive, experience-bound mode. Such individuals, showing the pattern depicted in mode 17, do not move in the world in ways likely to generate fresh new experiences for themselves, nor do they risk action in ways likely to test their speculations, conceptions, intuitions, or perceptions.

Some students are so totally involved in action and the generation of new experience that they exhibit experientially diffuse behavior unchecked by reflection, conception, intuition, or perception, as we have seen exemplified in mode 15. These students have an exceptionally difficult time developing the detachment and thinking needed to negotiate the typical academic setting successfully. Other students seem to develop well-articulated thinking modes with considerable detachment from active risk-taking and attention to inner experience, an opposite kind of mind–body or mind–action split (mode 17).

Modes 13 and 14 exhibit patterns for students who come to college with either a unidimensional mode of thinking (mode 13) with closure to risk-taking and inner experiencing, or an embryonic thinking pattern (mode 14 emphasizes either scientific or literary thinking) with closure to risk-taking and inner experiencing. Mode 16 exhibits a threshold pattern of a student beginning to think in an organized, integrated manner (either science-oriented or music- and language-oriented thinking) accompanied by an open risk-taking, inner-experiencing mode. Mode 18 shows a well-articulated thinking pattern for literary thinking which appears to be substantially integrated with the individual's propensity to engage in active risk-taking and openness to inner experience.

In Perry's terms, it is highly likely that students exhibiting patterns in modes 13, 14, and 15 are engaged in absolutist or dualistic thinking; students exhibiting patterns in modes 16 and 17 might be moving into multiplistic thinking; students exhibiting a pattern like mode 18 would be close to relativistic–contextural thinking and commitment.

By using the OPI, faculty persons can help determine that a particular student or group of students may not be making much use of one or another dimension that is critical for thinking in their discipline. The visualization of thinking patterns by the OPI can help teachers more consciously to explore and test with their students, by way of interviews, classroom observations, written papers, and exams, how students are thinking, what processes they may be using, and what processes they may be ignoring and leaving unused.

SEVEN ADDITIONAL OPI SCALES

The fourteen different OPI scales are each statistically and conceptually independent of the others. The scales are highly reliable and the inventory was designed to measure change. Thus far, we have described and discussed seven of the OPI's fourteen scales—primarily the scales that indicate different approaches to thinking. Two of the remaining seven scales have an indirect relationship to thinking since one of them, *Autonomy (Au)*, provides a measure of how ready an individual is to become independent while the other scale, *Religious Orientation (RO)*, indicates how free an individual is from dogma.

Persons who enjoy being or want to be independent and self-directing in their relationships with others and who shape their own ideas tend to score high on Au. Very high scorers, however, may be rebelling strongly against any and all authority figures. Persons scoring low on this scale tend to be "other-directed." They acquire most of their opinions and ideas from others, are quite dependent in their relationships with others, and find speaking their own mind and being by themselves difficult and upsetting.

The RO scale indicates whether or not the respondent exhibits a strong acceptance of a religious belief system. Persons scoring low on RO are likely to exhibit a strong, unshakable adherence to a fundamentalist, "true-believer" religious belief system. They tend to belong to some organized, group-endorsed form of religion; they take part in religiously oriented activities on a regular basis. They filter and judge the observable world around them through an a priori established belief system. Moderate scorers usually have an identifiable religious belief system or set of religious values, but they tend to be more self-aware and less rigid in their application of these beliefs and values. Persons scoring above the mean tend to have developed a well-examined *personal* religious belief or value system. They tend not to engage in group-oriented, organized forms of religious activities. Their observations of the world and their beliefs have interpenetrated each other and through reflection their beliefs have become more flexible and reconciled to each other. Very high scorers tend to be antireligious, even prejudiced against religion and religious values.

The Autonomy and Religious Orientation scales are important for gauging a student's development. Students who are dependent on others for their ideas and sense of validity or who are caught up in political, religious, or other dogma or ideology may not be able to develop the basis for independent, critical, flexible, and creative thinking. They may not have developed to the point at which they can see and trust themselves as their own touchstone for "truth." A reliance on receiving truth from others is stagnant and does not promote the necessary individuation of the basic thinking–knowing processes.

The *Social Extroversion (SE) and Altruism (Am)* scales, when used together, indicate features of an individual's interpersonal style. The SE scale measures social extroversion versus social introversion. Higher scorers on this scale tend to seek out and enjoy considerable social interaction with others. Low scorers tend to prefer small groups of people or one-on-one relationships and encounters, and they can enjoy and feel comfortable with solitude. Persons scoring in the middle enjoy social encounters in both large or small groups and their own solitude as well. The Altruism (Am) scale indicates the extent to which an individual feels good about, likes, trusts, and enjoys other human beings. High scorers want to help, serve, or please others. Low scorers tend to distrust other people, even to dislike them, and to feel alienated from them. Persons scoring near the middle on this scale may be more likely to relate to others with indifference rather than with trust and liking or with some suspicion.

Knowledge of a student's interpersonal style may help a teacher to relate in more effective ways to a given student. Students high in sociability (high SE) may need to be encouraged to find quiet times and places for reflection and concentration. A student's liking for and interest in people (high Am) could provide the teacher with a motivation for finding the ideas and conceptions that are likely to stimulate the student's curiosity and involvement in learning. Students low in sociability (low SE) and at the same time indifferent to (moderate Am) or alienated from (low Am) other persons provide a particular challenge to teachers and institutions.

The remaining three scales consist of the *Practical Orientation (PO)*, *Masculinity–Femininity (MF)*, and *Response Bias (RB)* scales. The Practical Orientation scale reflects the individual's position with regard to career goals and the utilitarian, pragmatic aspects of life and learning. (Low scorers usually show an interest in ideas apart from their practical consequences.) The Masculinity–Femininity scale (high scores indicating "masculinity" and low scores, "femininity") provides a measure of what now are the "older," more traditional notions of "male" and "female" roles in American culture. The Response Bias scale indicates, for high scorers, a need to take account of and please others, and a generally positive self-image, whereas low scorers tend to lack in self-confidence and have a poorer self-image.

These scales may provide clues to student learning. A student scoring high on the Practical Orientation scale may need additional help to see and appreciate the value of learning in ways that are not immediately pragmatic or career-related. Students scoring high on "masculinity" or "femininity," as traditionally defined, may need opportunities to express and think through their ideas on the characteristics of men and women, so that a woman student may come to think it nonthreatening to go into engineering or science or a male student may reconcile his idea of masculinity with his interest in literature, poetry, or the dance. High scores on the Response Bias scale, especially if obtained by young people leaving home for the first time, may indicate that the student's interest in a field of study, a career, or a way of behaving is directly traceable to the student's desire to please a parent or peer. Low scores on RB suggest that the individual may experience a lack of self-confidence or some feelings of inferiority.

RECOGNIZING AND DEALING WITH INDIVIDUAL DIFFERENCES

As we have indicated, the OPI was designed to be able to measure change in individuals over time. Some individuals enter college with quite embryonic thinking patterns (see modes 14, 15, 16) and over a shorter or longer period develop much stronger and better-defined thinking modes.

Some individuals enter college with a closed emotional pattern (mode 11) and gradually evolve toward a more open emotional pattern (mode 10). Other persons arrive with a particularly well-defined thinking mode suited to the study of physical science and then become interested in the social sciences, and after that in art and esthetics. Eventually, such individuals might be able to coordinate these more partial modes of thinking into a more complexly coordinated thinking pattern. Research with the OPI has shown that changes in thinking or emotional–motivational patterns do not occur quickly. Taking the OPI every month or so is not likely to reveal much change. Profile patterns tend to remain stable from year to year *unless* the individual has encountered experiences or well-designed formal learning situations that are new, powerful, sustained, and different enough to effect change in the individual's mode of looking at the world. We have seen such changes in both students and faculty.

One of the factors preventing faculty from teaching as effectively as they might is neglect of student differences. Though students are not all alike, teaching continues on the assumption of a common denominator that, when found, will enable the faculty member to reach most of the students. Those faculty who have given up aiming for the middle range of their students have resorted either to addressing primarily those few students who seem likely to catch on to their particular perspective and level of thinking or to focusing on those students who need the most help to make it through the particular course. Some faculty have given up altogether on determining a strategy for coping with student differences and simply run their course on a sink-or-swim basis, counting on the "objectivity" of their grading system to maintain "standards" and thus avoiding the fact of student diversity. As the numbers of students in college classrooms have risen over the years, the probability and the possibility of attending to student differences have decreased. When classes are small, and some give-and-take discussion is encouraged between the teacher and the students, it is more difficult to overlook differences among students. But with large classes and the use of the lecture method, the fact of individual differences is much less evident and these differences can be rather easily ignored. The approaches we have suggested can make it possible to understand more fully the importance and meaning of observed differences and, in light of that understanding, to begin taking them into account in planning individual courses, the curriculum, and the institutional environment.

7

Tools for Understanding Students: The Interview

Teachers have always used data of some sort to assess their impact upon students—among them tests, more or less casual verbal comments, and end-of-term questionnaires. None of these have usually been sufficiently in-depth about how students learn nor have they offered substantial guidance for improving teaching practices. The interview can provide such guidance, and it can substantially enlarge our knowledge of how students learn. For most college professors, the interview is a tool for the use of which they have had no previous training. This chapter gives some basic description of how interviewing skills might be acquired. Practice will improve the art. We ask the reader to bear with us as we go into the necessary detail. Some of the statements will take on enhanced meaning as readers engage in their own interviewing. Much of our own knowledge of classroom practice and of how students learn has come from interviews with students. In recommending the interview as an investigative tool we address ourselves not primarily to researchers, but to professors who want to acquire increased knowledge of students as a base for their teaching. But we see no hard-and-fast distinction between practice and research. The professor's increased knowledge of student learning is likely to help build our budding science of student cognitive style and development as well as to improve teaching. An attempt similar to ours is being made in medicine, where an investigator has argued for increased knowledge of patients brought about through more careful listening by physicians to their patients (Jay Katz, 1984).

INTERVIEWING, LISTENING, UNDERSTANDING

The interview is a neglected tool in the pursuit of knowledge. Interviews are, of course, widely used, and their principles and techniques are well described (see, for instance, Kahn and Cannell, 1983; Stewart and Cash, 1985; Survey Research Center, 1976). Interviews are used for hiring and screening people, for journalistic information-gathering, for psychotherapy. They are a tool in social science inquiry—an embattled tool, as many investigators give preference to more "objective" instruments, such as the questionnaire. The interview is often thought of as an auxiliary instrument, but a different picture emerges if one asks oneself about the place of listening, that is, active hearing, in human life. No one would wish to deny that being able to hear what other people are saying, to become aware of the thoughts and feelings behind what they say, is an essential human competence. Yet training in that competence is rarely spelled out. We take for granted the emphasis on expression in our schools. Courses in writing, for instance, recognize the desirability of being able to say well what one thinks and to learn to think better through practicing expression. No corresponding attention is being given to listening. There are no generally required or recommended courses concerned with developing listening skills. The fact is that we listen badly, that we do not hear what other people are saying to us. Moreover, what people say is readily distorted through the lenses of our own wishes and preconceptions. Even scholarly discussions show often enough a lack of understanding of what a peer in one's own discipline is trying to say. Probably a good many polemic exchanges in scholarly journals, not to speak of argumentative discussions in newspapers and magazines, arise in the first place because the thrust and the details of what one person says are misunderstood by the other person. In personal relationships, notably between spouses or between parents and their children, we often find a flagrant lack of competence for hearing what the other person is saying.

The interview can considerably sharpen our skills for hearing. If properly used, it allows for the temporary suspension of one's own belief system, judgmentalness, preconceptions, and other dispositions by which we filter and may distort information from the external world. It allows us instead to enter into another person's world and to see that world in her or his terms. The interview thus can be a powerful exercise in objectivity, transcending the limits and enlarging the scope of one's own subjective ways of perceiving and evaluating. The interviewer is no passive camera. What he or she hears does not fall upon a tabula rasa, but upon a mind that, while entering into somebody else's construction of the world, is affected and challenged, at time deeply, in its own sense of people and things. The interview may put into question some very cherished beliefs. Indeed, there is a double power to the interview: It allows for an expansion of understanding of what other people are like cognitively and emotionally, and it makes possible a gradual modification of one's own self—an altered belief system, a different way of feeling, a different disposition toward action.

We may interview just one individual, several students, or even a whole class. For the interview to lead us into somebody else's world we must guard, methodically, against the tendency to steer our respondents, even if subtly, toward saying things that come from our world rather than from theirs. Acquiring competency in interviewing is precisely the overcoming of such subjective imposition. At its most skillful level, the interview goes beyond eliciting what the interviewees might already have thought or articulated before we meet with them and enables them to achieve articulations about their situations and themselves that go beyond their previous knowledge or even capacities. Not only the interviewer but also the interviewee finds out things that were unknown when the session began. But that capacity to elicit somebody else's thinking is conditional upon a process by which the interviewers themselves actually think, and modify their thinking, as they proceed in the interview. Professors learn much not only about their students, but also about themselves.

The challenging nature of the interview makes it also a teaching instrument. For instance, students who are interviewed regularly by their teacher in the course of a semester can learn much about the ways in which they think or learn, and this articulation may modify considerably their ways of learning. The interview raises what is implicit to the level of awareness and this leads to fresh experimentation, then to reflection on that experimentation in a further interview, and so on in a continuing cycle of new thoughts and experiences. The classroom, homework, motivation, and learning style may be affected in fundamental ways. What we are after is gaining a sense of the students' world that can serve as a guide for our teaching and their learning. This includes obtaining a picture of the great differences in learning ways among our students. We are not here focusing on the counseling or therapeutic uses of the interview. But this distinction is not easily made. As thinking and instruction are never affectless, one cannot, in the long run, do a complete interview without having an adequate sense of one's own emotion and the interviewee's emotions and how these affect learning.

LEARNING TO INTERVIEW — THE INTERVIEW SCHEDULE

There is, or there should be, no set way for conducting interviews. If the interview is the creative instrument we have said it to be, the individual interviewers must find their own style. The process of discovery in interviewing, as in teaching, involves a distinctive use of one's own person. The interview is a relation between people, and the interviewer's attention and understanding can lead interviewees to open themselves more fully. To practice the skill of interviewing one might start with one's own or somebody else's tape-recorded (or videotaped) interviews and *discuss* them with one or several other colleagues. Role-playing (both the interviewer and interviewee roles) can be helpful. After one has done one's first interview or interviews and listens back to them, it is good to bear in mind that many people are self-conscious when they hear their interviews for the first time. Some people are overly judgmental, and anything "bad" seems magnified. It may be advisable to have this first listening shared with an experienced interviewer who can provide perspective. It is good for the beginner to know that even experienced interviewers, when they listen to their own interviews, find that they have not followed up some important clue or have been asking "leading" questions that influence the response unduly.

The first step in preparing an interview schedule is to ask oneself what question areas one would like to explore. For instance, we may want to know how students respond to their teachers, to the classroom, how they prepare at home for their classes, for tests, how they go about writing papers. It is probably a good idea not to fix on the questions too specifically at first but to do several rather open-ended trial interviews in which the interviewer keeps in mind the question *area* he or she wants to explore and asks questions in these domains. This approach often gives important leads to how the students themselves think and respond in the areas under investigation, what kinds of questions seem to work well and are elicitive. Often as well it generates new questions or question areas one did not previously think of. At the end of each exploratory interview it is a good idea to tell the students what the intent of the interview was and to ask them for suggestions about what they might ask if they were to conduct such an inquiry. We have found the students' responses to this last query often highly valuable.

After these preliminaries one can work out an interview schedule with a more definite set of questions. It is important to ask the same questions of differing people to achieve comparability. But it would be missing out on the opportunity of the interview as an instrument of discovery if one did not follow up clues and ideas that arise in any specific interview. At the minimum one learns more about the individual student, but not uncommonly one student's articulations can open up new domains and describe things that are true not just for himself or herself but other students as well. Going beyond the predetermined questions can be one source of fresh discovery.

The interview has its own inherent structure. It is desirable to taper off at the end so that the interviewee does not leave the session in a high state of tension. But it is usually quite possible, if not desirable, to have the casual talk at the beginning reduced to a minimum. One can state in a few words the purpose of the interview (or the project of which it is a part) and then launch into the first question. One may add that the interviewee will get a good idea of the intent of the interview or the project through the interview itself, and that there will be opportunity to ask questions at the end. Obviously one should not raise the most sensitive issues at the beginning. If the interview is tape-recorded, as it is useful to do, one should ask for permission to record and may say that the interview is confidential. We suggest keeping the request and the reference to confidentiality very brief; a long explanation may arouse suspicion and, given our commitment to confidentiality—which of course must be kept strictly—we can expect trust from the student as well. It is not necessary to hide the recorder, but one might place it in such a way as to minimize obtrusiveness. Proper attention should be paid to the quality of the recording. The interviewer should try out the equipment beforehand in the location where the interview will take place and should keep in mind extraneous noises—through open windows, from fluorescent lighting, radiators, and the like. For relistening and for transcribing, the quality of the recording is crucial; otherwise interviewer or transcriber will have a grueling time.

THE INTERVIEW PROCESS

It is important to begin the interview at the agreed-upon time and not keep the student waiting. At the start of the interview one may ask some background or general questions, for instance, about some previous courses that the student has taken. Sometimes if in the response to an early question one gets clues to some deeper thoughts or feelings of the student, one may make a mental note and come back to them later in the interview when more of a situation of trust and expressiveness has been established. It is a particularly good idea for the interviewer to talk very little at the beginning of the interview so that the *student* gets into the frame of mind of talking. Throughout the interview it is desirable not to rush into the next question. Sometimes the student is catching his or her breath or is hesitant, and if the interviewer waits, the student will say it. This is particularly true in regard to things that are more difficult for the student to say. If the interviewer does not wait, the student may get the idea that the interviewer does not want to hear about it or is embarrassed about it. Learning to be silent can be difficult for the teacher turned interviewer.

It is a good idea to take notes during the interview even though it is being tape-recorded. It has the advantage of obtaining an immediate written record of the interview. On the basis of this record interviewers can decide which portion of the interview they want to listen to again or which portion they want to transcribe (on the assumption that it is often too costly or not necessary to transcribe the entire interview). Some people can take notes and still keep looking at the students and remain attentive to them. Others find this difficult, particularly when they have not had much experience. One may, therefore, want to take only very brief notes. This allows one to have an "outline" of the interview and to find the appropriate place on the tape. One might want to take no notes at all and write from memory right after the interview. Or one might relisten to the interview and take notes then. For training purposes relistening is very useful. Even very experienced interviewers discover how much they missed during the interview itself. If one has taken notes one may discover that some of the things one wrote down have changed or even distorted what the respondent actually said.

An interviewee will rarely object to being tape-recorded. Equally rarely, a student may during the interview express anxiety about being recorded, perhaps because the information he or she is giving may seem "sensitive" for a variety of reasons. If that happens, the interviewer might suggest turning off the recorder, perhaps to be turned on after this particularly embarrassing or difficult portion of the interview is over. It is desirable to keep the tape recorder going even after the formal interview is over. Sometimes important things are said then. It also deemphasizes the use of the recorder. Students who are more strongly conscious of its use may reveal their concern by referring to the recorder during the interview, or they may call attention at the end of the interview to the fact that it is still running.

In conducting the interview, the interviewers will usually have the list of questions in an easily visible position (unless they have memorized it). On such lists the questions usually are numbered and arranged in some topical order. But at any time in the course of the interview a student may bring up matters that relate to a later question on the list. In this event it is desirable to stick with the interviewee's sense of sequence and not be concerned with the order of questions on the form. The more spontaneous the interviews, the more likely one is to get more revealing information. The interview should flow as much as possible like a conversation and not like a barrage of questions.

In each question area one probably should start with a rather vague and general question. For instance, one might ask generally how the student felt about a class session or why she or he chose a certain course, or how she or he would describe a certain teacher. The advantage of vague over more specific questions is that the interviewees get less of a clue about what the interviewers may want to find out and hence prevents them from structuring their responses in the direction of what they think the interviewers want to hear. Particularly at the beginning of an interview, many students have a desire to please by giving the "correct" response. In reacting to a generally phrased question a student may ask that the question be more specifically formulated. On those occasions one might respond by reformulating the question equally generally, but in different words. Usually that is all that is required. If a student still asks for more specificity one can simply suggest that she or he do as well as possible with the question as worded. Students' requests for more specificity may be attempts to "psych out" the interviewer or may simply be a way of catching their breath before they begin to talk—or perhaps these are indirect requests for reassurance concerning what they are going to say.

Students often are marvelously explicit even in response to vaguely formulated questions. Such questions have the additional advantage that they may lead students to go into areas that the interviewer has not thought of, and they serve the primary purpose of the interview to find out what is in the student's thoughts and perceptions. Nevertheless, we want to obtain answers to specific questions. Regarding these questions, the interviewer may wait for the opportunity when, in the flow of the interview, they are most opportunely and least disruptively asked. If interviewers are not bound to the sequential order on the interview schedule, they will be surprised at how much students will turn on their own to appropriate areas, to the point at times of giving answers without the question's having been asked.

Ideally the interviewer asks as few questions as possible and the student talks as much as possible. This does not mean that the interviewer becomes a passive recording device. First of all, the interviewer is alert intellectually to the ways, often different from his or her own, of the student's construing the world. This alertness leads the interviewer to formulate probing questions that prod interviewees to levels of articulation they have not previously achieved. At its best this becomes a cooperative enterprise transcending the sort of preset question–answer format that would separate interviewer from interviewee. Second, the interviewer's attention is an important incentive to the student. The chance to talk to an *interested* adult, a professor, in itself provides a not-insignificant encouragement. At such points where the student expresses some salient feelings, one might indicate that one understands them and is moved by them. Similarly, as the student talks about some problems and dilemmas, it may be well to let the student know, through gesture or a few words, of one's empathy for them. To be understood is an important human experience, one not had as often as desirable, and the interview can be an important vehicle. It is wise, however, not to *agree* too readily with students, for instance, with their expressions of protest or complaints. First of all, it may take a while before we really know the bases and possible legitimacy of their complaints. Moreover, students may have a more or less dim sense of the partiality of these complaints. If interviewers confirm complaints too readily they may undercut the students' possible efforts at redress, at taking more responsibility upon themselves; the interviewer may thus encourage a student's tendency to blame other people or external circumstances. It is also good to remember that ambivalence frequently characterizes human emotions. If the interviewer agrees with one side of the ambivalence, the student may lose sight of the other, for example, in the case of conflicting feelings about friends, parents, or teachers. Interviewers for their part are by no means neutral observers. An interviewer's disapproval or rivalry, or paternal or maternal feelings can detract from objectivity, distort a student's responses, and even adversely affect the student's sense of self. Interviewers must become adequately conscious of this aspect of their role and they might seek help from a knowledgeable colleague to recognize what in psychoanalytic language is called the countertransference.

The interview can generate a high degree of involvement, and students may talk about certain intricate problems in depth and with tension. Hence it is good to plan for a leveling off toward the end of the interview and to conclude the interview with one or two questions that are relatively unburdensome. In addition, particularly at the end of a first interview or a one-shot interview, it is desirable to ask the student whether he or she has any questions of the interviewer. It may bring something out in the open that has been of concern to the student and that he or she has not dared or not seen an occasion to say. Moreover, sometimes this question leads the student to ask some further questions about the interview and to make some particularly revealing comments. Students may also ask about the purpose of the interview. One should be rather brief in one's initial response. The temptation for the interviewer is to give rather long and wordy answers. But the students usually are not very interested in the details. In the rare cases that they are, they will usually let us know. Their questions may instead be concerned with finding out how they compare with others, whether they are "normal," and so on. In such cases a brief reassuring response may be all that is needed. One may also ask the student for a reaction to the interview situation; this will allow the student to ask questions stirred up by the interview. If it was a one-shot interview it may be desirable to offer the opportunity of a return. At the end of this chapter we provide a sample of interview schedules for a professor who wants to make an initial exploration of the nature of teaching and learning.

In chapter 2 the approach we describe calls for repeated interviewing of the same student. Professors we have worked with have at times balked at this investment of time only to find themselves eventually richly rewarded for the effort and quite willing to give the time. Several interviews with the same persons have advantages over one or two. People often begin to open up more deeply only by the third interview. A certain trust in the interviewer is established and the student has learned more about the art of self-expression. It is wise for the interviewers to review their notes of previous interviews so that they do not disappoint the student by not remembering something that was said previously. Such reviews also alert one to gaps in what the student has said and to areas that are particularly interesting for further exploration. For repeated interviews with the same student the structure of each interview should be flexible. One should keep the major question areas in mind and may go into only some of them at any one session. Question areas include the following: the student's reactions to the immediately past class session, perhaps certain salient episodes in it; reactions to the teacher's and fellow students' contributions and behavior during class; the student's ways of preparing for the class; for tests; ways of notetaking; of writing papers. One should not confine oneself to the classroom alone. Questions about the student's dormitory life or life at home or at work can be very revealing about his or her ways of thinking and learning. Often enough only an isolated portion of the student's mind is engaged in the classroom, and capacities that may be very useful for learning are fenced off in the extracurricular part of life.

As thinking is heavily dependent on and intertwined with the emotions, the exploration of the student's attitudes and feelings are highly relevant. Some exploration of the student's aspirations, relations with friends and parents, attitudes to authority, and sense of responsibility will tell us something of the cast of the student's mind, its sophistication and complexity. It will teach us something about the student's incentives for and resistances to learning. Impulse-driven assertiveness, fear of expression, anxiety about competence, lack of courage, fear of failure, fear of success—all these can stand in the way of cognitive skills that are "waiting" under the surface. The interviews may encourage some students to bring up more deep-seated emotional problems. It may be useful for the interviewer to be able to talk to a counselor or psychotherapist about these problems. It is desirable for the interviewer to have the names of one or two competent counselors or psychotherapists to whom a student can be referred if he or she so requests; but it is wise to wait for such a request or its near-expression rather than to suggest it.

To gain an even more complete sense of the student's thinking it is useful to collect other materials and to utilize them for one's ongoing interviews. Thus the interviewers might ask at appropriate times for copies of the student's tests, papers, and class notes. They might take their own notes of the student's behavior in the classroom. They might ask the students to keep a record of their responses in the classroom, how they do their homework, or their reflections on the contents and processes of the course.

ANALYSIS OF THE INTERVIEW RECORD

The interviewer's analysis of his or her records is a difficult task. The high costs involved usually prevent systematic coding of the interviewer's notes or of partial or whole transcripts of the interviews. The conventional coding procedures, moreover, may be not appropriate, except perhaps for limited portions of the record. The thrust of the interviews here envisioned is heuristic. The aim is to obtain articulations of how students go about their various learning tasks in and out of the classroom. In a series of interviews with the same student, the same question areas will come up repeatedly, but the questions will be asked in different ways, hopefully each time in a deepened way based on what was said in prior interviews. The students in the intervals between interviews are likely to have done reflective work of their own. Further opportunities for analysis and conceptualization come from comparing different students along the same dimensions and by comparing the students interviewed by one professor with students interviewed by others.

A form of "content analysis" seems most appropriate to the data generated through the methods here described. Interviewers might begin by differential *underlining* of the student's responses. This will lead to a first categorization of the data. They can then ask what descriptions of processes are furnished under a specific category. From these they might proceed to seek explanations. For instance, they might find that in response to certain situations student attention in class begins to wane. The data also may contain student descriptions of other situations that lead to increased student attention. Putting these data together may permit a plausible explanation of the factors involved.

The explanation will be confirmed and redefined if the teacher tries a new approach in class. This interaction of interviews and classroom practice is a useful way to generate fresh knowledge. A simple illustration of this process is one teacher's discovery (see Aaron Carton's description in chapter 5) that his not leaving enough "pauses" or time for assimilation in his presentations caused many students' attention to fade. The first clue to this phenomenon came from one student who remarked that the teacher's going to the blackboard and writing on it were welcome occasions because he used the extra time for assimilation. The teacher in turn tested the hypothesis by varying the pace and substance of his presentations.

Interviewing is a highly active process, first in the doing and later in the interpretation. Our interviewees are not easily able to articulate some of the things they are thinking and feeling, and they need help to reach such articulations. Furthermore, our interviewees are not easily able to articulate for us the structure and dynamics of their learning processes. They may give us the raw materials out of which we, with their help, can construct articulations, concepts, and theories; but we will not get the raw materials unless we ask the appropriate questions and stimulate and prod our interviewees to give us descriptions in detail and depth. The analysis of the interviews requires the interviewer's interpretive imagination. For instance, a student will not tell us that his thinking is "dualistic," but out of his detailed descriptions such a category can be furnished. Perry's work is a good instance of successful categorization of interview data. The approach described in this book has the advantage of getting the data from students continually while the course is progressing, rather than having them reflect on their coursework after it is over.

INTERVIEWING AND THE CURRICULUM

After having talked about the spirit and the mechanics of interviewing we raise, in conclusion, a curricular question. The interview is a prime instrument for developing listening skills, and listening is, as we have suggested, one of the major human aptitudes, the complementary domain to expression. Why then is listening — in the sense of active hearing — not given a larger place in the curriculum? We take the teaching of writing skills for granted, but why not the skills of listening? Perhaps the answer lies in the fact that defects in listening, an "inner" process, are not as easily visible as defects in writing, even though the effects of not listening are if anything more injurious. Some attempts to help students learn to listen are made. For instance, when we ask them to describe the argument of a chapter or book, we encourage and test something of their listening skills. But such attempts are often rudimentary. Few professors ever look at their students' notebooks or ask students for some rendition of what was just said in class. If professors inquired they would soon discover many deficiencies in listening, which might move them to enable their students and themselves, to learn how to listen better.

If listening were to have a larger place in the curriculum the interview would emerge as a major tool. The interview can bring thoughts and feelings into the open and can lead to new levels of articulateness. The interview can enhance the learning capacities and self-reflectiveness of *both* interviewee and interviewer. The practice of students' interviewing fellow students as well as other people in different domains of life can become a source of enlarging knowledge and sophisticated empathy and understanding of other people. In giving the interview a place in the curriculum, one should, however, not repeat the mistake made with writing and locate the teaching of interviewing in a special course. Rather, interviewing skills should be taught in several courses, for example, history, psychology, and linguistics, where interviewing would serve different purposes and where the complexity of the tool would allow it to take on different forms and develop in the context of different methodologies.

Being able to listen to oneself is a prime condition of successful achievement of personal identity. Being able to listen to others is a prime condition of harmonious social intercourse and, moreover, it helps us to transcend the narrower boundaries of self that are the inevitable effects of a particular upbringing. Understanding what fellow investigators are saying is a condition of building one's own progress in knowledge on the work of others. These are essential aptitudes, and making interviewing a more deliberate part of the curriculum would allow us to address ourselves more effectively to their cultivation.

SAMPLE PLAN FOR INTERVIEWING STUDENTS AND FACULTY AND FOR CLASSROOM OBSERVATIONS

The following is a three-part sample plan for an initial exploration of student learning and faculty teaching. The plan consists (1) of interviews by a faculty member with one or several students taking a course, (2) an interview with a colleague prior to observing the colleague's class, and (3) classroom observation and interview of the teacher afterwards. All questions are samples; they may be added to or omitted to fit the needs of the inquirer.

(1) Student Interviews

Ask for age, class, and major of student, and note sex.

1. When you first came to this college, what were your expectations? To what extent have your expectations been met, and how? Have they been modified, and why? (Expectations may be academic, personal, social, etc.)
2. Can you think of a course that was particularly meaningful to you and describe it for me (teaching, contents, procedures, requirements, grading)? *What* did you learn in that course and *how?*
3. Please describe to me your current course (the course under observation): contents and procedures, the professor's ways of teaching, and the nature of your fellow students' participation. In *what ways* do you go about learning in the course and *what* do you learn? (Be sure to ask about the ways in which the student studies for the course.)
4. What two or three major changes are most desirable in this course and why? What would help you to learn better and develop better?
5. When you think of your experiences in different college courses, can you list some dos and don'ts that might enable a student like yourself to learn better?
6. What do you do outside of classes and studying? What activities interest you particularly, and why? Can you tell me what relations you have with fellow students and other people? What do you do together, particularly with your closer friends? What do you talk about with your friends? Do you have a paid job and/or did you have one last summer? What benefits, other than money, do you derive from having a job?
7. In what ways are you different, academically and personally, from what you were when you entered college? What made you change, and how did it happen?

8. What would you like and what do you expect your life to be like ten to fifteen years from now? How does college serve the objectives you have set yourself for your later life? What contributions would you like to make to society, and which do you think you will actually make?

9. What two or three major changes are most desirable in this college, and why? What two or three things are particularly good about this college, and why?

(2) Faculty Interviews

Contact a professor you know or don't know, someone from your own department or from another department. Explain that your purpose is to learn about classroom teaching. Ask to interview him or her, and say you would like to observe a class and interview one or several students from the class. You may wish to ask for an interview *first* and during the interview ask about visiting a class and interviewing students.

1. Thinking back to your own undergraduate education, can you select a teacher from whom you learned particularly well and describe for me how he or she went about teaching and enabling you to learn?

2. Can you tell what your teaching was like when you first taught? What changes have you made in your teaching and why?

3. In regard to a course you are currently teaching (that is, the one the interviewer plans to observe), can you tell me (a) what your objectives for this course are and how you go about realizing them; (b) what you think is particularly important that your students learn; (c) how and in what different ways your students respond to your course and how they go about mastering the materials of your course; (d) how you determine what you are achieving; and (e) how you go about improving your teaching (in terms of student learning)?

4. Please give an example of a successful classroom hour in your course and describe it in some detail. Please describe an unsuccessful class hour. What do you do when a class goes wrong and how do you define *wrong?*

5. In your years of teaching, what changes have you observed in students and the ways in which they learn?

6. How is your teaching related to your research and scholarship? Are you different in the two roles?

7. What satisfactions do you derive from being a teacher? What are the dissatisfactions? What suggestions do you have for your institution so that it can become a better place for teaching (student learning)?

(3) Classroom Observation and Interview
with the Teacher Afterwards

Try to arrive a few minutes before the beginning of the class to observe student attitudes, moods, and what they are talking about. Seat yourself where you have the best view; try to be in a position where you can see the faces of the students. When the class is in progress, observe contents (for example, organization of material), methods of presentation, pace, rapport with class, and affective components (for example, concern, distance, humor, sarcasm). Watch student behavior in relation to what the professor does at any moment. Even in a straight lecture one can observe when students take notes, when they are restless, when they look at the professor; one can watch their various postures, moods, energy, relations with each other. When students ask questions and when there is discussion, the materials for observation may get richer. Always have regard also to the differences among students in the same class. Take notes on the content and process of the class. (This paragraph largely repeats suggestions made in chapter 2.)

Try to arrange to talk with your colleague about the class afterwards, preferably immediately after (you might walk back together to your colleague's office, have lunch together, or the like). You might begin by asking about your colleague's reactions to the particular class hour. (The vagueness of the question might elicit his or her perceptions and preoccupations). You might explore what your colleague intended for this particular hour, to what extent your colleague feels, and on what evidence, that these objectives were realized, what perceptions your colleague has of the students' reactions and learning during the hour and in the course as a whole. It is probably best for you to make as few affirmative statements as possible and to cast much of what you say in question form and in an exploratory mode. Your classroom observations and your student interviews should provide a rich source for questions. If you engage in observations and interviews repeatedly, you may over time be able to help your colleague and yourself to reach more complex articulations of what you do as teachers.

The classroom is such a varied phenomenon and observers bring forward such varied questions about it that you may soon find yourself stimulated to conduct your observations according to a partially or wholly different scheme than the one suggested here.

8

Interviews about Teaching and Student Learning with a Biologist and a Political Scientist

At the end of our Ford Foundation project we interviewed all faculty participants about their teaching. The interviewees gave us, each in turn, a distinctive account of how they seek to enable their students to learn. This chapter offers somewhat abbreviated versions of two of the interviews, and they have been slightly edited for readability. They exemplify that interviews can be an opportunity for faculty to reflect on and articulate what they do in their work with students, and they can serve as a source of knowledge for colleagues and groups of colleagues who wish to develop the practice and the theory of learning and teaching. We first reproduce the schedule of questions we followed, flexibly, in our interviews.

INTERVIEW QUESTIONS

1. How did you get into your profession and into teaching?
2. How is your teaching now different from what it was when you first taught?
3. How would you characterize your students and the differences in their learning styles? What are the differences in the ways in which you teach nonmajors and majors?
4. What do you think is particularly important that your students learn? How do you go about teaching (that is, make possible for your

students to learn these things?) What cues do you use to assess how you come across to your students? How do you assess (evaluate) your teaching on a day-to-day basis? How do you go about improving your teaching (student learning)?

5. What do you find most difficult in teaching? If a class goes wrong, what do you do? How you define *wrong?* What do you like most in teaching? Does "overload" interfere with what is essential in your work with students? Can this be remedied, and how?

6. What preparations do you make before you meet a class?

7. How is your teaching related to your research and scholarship? Are you different in the two roles?

8. Why do you teach? What would you rather do? If you were not in this profession, what might you do?

9. Can you give me a brief sketch of your philosophy of education? Does your teaching live up to your philosophy?

10. What have you done as a participant in the Ford Foundation project? What has the project done for you? What relevance does it have for yourself and your college in the future?

INTERVIEW WITH J.L.*

The beginning of the tape was accidentally erased, and we summarize it from notes taken during the interview. The interviewee started out by saying that when he was in graduate school his primary goal was to be a research scientist. He comes from a family of scientists; his being a teacher is a byproduct. In his teaching he wants to convey to his students both what goes on in the lab and the intellectual excitement of science. He finds that teaching offers scientific benefits, too, because going over basics allows him to rethink fundamental questions in his field. His teaching method is influenced by the fact that in college he started out as a theater major and switched to biology. He thinks that his acting background is helpful in his teaching because he knows something about the mechanics of speaking in front of people and about imparting information that is interesting to an audience. The course he was observed in was his first major teaching task, and he was still working out the mechanics of the class.

At this point the tape begins.

How long have you been teaching?

It will be two years at this institution. I did only spot lectures before; I was a teaching assistant. I have not had any major teaching experience. The

---

* J. L. is an assistant professor in a biology department.

course I taught under the Ford project I did in a different way toward the end, based on the feedback that I got from the interviews and from talking with my colleague. From the students I got useful information about when they paid the most attention and what was most effective in terms of their understanding the material. I interviewed two students, and they were very different students. One was clearly more interested in having all the little pieces put on the table and arranged in the right order and not having to worry about analyzing anything: She wanted things pieced together; she was very mechanistic in that way, perhaps out of fear of using her imagination or creativity. The other fellow was just the opposite. He had this intense problem with memorizing—hated learning by memorizing—and really wanted to do the paper that I assign in my class because he thought that doing a paper was a great way of understanding something. He may have had some fear of being put on the spot to memorize things, whereas the other student had just the opposite problem.

Both of them, in spite of their differences, said that the way that they learned the best and the times when they found themselves paying closest attention in class were when a story or a history was being told and they were taken from A to B to C to D, and it was put in a very human and contemporary context. These were the things that they really remembered and they were the most interesting. I played with that in class and now I can watch and literally see people nodding off when I am not doing it and I see people at the edge of their seats when I get to the punchline and hold back and ask them a question. It is something I never realized was so important. To speak as though someone is listening is something teachers may not do. They may present facts and give a list of information, but they are not speaking as if someone is out there. I know from my theatre background that you can't get away with that—when you are playing to an audience you have to appeal to them. You can't just get up there and give them some information. So, to appeal to my students, I now try to present a coherent story based on the work of other researchers. That is really helpful.

Where do you get the information?
I look at the original papers and see who did what and when.

You talk about giving a more dramatic background. What do you mean?
Once in a while I get into a subject such as dueling it out for the Nobel Prize. I talk about how a particular person moved from a base of limited knowledge to a better understanding of the subject, and how different research groups came up with different information on the same problem. This is essentially how modern science works. Everybody looks at different aspects of the same problem, or attacks the same problem by different methods, and tries to collect information that will verify or argue against

the current working model, which has changed ever so slightly. To look at it as a dynamic process is very different from just presenting it as static. The students can see how one group of researchers trying to solve a problem came up with an explanation that didn't quite agree with another group; these researchers said, Maybe we can explain it in *this* way. Or person A found out this side of it and person B found out that side, and when they got together the answer began to make some sense. Or one person realized that another person was working on the problem and was mistaken by using this technique. [In a prior discussion this professor reported that early in the course he was observed in he told the students the history and processes of the research efforts he himself had participated in. When he noted how these accounts aroused the students' interest he began to gather the requisite information on other research topics.] Real science is a continuing, evolving process. When you treat it like a process, it becomes more truthful, more real, and more vivid for the students, and they will understand it much more than if they are presented an antiscientific approach according to which they are just given lists of things and asked to memorize them. And yet that is the way most science courses are taught.

How come?

I think there are a number of factors that lead up to this. I don't think that it is any one person's fault. There is a very nasty symbiotic relationship between students and teachers at certain universities. Students come in having been prepared in the sciences by very primitive teaching methods, based on the idea that in science they somehow have to get the basics first. This is analogous to having to memorize the letters in the first grade. I think that science students are kept at this learning level for too long; hence even though they may be seniors in high school, they are still learning this way, instead of an active, reasoning, scientific, analytical approach. There also is a very, very profound pressure on these kids, which they put on themselves and which their parents put on them—to go to medical school. Three-fourths of the students that we get are going to medical school; it seems like that to me and this pressure makes for a profoundly different student. Their motivation is intense, completely different from other students', and as a result they are very uptight and very nervous, and in a way their minds get closed. They are fearful of not being able to get the important stuff, so they cannot deal with anything that they feel is extraneous. They are panicked by not having things listed out in front of them so they will know what they are supposed to know. They are also panicked by the thought that there is no limit to what they have to know. Both of these panics are very antiintellectual. They come to college with these attitudes and they are reinforced by their peers.

On the other side of the coin are the teachers. It is so easy for them to fall into the trap of giving the students what they want, giving them an A for doing what is not really A work, while they are not using their scholarly abilities and are not interested in the subject matter. Students do not realize how interesting it can be when they actually get into doing and finding out something and making it their own. When they make some information their own, synthesize something new, it becomes an active process, very different from just taking information, holding onto it for a while, and then regurgitating it.

Have you been able to break into that?

I don't really know. I don't know when they're just giving lip service to me and when they really have broken out of that mode. We are talking about some very smart students. I lay the blame on the teachers when they give the students essentially what they are asking for because that is the easiest thing to do. These teachers don't have to go out and do more work for their teaching, so they have no real incentive to teach well, especially at a large university. Particularly the younger assistant professors are not in any way, shape, or form ever judged on their teaching. Under those circumstances, people may do the least amount possible to get by. Out of self-respect and pride, most people will do a good job anyway. But it depends. I feel myself that I am being tugged in the opposite direction. I know darn well that my research is all that counts according to this university. To be said to be the best teacher in some departments is equivalent to the "good sport" award on the basketball team, given to the guy who is on the second team and probably never gets into the game. That is an unwritten attitude in a lot of departments and as a result undergraduate teaching suffers. But even so, at this university I don't see a lot of people slacking off. I see people in this department taking pride in their teaching.

How would you characterize your students and differences in the ways in which they learn?

I think that one of the two students I interviewed was more of a fact monster than the other. I think she was more interested in having things ordered as a part of a puzzle put together so she could see how it worked. In that sense, she was leaning toward a process or mechanistic approach, and in that sense I don't think that she was the classic "just give me the facts" person. She recognized her limitations and said she was working on being more analytical and more creative in her approach. You could tell with her that it was a clear-cut case of her being insecure about her abilities and even fearful of taking part in a class discussion. If students are like this, it is out of anxiety. It is unfortunate, it gets in the way.

Have you found this to be more often the case with women students?

No, not really. The reason I think not is that perhaps there is even more pressure on some of the male students, from their parents and from themselves, to go to medical school. I have seen that some of my women students are less encumbered by these types of anxiety and perhaps come up with more interesting approaches. This is not to say that in some cases they are not as driven. Quite the contrary. They just come in with less of the baggage, and they are sometimes more able to perform as scientists.

Is there anything that you have tried in order to tackle your students' anxiety?

Yes. I try to have them do things that tap their intellectual abilities without putting them on the spot, like writing a paper. I think *that* is the main reason why I emphasize the paper so much. Most of them have never written a scientific paper or a paper for a science class. Many go for four years without ever having used more than maybe a couple of textbooks from the library, which is shocking. We have all these stacks and stacks of journals and all the information you could ever want and hardly any of the undergraduates ever learn how to read a journal article before they leave and that is something that I virtually force them to do. I have them write a paper and I have them analyze at least two or three primary scientific papers. So they have to understand how to read literature, how to put it together and make some model, how to analyze data, and most of all to get over the intimidation of reading what scientists publish. One of the first things I do in the class is announce that the students are going to be able to read papers before they are done, and I try to explain to them that most scientists cannot write very well. I show them examples illustrating how badly people do things, either in the lab or in writing. They find that rather amusing. Also on tests I go right to journal articles. I pull out some data and I put them on the test and say, explain this. They are shocked afterwards to find that that was what I had done, and you can tell that they feel proud of themselves that by hook or crook they have finally been able to understand something that was written by a scientist. I think they feel less removed from the actual scientific process if they have been forced, not just under the gun but at their leisure during the term, to sift through original works.

Could this be done with lower-division students as well?

I don't really know. You would have to be a lot more careful about the kind of things you would have them read.

It seems to work with the upper-division students?

Most of them. Some students miss the mark entirely. They can't get over the intimidation, the fear. Or they try to laugh it off and say that this isn't really what is required to go to medical school, so they say that they are going to do the least amount possible to get through this assignment. One student actually stood up in class and said: "Are you telling us that this paper is going to be one third of our grade?'' That guy I lit into. I really got mad that time because he was making the utmost antiintellectual statement: What does reading stuff in scientific articles have to do with understanding the material? Why can't you just tell us what it was about?

What happened with the student?

He went to medical school. He wrote a paper by going to a chapter in a book that summarized findings from a bunch of other papers. He never concentrated on articles; all he presented to me in his paper was on the one person who wrote the chapter and who of course quotes himself as scientists usually do. So the paper was horrible. He never went into any issue except to regurgitate what this fellow had said. I gave him the lowest grade in the class. He probably couldn't have cared less because he was already going to medical school.

You said that the paper assignment reduces anxiety.

Yes, for some students. They feel that they don't have to be put on the spot for a test, that they can accomplish something well at their own pace without being put under the gun and can show me how they can do something like this. Some students don't want that because they want to concentrate on what they feel is important and not be confused by anything extra. I give them a little bit of the old ''just give me the facts, mam'' approach, just because it is a rock that they can stand on. They say to themselves that at least they will get this portion because they know exactly what the teacher wants. I do it to reduce their anxiety, like giving them an anatomy diagram and asking them to point out the following things. There is a place for that. They do have to learn the vocabulary; they do have to learn certain very basic processes. Sometimes I just don't have the time to tell a story about the evolution of the research. So a good portion of my course is still that way. When I started out with my class in the Ford project, I was almost forced to go back and teach that way at the beginning because of my own inexperience in teaching. I have progressed the way that students might progress in the course. I think I will teach the course very differently next year.

What do you think is particularly important that your students learn? How do you assess on a day-to-day basis what they learn and, in light of it, how do you change your ways of teaching?

I perhaps don't get as much feedback as I should as the course progresses, but my main sources are how they do on the midterm and when they come in during my office hours to go over class notes and talk about how their papers are progressing. I make sure that they see me about their papers. I require them to come in. It allows me to get to know the students, to talk to them, and I make sure that they focus on good papers and are not going to get lost in the wilderness just because they don't quite know how to put the paper together. It is a difficult thing for them to do the first time, and I want to make sure it is a positive reinforcing experience instead of a catastrophe. I have undergraduate and graduate students who work in my lab and who are sitting in on the class, and they are almost like my spy system. I can tell from them whether I am leaving anybody in the dust or talking through my hat. I don't think they realize they are used in that sense, but I can understand a lot of what goes on in the class by personal contact with these students.

Did you suggest that you would like to have more feedback?

My initial reaction was that maybe I don't get enough feedback, but now that I think about it maybe I do.

How do you use it?

I think about it and ask: Am I going too far out, away from what I really wanted to do in the course, or am I just rehashing some stuff that they may have had in another course? Am I talking about things that perhaps they cannot sink their teeth into because not enough is known about it at this point? Or, on the other hand, am I just going over some basic physiological process that is redundant?

But you also seem to pay a fair amount of attention to process, for instance, when you identify anxiety.

I do — when students come in and they are particularly upset or anxious or curious or in one way or the other there is some extreme thing that sticks out at me, and I realize that something that I am doing could be done in a different way.

What do you find most difficult in teaching?

Striking a balance between students' not wanting to be confused by too much complexity and students' becoming easily bored and uninterested because there is nothing that is taxing their ability to think.

What preparations do you make for your teaching before you meet a class?

I will do a lot of reading, take some notes on the reading, make a quick outline. Then I will sit down in front of a computer and give a lecture off the top of my head. I won't use it, other than as a guide.

How is teaching related to your research? Are you different in the two roles?

I am fortunate in that I am teaching courses portions of which are some- what close to my research area, so the process of teaching is very helpful for me in keeping current on the fundamentals and the more sophisticated levels and the ways they relate to my own research. Teaching keeps you crisp; keeps you primed; keeps you thinking; keeps you sharp; keeps your perspective. When you are talking about things that are not exactly in your area, there are certain mechanisms and certain processes that are basic and underlie all aspects of biology that you lose sight of, but there are also some that might apply that you might not think of because they were used in a totally different area—a fresh insight, perhaps, that you would not have thought of if you were not keeping current on some other area.

Can you make a comparison with researchers in your field who are not teaching? Are they missing something?

If you are not doing some teaching you become very myopic in a lot of ways. I saw it in myself. When I was a post-doc I was at an institution where it was all research and very isolated from a university campus. After two and a half years there I felt as if my intellectual capacities in some sense were stale just from disuse. No matter how many group meetings you have on research papers and whatnot, it just doesn't take the place of hashing over things and looking at a broader context and looking in different areas. There is something about the rich atmosphere at a university campus that cannot be replaced. Also to have young, naive, but bright minds running around and asking all sorts of questions is a thrill a minute. They will ask nineteen outrageous questions and the twentieth is always going to be a real zinger because it is something you wouldn't have thought of before. You have the inhibitions that you have developed over ten or twenty years as a scientist. You need the intellectual exercise to stay intellectually fit and when you concentrate exclusively on your lab work for three months and then you sit down to write a paper, you lose sight of a lot of things, and you are not actively putting things together and synthesizing things.

You are making a powerful argument in favor of teaching.

It cuts both ways.

If you were not in this profession, what might you do?

Sometimes I call myself a researcher, and sometimes I call myself a university professor when I think of myself as a teacher. If you ask what I would do ideally besides research, I would say teach. If you ask what I would do besides teach, I would say research. If I were not here, I would probably be at a drug company doing research or at an undergraduate liberal arts college exclusively teaching. Perhaps I would be working for a biotechnology company.

Anything outside of the sciences?

I don't know how realistic it might be for me. In a lot of ways I have made choices that are definitive. I have always wanted to write.

You didn't mention the theatre, is that a past option?

As a hobby, but not as a profession. I don't have the desire to satisfy my ego on stage as much as doing something like writing a play and using my composing abilities.

What is the appeal of teaching at a liberal arts college?

The teaching. I enjoy teaching. I could get in on some research and perhaps try to start something in a small way, at least keep up on the literature.

If somebody chased after you from a liberal arts college, with a lot of inducements, could they get you?

I doubt it. I love the research here and the interactions with my colleagues too much. I am having too much fun with my research, and I am far too interested in that to give it up for long.

Can you give me a very brief sketch of your philosophy of education?

As succinctly as I can put it: Learning the process of science, learning to learn. I do not believe that you can "learn" somebody. I think that people have to educate themselves, and that teachers are here as moderators. It is unfortunate that especially these days we are seeing students come in with the mentality of facts per buck. What I say are obviously lofty ideals that have not as much basis in reality as one would want, but if we can strive toward teaching students to exercise their scholarly capabilities, we will have done something. If we sit them down, and given them a textbook, and rehash what is in the textbook, we haven't taught them anything.

Can you give me a brief sketch of what you have done as a participant in the Ford project and what it has done for you?

I have interviewed a number of students and talked with them about my classes, and for me it has had a very positive impact. I can now put my finger on what exactly it is that makes a class work and what it is that allows a student to take part in a class and get something from it. It was especially informative for me as a junior faculty member. Starting out to recognize these things early will get me into some very good habits. Instead of doing things by instinct, I now can recognize some things that I am doing well and perhaps get rid of some things that I am not doing well. It has helped me a lot in interacting with students, having ways in which I can more effectively communicate with them and understand whether the things I am doing are having an influence on the class. Paying attention to what I am doing is probably the most important thing that I have learned. It sounds so simple but it is so basic: being aware of what you are doing. Just the act of analyzing what you are doing goes a real long way.

Where do you go from here?

This project has helped me put in perspective just how I keep a class in a certain state, and that, on a miniscale, is a scientific pursuit. It is a model that will get changed here and there as the years go on. It is almost like these movies where they take a piece of clay and in each different frame mold it a little differently so that things move forward. That is how I look at the class now. Within that piece of clay or entity there are little rings that intersect and those rings I can identify as stories. Students want a logical progression of how, yes, and putting together a puzzle, yes, but they want these told in the context that they can understand, and that is a story with a beginning, a middle, and an end that leads to the next story that has a beginning, a middle, and an end, and so on. Also my task is getting the students to become a part of it. I asked some students what they are going to remember from my course five years from now, and they all said that they would remember what they did for their paper. What they took on themselves is going to have the best and most profound impact.

How useful was it to observe your colleague?

I learned some basic mechanics from my colleague in the project by watching him. For example, I never used the board effectively. I wrote words that I was talking about and underlined them and that was as far as it went. I also did not pace myself very well in a lecture. I would go too fast or too slow, and I learned from looking at my colleague that I was doing that. He is a good lecturer and the students were very comfortable with his style.

How was it having an observer in your class?

Because it was the first couple of times that I was teaching, it made me extremely nervous to have him there. It was almost like having my pants down in public. But I got used to it. I was nervous enough already starting up a class for the first time and getting it going — because I didn't have the experience of teaching. I am not sure that having someone from outside of the department observing me would have made a difference. Even if less so, I would still have been anxiety-ridden.

Is there anything about the incredible demands on professorial time that could be eased?

No — it is sad but it is true. Given the rigors of getting tenure, of getting grant money for your research, the only possible solution is to reduce the teaching load. You could then pay more attention or do a better job in a fewer number of courses. On the other side of the coin, research competition for money is just as keen as ever, if not worse. You are on a much faster treadmill these days than you were fifteen years ago. You can tell *that* by the research papers that come out. It used to be that you would spend two or three years on a single study and publish a tome. Now you just have to publish, publish, publish.

The thing that gets me is that people's perception of the university professor is so distorted. While we are under all these pressures, the outside world looks upon the university professor as the person who maybe doesn't know where he put his shoes last night and rides the bicycle to work, the absent-minded genius who doesn't work all that hard. He sort of cogitates in the back room while smoking a pipe and every once in a while will come out and give his blessing to the class. A news magazine this past issue talks about the financial crunch at universities. They get to the part that university professors on the average are paid so and so many dollars. While this doesn't seem to be much and maybe they have a beef, the article says, professors do not seem to work very hard to get these salaries. Some study said that they are only teaching a certain fraction of the time and have to work only nine months of the year. I was livid, just livid that this is the stereotype. If the people only knew what my daily schedule is and how my wife and I have to make an appointment to see each other at ten o'clock at night. The perception is very different from the reality.

But I have to say, in fairness to the system, that we are being paid by government grants to follow our intellectual curiosity. Somebody could even call it a hobby; I wouldn't. What we do is part of a whole that will bring us to a point where we can improve our health, our quality of living. Each research project adds to that whole. I am firmly in favor of having basic science research as a way of getting to clinical and world global improvement. Nevertheless, if one of these projects were not there, the world would not suffer, and we are after all competing for money that will allow us to do what we enjoy doing. So I don't think that there should not be competition. I think that perhaps there should be more awareness of what younger faculty go through and the pressures that they face. The years immediately preceding tenure can be very stressful, especially at a place like mine where a lot of people don't get tenure. So on the one hand there is a real ecstasy in doing research and I cannot think of anything that is more pleasing outside of love and sex. At the same time, research is the most difficult thing to be able to get yourself in a position to do. It is sort of agony and ecstasy. As long as the ecstasy is still there, I will put up with the agony. At this point I would say that my agony level is low because I am enjoying what I am doing so much and I have been successful in getting research funds. I think that if I were strapped for research funds, couldn't support my graduate students and therefore couldn't do the science, I wouldn't be nearly as happy as I am now. I would consider going somewhere else and doing something else. In that sense, the university has been very supportive. They have given me a good lab, they try to make it easy for me to go out and get funds. There is good and bad from the system, just like, any system.

I want to thank you. I very much appreciate your participation in the project. It gave us much pleasure. I am happy that the project has been of help to you in your work with your students.

INTERVIEW WITH KATHERINE HOPE*

My first question is, how did you get into this profession?

The reason I got into this profession is my college advisor. I am very close to him, he is like a father to me. I took one of his courses. I liked him a lot and he for whatever reason picked me out and decided that I should do something of significance. I took a lot of his classes and did special projects with him. Last year in my department we did a little study to see how many women go into political science. We talked about how we could increase the numbers of our students who go on to graduate school in political science. One of my male colleagues interviewed all the women professors in the department and every one of them said that basically the reason they went into political science was that at some point in their undergraduate career they had a mentor who was a political scientist, who acted as a role model and encouraged them to go on.

Was it a male mentor?

Yes — I am not sure, but I think almost everyone had a male mentor. Given the proportion of males, this is not unusual.

Is your teaching different now from what it was when you first taught?

Yes. I do less lecturing and more teaching by asking the students questions and through discussion. There are still many times that I resort to lecturing. My institution has a preferred teaching manner that is oriented to discussion and participation by the students. I think that using discussion is a matter of my gaining more confidence. When you start teaching, you want to have your lecture all nicely structured, and you hope it will fill up the seventy minutes. Because you are not confident enough, you don't know what will happen in the classroom, how long it will take to present the material, what is difficult and what is easy. As you gain experience, you are more spontaneous. You know what you want to do and you go into the classroom and feel more comfortable trying different methods to achieve whatever end you have.

---

* Katherine Hope is assistant professor of Political Science at Wellesley College.

Lecturing is easier?

You have more control. If you want to convey a certain body of information and make sure that you get through it all and that it is understandable, it is easier to do in a lecture form. On the other hand, if you open up to a lot of student participation, you will get comments you don't expect, and it is sometimes hard to pull out of them what you want to pull out. For some things I teach, especially in my introductory course, there aren't any really appropriate readings, or at least readings that are at their level, or short enough that students will bother to do them. This means that the burden is on me when they haven't read an article and I want to extract the points; I have to be more creative and more skilled to convey the material if I am not just to lecture at them.

Do students tend to be less likely to read longer pieces?

I think they are more intimidated by longer pieces. I am teaching a seminar this semester, with a good group of students. At one point when I gave my assignment for the following week, one of my students raised her hand and said, "Do we really have to do all of them?" Length is one factor and the other is difficulty. You give them a long piece and if it is sort of story-oriented, they will probably go through it. If it is a long theoretical piece, they will probably find it discouraging and may be less prone to read all the way through. Our students are very diligent. They tend to do most of the work and most of the readings. It is quite impressive. They feel as if they must read every single word of everything that is assigned. It seems to take them a long time. One of the most important things I learned in college was how to cut corners, what you did and did not have to do. It is not that I didn't do the work when I was an undergraduate; in fact much of it I really enjoyed. But here the students seem much more diligent. But to some extent you see a change as they get older—the seniors to some extent have figured it out.

I had one student call me up on the phone one time in a panic because she couldn't figure out how she could possibly read every word of every assignment. I suggested to her that she didn't have to read each and every assignment thoroughly. She wanted to know which ones she didn't have to read, but I wouldn't tell her. My philosophy is that this is part of what you learn in college.

Have you ever discussed this with your whole class or only with individual students?

Individual students, but never a whole class.

When you talked to them, did they catch on?

I think some of them grasped the idea, but they didn't seem to understand how to go about it.

It may be something worth thinking about. The students would learn that it isn't a way of shortchanging themselves but learning a way of reading that allows them to get at the material. Turning to a related matter, what is the relative importance of conveying information versus helping students to acquire skills?

You teach the course because you want them to learn certain information. I feel it is especially important when I teach my Introductory American Government course. Because colleges are not big on teaching civics or trying to produce better citizens, I feel that some basic knowledge of how American politics and government operates is important for citizens. They should be more informed so that they can make more critical choices. Politics and government have a major impact on our lives. On the other hand, I also think it is important that they learn process, that they learn how to learn and how to think critically, that they learn to ask questions. The other thing I am big on, which they hate, is how to write. I downgrade them for poor writing. Whatever you do in life you have to know how to communicate either orally or on paper. When I was in college, I took a writing course and the teacher said that the reason it was so important to learn to write was that clear writing was the reflection of clear thinking.

Has the amount of information you want to convey changed?

In some ways it has. For example, in my introductory course I have had to reduce the amount of material I cover. It was clear to me from the first time I taught the course that I tried to cover too much material. Recently, I have given up, I have dropped a couple of topics.

How would you characterize your students in regard to differences in learning styles? Are there differences between majors and nonmajors?

Overall, the students that I see are not that interested in theory; they are very interested in practical or real-life stories and don't often see the linkage between theory and real life. A majority of students are like that, although some are less troubled by theory or actually enjoy theory. I do not see that big a difference between majors and nonmajors. By the time you get to the upper-level courses, you are dealing primarily with juniors and seniors. They are much more mature, they know a lot more and have a substantive background in the field. That's fun.

What do you mean by more mature?

They are older, able to think a little more on their own, better able to make evaluations on their own, more likely to try anyway. In my upper-level courses, we are more likely to have a situation where before we even start somebody will raise her hand and tell me she hates the reading. She just totally disagrees with the author. In my introductory courses, I usually don't find that. We start to discuss something and maybe once in a while somebody will put up her hand and say she doesn't like it. But it is hard to get students on that level to express disagreement; maybe they get a little more confident by the time they are juniors or seniors.

You still see much of a nontheoretical approach even at the upper level?

Yes, and even with some of my best students. Some students say to me that they don't see the value of theory. It is too abstract; it is not related to real life. Some of them even go so far as to claim that if you try to apply theory in real life, it doesn't work. It is just a series of abstract generalizations that is up in the clouds somewhere. It doesn't help you in real life or help you to understand what a real-life executive is about. On the other hand, a student called me recently. She graduated last year, works for the United States Department of the Treasury, and asked me to send her a copy of a reading in our seminar because she had given away her only copy. She told me that some of the things that we learned in class she could see operating in the treasury department. She was very pleased that some of the matters we had talked about, executives in American politics, she saw right there in Washington. So maybe later, students will see that theory and reality are more related than they think, and it may be that they don't have much experience with reality or theory because they are young. One of my colleagues and I like to talk about a recent report that suggested it may not be until people are older than college age that they have the skills or the ability to acquire wisdom, that is, to acquire a higher stage of knowledge. It may be that for a lot of people eighteen to twenty-two is still too young to deal with theory.

Do you think that more could be done to help students see the point of theory?

I guess you just keep trying. You try to persuade them that there is a relationship between theory and real life, and you provide examples. One of the things we are doing this semester in my seminar is reading a book about the Reagan presidency. If you read this book, you will understand why the Iran/Contra affair occurred. The book is not big on theory, so I try to use it as an example of some of the theoretical concepts we are talking about. I try to illustrate how if a particular theory is followed, it makes for a good executive, or if it is ignored, it makes for a bad executive. It might be helpful — although it is not easy to do — to have alumnae come back periodically. If an alumna said that out there on the job she actually saw some of the things happening that we talked about on a theoretical level, that might impress them. One of the things I say when emphasizing the importance of writing is that it is a "real world" skill. I often use the example of a student I had who had a summer job between her junior and senior years working for a consulting firm. She actually got a couple of articles published in trade journals. She was pleased to find that the consulting firm was very happy with her because she could write. She told me how worthwhile it was to have had to rewrite her papers. I guess you just keep harping at them and you hope while banging it into their heads that even if they don't realize it at the time, a year later they will realize it is important. There were things that I studied as an undergraduate that I didn't fully appreciate until a couple of years later or even now, ten years later.

Sometimes I say to my students that something we are discussing probably sounds boring or insignificant to them. But I don't think it is. For instance, one of the things we talk about both in my presidency course and my executive course is an article about organizing the White House for decision making. It provides three models of how you organize it so that the chief executive can make the best decisions. I will grant you that this is a somewhat boring topic, even for me, but thanks to recent events in Washington I can point out to them that, though this may sound boring on its face, look what happens when you don't pay attention. I say to them, read this article and understand what went wrong.

Do the students read the newspapers?

I think very few really read the newspaper. As an assignment I asked them to watch the State of the Union address. I don't think they keep up on current events. When I was an undergraduate, I didn't keep up on current events either.

Did your students watch the State of the Union Address?

Yes, I am amazed about how many of them apparently did. We had a reasonable discussion the next day, and I did tape the State of the Union address and showed parts of it in two of my classes. I have a VCR at home and I think this is a great technology for teaching political science because there are a lot of events that occur and the press is always there. For example, in 1988 I plan to tape presidential debates and things like that. You show it for a few minutes, so they can get a taste of what happened, and it promotes some good discussion. You cannot count on them to have read the paper or watched TV. If you make an assignment, I think some of them will make some effort to watch even if they sit there and read something while the TV is on.

What do you think is particularly important that your students learn?

There is some substance that I want them to learn. I am notorious for being a hard grader, in part because I expect them at least for the exam to have learned the substance. I don't necessarily expect that they are going to retain it for the rest of their lives. I hope that they learn that certain questions or issues are important in this society and that they should not take the nature of our political system or what our leaders do for granted. They should understand that the nature of our political system has important implications for their lives. I want them to be at least somewhat more informed and questioning about the system and about their leaders. I want them to learn how to learn. There is too much to do in life, there are not enough hours in the day. So I want them to learn how to figure out for themselves what is important for them, what you have to do to get by and what you don't have to do.

How do you get that across?

The first thing I do is give them a lot of work. I have pretty high expectations of how well they will do their work. When they come and complain, most of the time my reaction is that they have to figure out what is important and what isn't so important. I try to give some suggestions along the way. I do some one-on-one counseling. I have students come in who are having trouble. I try to be helpful, but I am not sure how to do it. I had one kid who bombed the midterm in my introductory course this semester, and I know why. She hardly wrote any notes. I would be saying things that I knew the rest of the class would be scribbling down madly, and she just sat there looking at me as if she weren't paying attention. We talked about that.

Did she say why she didn't take notes?

She claimed not to know how to take notes and figure out what was and wasn't important. I went over that day's lecture and I told her what I thought was important and what I thought should be in her notes. I also suggested that she might want to compare her notes with students or friends in the class and see what they had taken down and what they hadn't. We also went over the midterm, and I said: Look, here are the kinds of questions I ask. What would you need to know to answer these questions fully? We talked about what good answers would be and talked about whether she had the requisite information in her notes. In some ways I was at a loss about what to do, other than perhaps creating little exercises for her, where I would give a lecture or have her listen to the recording of a lecture and she would take notes and we would go over them. She does seem to be taking many more notes the second half of the semester. I don't know fully what to expect of her on the final. There are still some times when I look out there and I think that she should be taking notes and she isn't. I had told her to come back. She said that she was going to talk to some friends in the class and start comparing notes with them and get a sense of what they thought was important to take down. She hasn't come back.

Do most students exchange notes with each other?

Some consider that a violation of the honor code. As far as I am concerned, they can exchange notes. I don't see it as a violation. The dividing line gets a little fuzzy and sometimes they err on the side of being too strict. If they want to collaborate, if they want to go over their notes together or study for an exam together, that's fine, that's great. By talking to each other they learn more.

Getting students who are behind in their work together with other students would seem to be a very good idea.

It's a good thing that students can work with each other; sometimes, I think, they find coming to the instructor intimidating. Apparently, I can be intimidating to some people. On the other hand, they recognize that I am closer in age to them than many of my colleagues. So in some ways I have a different relationship and a different kind of rapport with them, certainly different from my male colleagues and even from my older female colleagues. In some of my older female colleagues I see a more maternal relationship; as if they are going to Mom and she will solve their problems. They can identify a little bit more with me, and in some ways, I think, they feel more comfortable coming to me. I am closer to being a student; they know that I have been here only a couple of years. I look very young. But I obviously intimidate some students because they do not come to see me, and I can tell it also from reading my evaluations. I had one student complain that I was extremely accessible but that I didn't force her to come see me. It seems that this kid was somewhat intimidated.

What cues do you use to see how you come across to your students, and how do you assess your own teaching on a day-to-day basis?

I think I come across as reasonably friendly and accessible. I try to be friendly, try to demonstrate a sense of humor, be sympathetic to them, at least to some extent. On the other hand, I make it clear from the beginning that I have pretty high standards, that I grade strictly. I have a rule that papers are due by the deadline. I say to them that if they turn something in, they have fulfilled their part of the bargain. They then have the option of rewriting their papers. If they rewrite the paper and get a better grade, that is the grade they get for the assignment. There is no averaging and they can rewrite it as many times as they want until the semester ends. I try to make accommodations in these ways. I try to strike a balance between being firm, somebody who is a tough grader and sets high standards, and trying to do it in a nice way, not being so harsh that I am unsympathetic to their problems and what they want.

It somewhat varies with the size of the class. I feel that in my introductory class I have to be a little more strict because I have many more people; if I give everybody a special deal then I will never get my work done. What they don't appreciate is that every time one of them gets an extension on a paper that is more work for me. I have scheduled my semester to be able to get all this stuff back to them on time and I cannot do it if they are turning in papers at any old time that they feel like it. In my upper-level classes, which tend to be smaller, say ten to twenty students, I am more flexible.

How do you ascertain how much your students have learned?

I look to the exams, especially the essay questions. I try to frame questions so that they have to take a theory that we have been discussing and apply it to a new situation, often current events in American politics, or where they have to take materials from several parts of the course and put them together, usually in some way that we have never tried before. I also consider comments in class, the student who raises her hand and takes what we are talking about in class and relates it to what a public figure just did. I read their papers and they come in outside of class and I try to get some feedback there. I read their evaluations and see what they say.

What do you find most difficult in teaching? When a class goes wrong, what do you do, and how do you define "wrong"?

That is tough to define. You go in there and you feel that it is not working, either they are staring at you as if you are from Mars or they are all asleep. I define a wrong class as one in which I get no response or get a wrong response.

Is it because of you or because of the kind of day it is?

Sometimes it's me. Sometimes it is the day. Sometimes it is the class. Sometimes it is the way I interact with them. Sometimes certain material turns them off. You hit it off with certain classes, you get a good response almost all the time. Other classes just do not work. You can struggle all semester and you do not feel that you are making contact, that anybody out there is alive and listening. When I was in college I had a professor who said that he was relieved to see that there were still a few intelligent students out there and that he was glad that I was in his class, because he ordinarily felt that he was talking and no intelligent person paid attention. I can now understand that. A lot of it is intangible.

Another example of things going wrong is when you given an exam and you get back something that is totally off the wall. Then you have to ask yourself what happened—what did I do wrong? Among most of my colleagues here there is a tendency to blame oneself first; more so perhaps than we should. Maybe the students share some of the burden, maybe it is the general system, maybe we are all too overworked at a certain point in the semester, or maybe it is just a bad match that semester between professor and students. When a whole class seems dead or when certain classes do not work well all semester you try different techniques: more discussion, less discussion, debate, lectures, anything you can think of to catch their attention. When that doesn't work, you keep trying and floundering and you get more frustrated. It is not completely clear to me what you can do in these situations. Sometimes I think that the students don't perceive it as being as bad as I do. If I am dying up there and then I get the student evaluations, I find that some people in the class will complain and the rest will seem very happy.

In one of my classes there was a big difference between the students' OPI profiles and my profile. I am high on the first two cognitive dimensions, the TI and the TO, and they were all low on theorizing. Where I was up, they were down, and vice versa. There were a lost of students who had very low scores; their profiles were sort of embryonic. I was ready to commit suicide—I was so frustrated with them. My observer noticed it when she visited my class. She said that the spark is not there. This semester I teach the same course and I walk in the door and the students are going already.

One thing that might be important, especially in a small class, is the dynamics among the students. It is clear in the class that I am teaching now, a number of the students know each other and they get along pretty well. That adds a lot. It is not just that they are comfortable with me and my reactions to them when they talk, but with the reactions of their peers. They are good buddies, they are having a good time. They are more free to express themselves because they know their peers are going to be accepting of what they say.

That is interesting. That may give us a cue for other classes where we might try to get something similar going among the students.

That has struck me lately. In my first semester here I taught a class that was spectacular. I did nothing. I just walked in and had a great class. I think it had a lot to do with the dynamics among the students; most of them seemed to know each other. They were a vocal group and I thought that in many ways they were self-teaching. I set the agenda for the day and then they ran with it. I got great evaluations but I thought it wasn't me, it was them. It was a fun class for me to participate in because the students were so good.

And you participated?

Yeah. It was more equal participation than any class I have ever taught because these guys were really good, the sharpest class I have ever had.

What preparations do you make before you meet a class?

If it is a new lecture, it takes forever. Otherwise I pull out the old notes and decide if they need to be modified or updated. Periodically as you teach a course, there are certain sections you have completely to redo. If I am starting a new lecture class from scratch, I easily put in ten to twenty hours just to be ready to say anything in that seventy-minute class. If it is the introductory course that I have taught many times, it is just a matter of changes here or there and I spend maybe a few hours on them, two to three hours.

How does your teaching relate to your research?

Sometimes I wonder. My fields are urban politics and also executives. I am writing a paper now that is related to urban politics and also gets into my interest in executives. The paper complements my seminar and even the course I teach on the presidency. In that sense they are related. But it is hard during the semester to get any research done. I am almost done with my paper, but again I am at such a busy point in this semester that the paper is on hold.

Do you feel that there is a great deal of difference between yourself as a researcher and what you are in the classroom?

Somewhat. In some ways, I feel as if it is a schizophrenic existence. In one way the research and the teaching complement each other and you are a better teacher because of the research. In doing the research, you have to keep up on the literature, so you are really up-to-date. You think about interesting questions and new ways of looking at your field and you can convey some of that in the classroom. On the other hand, teaching makes it hard for me to do my research. Much of my research involves having to go to interview people, whereas much of my class preparation is using the library or going over old notes. I think people regard me differently when I am playing the research as opposed to the teacher role. When I am doing the research, I am dealing more with people in the real world, and they regard me as a scholar. When I am back at the school, my whole world is much more oriented to students, and students perceive you first as a teacher. If anything, they probably complain that we spend too much time on our research or on tenure decisions, that there isn't enough emphasis on teaching. So it is a little schizophrenic.

What do the students have in mind when they think of you as teacher and as researcher?

When I am a teacher, I am spending time with them, I am worrying about them, I am oriented to them. When I am a researcher, they think I am not. I am away from the college, I am not worried about them. They have little or no sense of what we do as researchers. They cannot quite picture what we do.

Do you have the students do interviews too as part of their work?

I don't normally have them do interviews. In the seminar on executives, they have to write a paper on a real life executive. Some people have done interviews for that. It is tough to do. It is hard for them unless the person you need for your topic is right on campus.

What I wonder is whether there are situations in which they are more like you. That may help them to realize what your role as a researcher is.

Occasionally when working on my paper I am sitting in my office trying to write, when students have come by to hand in their papers. They will moan and groan or ask for help on the paper. So I will say that I sympathize. Here I am writing *my* paper. I have the same problem as you. There just aren't enough hours in the day, I agree wholeheartedly.

Why do you teach and what would you rather do?

I teach because I like it. I like it because I like contact with people. You meet lots of interesting people. I like it because sometimes you actually feel you are doing something. You are helping someone and making a contribution to society, you are educating a new generation. I like it because sometimes students come back and tell me that they have learned something. I do it because — to go back to my college advisor, he made a big difference in my life. I am not saying that I am going to make a big difference in anybody's life, but sometimes I think I may. College students are at an age where they are impressionable and maybe somebody will become a political scientist or do something significant in part because of what we do here.

Before you met your advisor, what were you going to do?

I had no idea. Before I started college, my senior year in high school, I used to change my prospective major weekly. My mother was having an attack. She wanted me to go to a liberal arts college. If you had a kid who couldn't figure out what she wanted to do, she could try all this stuff and it wouldn't be such a big disaster. So I had no idea what I wanted to do. I never, never, ever, ever thought that I would get a Ph.D. and become a political scientist. I didn't know what political science was until shortly before I started college. I never had heard of the field. When they sent me the college brochure to figure out a list of classes, there was this field called political science and it sounded just like what I was interested in. I signed up for the introductory course.

When did you encounter your advisor?

Sophomore year. He was on leave my freshmen year, and I had heard all kinds of stories about him, and I took his class because he came so highly recommended. I loved the course, thought he was great. The next semester I signed up for another course with him and basically took every course that he offered, plus some independent studies with him.

I had been thinking about being a history major. I knew I was interested in politics and government; I had always been fascinated by it. I had lived for about twelve years in Chicago as a kid and I found Mayor Daley and the machine fascinating. I knew that *that* interested me. I had no idea what I would do afterwards, I could care less. I was not career oriented at all. I thought maybe I would go to law school, but I really had not given a career any serious thought before I started college. When I entered college, I was assigned to an advisor as part of some scholar's program for students they figured had some potential. I had no ambitions whatsoever. This guy obviously had ambitions for me. He called me into his office during my first semester and asked me how I was doing. I said I was doing okay. He said okay was not good enough, okay would not get me into graduate school. But I had no ambitions of going to graduate school.

When I went to college, for the first time in my life, I wanted to try to get a sense of who I was and what I could do. I had always done well in school, but I always had people telling me I could do better. I would get these evaluations at midsemester, and the classic one was from my French teacher who would send this note home to my mother saying that her daughter was doing well, but that she could do better. I was getting an A in the course. On the other hand, about my brother, two years younger, the teacher said he was a joy to have in class. I couldn't figure out why he was a joy to have in class and I could do better when we were both getting As. So I figured I would go to college and find out if I could do better. And I *could* do better. I found out what I could and couldn't do, most importantly, because my advisor got hold of me at age nineteen and gave me a lot of guidance.

What made your teachers in school feel that way about you?

They knew that I could do better, in part, I think, because I was very quiet and very shy, so I would not talk in class. I think they wanted me to talk. I think they thought that I was putting in a minimal effort to get the A and I should put in more effort. I was the classic study in front of the TV set for half an hour before the exam. When I went to college, I was determined that I would not worry about grades; I wanted to find out if I could do better. I expected to get all Bs and Cs. I didn't know what to expect. In my family, while education was valued and I knew I would go to college, the reason you went was because that was the stepping-stone to a good career. There was no pressure about what to be. I just sort of went and I had a good time, learned a lot about political science, and about who I was and what I wanted to do. That is ideally what I want my students to achieve. It is not so much the substance but to find out what your strengths and your weaknesses are and to get a sense of what you want to do in life, to make some contribution hopefully in the society.

If you were not teaching, what might you do?

I would say I would be in government. When it came time to decide where to go to graduate school and what to do careerwise, I had a big dilemma about whether I should go the academic route or go into government.

What aspect of government?
Some policymaking position, probably.

Might you still do it?
I will do it next year. I have a sabbatical and I am trying to land a position in the state's budget bureau. It would be a policy analysis position or budget evaluation. I think the research will complement my teaching. I hope to use it as a basis for some publications on policymaking and state governments.

Can you give me a brief sketch of your philosophy of education?
I guess my philosophy of education is that I want people to learn how to think and how to ask questions and how to communicate on paper and orally. I am concerned about people's acquiring skills that they can use in all kinds of situations, on and off the job. I do want them to gain substantive knowledge and I would like an educational system in which all educated people had some minimal shared knowledge. I would like the educational system to provide the opportunity for people to figure out who they are, what they can do. I would also like the educational system to encourage people to have a sense of obligation to the society and to the community and to be concerned not just with themselves and making money—to recognize that there are all kinds of needs and problems in society that they should be concerned about, even if they are wealthy investment bankers. There are other people out there who haven't had the opportunities that they have had, and they have some obligation to those people.

Earlier you referred to yourself as having been shy in high school. Did you work on that? Or did you grow out of it?
I started to change around age sixteen. I started getting a little bit more confidence. I think the big change occurred when I was in college.

Related to your advisor?
When I was a junior in college, my advisor was asked to be the executive director of the platform committee for the Republican National Convention, and he offered me a job to work for him that summer. He needed somebody who could work very long hours for little pay and who would do the job. I matured a great deal that summer. I basically went from not knowing how to answer the telephone the first day to being able to organize subcommittee hearings. This twenty-year-old kid set that all up. My mother commented afterwards that she was actually impressed that I had turned out to be a reasonable, mature, poised adult. I received a lot of guidance from my advisor, and it was easier to take because he wasn't my

parent. He was like a father to me, he still is, but he wasn't a parent. I was given an awful lot of responsibility for a twenty-year-old kid, and his reaction was that I could do it. When people could come to him, he would send them to me. I had to deal with it, so I did.

What have you done as a participant in the Ford project, and what has it done for you? What relevance does it have for you and the college in the future?

It has made me much more aware of myself as a teacher and also made me more flexible about trying different teaching techniques. I think more about teaching in terms of what is the best way to reach my students. If things go wrong, I am less shaken by that and more likely to shift gears and try something else. I am also much more aware about the fact that students have personal lives outside the classroom, which have such a big impact on what goes on inside the classroom. While I knew this before, the program brought it home to me. It has been interesting to use the OPI and have this sense that there are different cognitive patterns, and that I may or may not match up with my students. There are times when I may not have as good a rapport with my students because of these differences, and I can try different techniques — it doesn't mean that I am a total failure as a teacher. Sometimes when you blame yourself, you can get very discouraged. To be a good teacher requires an awful lot of energy and enthusiasm. When you start getting discouraged, it becomes just a job and when it becomes a job, you are not going to be a very good teacher. It has been good to be able to talk to other people about teaching. It is so rare to have that opportunity. We worry a lot about teaching, but even my institution provides few resources to help you improve your teaching. None of us are taught how to teach in graduate school. So you are groping along, and it is nice to have other people groping with you.

Observing a colleague is how I decided to use a reading evaluation form, and it has worked very well. It is a form that the students have to fill out for each week's reading. It asks a few not-too-earthshaking questions, like what did they find most enlightening or interesting in each reading, what did they agree with or disagree with, what would they like to have discussed further in class, what could an executive learn from each of these readings. There is a question about what they liked most or disliked most, and why. I get really interesting feedback. I am getting evidence that they like real life stories; it confirmed comments that they had made outside of class and their performance on exams. One of my colleagues in my department heard about the reading evaluation form, and he is going to try it. He has been frustrated because his students haven't been reading all of the material in advance. I wish I could say I had some kind of magic formula that I could rely upon or that I now knew what to do in every situation. I am more aware of all the problems and all the possibilities.

There really aren't any formulas, but continued inquiry increases our knowledge about how to help our students learn. To speak of the future, Where do you think you and the college might go from here?

For me it will be a matter of continuing to explore things that I have learned or become aware of, how to deal with students who just don't respond to you, how to deal with students whose style is very different from your own. I think about playing with some of what I have learned, trying it in different situations, seeing how it works out, further developing the art of teaching. For the college, I am not sure. I would say that one thing to think about would be taking a number of the smaller questions that have been raised by the study and pursuing them, having individual faculty members or small groups pursuing them. For me, it could be dealing with those difficult students, the ones that you cannot reach, the ones who never say a word in class, whose profile is completely different from mine. Or we could explore learning how to learn. I would like us to continue meeting together to talk about teaching and about problems in teaching. It is good to learn that one's problems are not unique. This is one of the things that I have discovered. I am not the only person who has had a whole class that seems flat for the whole semester. It is a relief to find that out; I can stop hitting my head against the wall. I don't feel this incredible burden that I have failed, that something is wrong with me, when in reality I am probably not a bad teacher.

Katie, many thanks. We have covered a lot together.

9

Reenvisioning Undergraduate Teaching

Mass versus Elite Higher Education. In the first chapter we suggested that this is a time in which the university as we have known it since its European beginnings is being replaced by a new and quite different type of institution. Traditional ideas about learning and scholarship are in a profound state of change. Martin Trow in a challenging article entitled " 'Elite Higher Education': An Endangered Species?" (1976) deals with the expansion of mass higher education in the period after the Second World War. He says that the large undergraduate colleges of the huge state universities "admit students of modest academic capacities and interests and also of modest ambitions" (p. 369). He sees only a relatively small number of institutions whose students remain dedicated to the pursuit of scholarship and science. Trow's definition of elite higher education is of special interest. He characterizes it as being distinguished by high quality "in the relations between students and teachers, the duration and intensity of that relationship and its emphasis on the shaping of mind, character and aspirations of the students" (p. 369). Trow's is a very fine definition of the ingredients of good education. The question arises what education is if it does not meet the criteria enunciated by him. If indeed mass higher education cannot provide what Trow talks about, one might ask in what sense it is to be called "education." An answer that some would call realistic is that the elite and mass institutions satisfy two rather different kinds of needs: the needs of those students who are oriented to and capable of contributing to the preservation and creation of advanced knowledge and those for whom institutions serve economic and social needs, allowing them to acquire occupational skills with perhaps a modest amount of general cultivation and citizenship skills thrown in. But to say this would neglect the fact that the elite institutions produce only a fraction of students who will serve the preservation and creation of the higher knowledge. For most students the elite schools are vocational too; such schools prepare them for the more prestigious and remunerative professions and confer on them status useful for business, professional, and political careers.

There is a special challenge in Trow's definition. The challenge is whether mass higher education cannot have the qualities or more of the qualities that Trow enumerates. Perhaps the work reported in this book points out some of the means thereto. The university has in many ways done little to adjust itself to changes in its clienteles and to reenvision its mission. A cardinal principle of education, implicit in much of this book, is the individualization of learning. The present curricular system in the mass institutions largely condemns students to being confronted with diluted, fragmentary, and overly abstract versions of the different fields of knowledge, bereft of a sense of the inquiry modes that underlay the generation of that knowledge and bereft also of making connections with the students' own knowledge and curiosity. Much in college can become "requirements to be gotten over with." The diluted versions of subject matter can be more or less easily mastered by students and repeated for exam purposes without their acquiring a clear sense of the meaning and thrust of the ideas that they are talking and writing about. Students can be subjected to sometimes frustrating attempts at gaining some grasp of basic concepts and operations involving much memorizing, and these students may end up thinking of knowledge as somebody else's possession and may feel a certain powerlessness or even a sense of failure when it comes to learning.

To turn this around, the mass institutions, and not they alone, will need to think about how to individualize instruction. This means that professors will need to know considerably more about the state of mind, the preparation, the cognitive and emotional dispositions with which their students enter their classrooms. Institutions will have to see to it that students work with teachers who get to know them well in small groups. Not every course will need to follow this pattern, but there will have to be a sufficient number and variety of academic activities being done in small groups. To have a sophisticated sense of the variety of their students' learning ways, professors will need to become more aware of their own learning ways. The methods exemplified in this book are one avenue toward enabling professors to acquire that kind of sophistication.

The Epistemology of the Disciplines. We found a strong correlation between the modes of thinking of faculty and the student majors in a given discipline. If different modes of thinking are linked to different disciplines, and these modes are partial, in the sense that thinking in one discipline may emphasize and highlight modes of thinking that in another discipline are deemphasized, and perhaps even actively discouraged, then it is important to be aware of how these differences are being presented to students. As we have suggested in chapter 3, many students fumble around during the first two years of their undergraduate experience and may be seeking a disciplinary channel that seems to be congruent with their interests and emerging modes of thinking. This situation raises difficult questions concerning what it is that faculty expect ought to happen to students during the first two years of college and in the years thereafter, when students might open up to a diversity of modes of thinking, so that they will be able to transcend the particular channels of whatever discipline or area of specialization they elect to concentrate in as a major. If faculty cling to the mode of thinking exemplified by their discipline, how will students be able both to learn the mode and yet be free of encapsulation by it?

In our work with faculty we have watched them become involved in examining their own modes of thinking and inquiring how their modes tend to fit or deviate from the predominant mode of thinking in their discipline. Such faculty found it possible to relate more flexibly and with increased understanding to those students who tended not to construe the world as specialists in the discipline did. Some faculty sought to enlarge their ability to think more flexibly and integratively by exploring a discipline different from their own. Sustained dialogue with faculty from other disciplines overcame initial difficulties of communication. Observation of a colleague's classroom and students helped them to understand other ways of thinking about and perceiving the world.

There are signs that concern about the methods and questions of the disciplines is beginning to emerge. Some faculty in the social sciences are engaged in self-questioning about the topics that they address and the forcefulness of results yielded by some current methods. Epistemology-minded physicists, chemists, and biologists are acknowledging the role of intuition and guessing in the "hard" sciences; hypothesis formation is being acknowledged as a creative act and closer to art than rule-following and amassing empirical data with insufficient attention to conceptional paradigms of varying scope. Proponents of humanistic disciplines are in an even greater state of uncertainty. Philosophy is divided, at times in bitter fights over whether one or the other way of doing philosophy is the right kind of philosophy. In literary scholarship, there is the continuing controversy about how the understanding and appreciation of literature is related to the lacerating divisions of schools of literary criticism. Historians are unsure whether history belongs to social science or the humanities. The studies that historians pursue seem to depend much on the needs and self-images of their societies; the recent emphasis on the private aspects of history, the way people of all social classes live their private lives, has been a result of the women's movement and the emerging definitions of gender roles, and it has opened up topics for inquiry that before lay below the surface of interest if not respectability.

Some, perhaps many, of the divisions among the disciplines may be questioned. Might not, for some purposes, a combination of philosophy, history, and sociology and/or psychology yield a much richer understanding than their current separateness? Would much not be gained by turning sociological methods upon the past and suffusing with them the sweep of historical research, inquiring into different and similar manifestations of present problems? Surely the understanding and power of philosophical concepts would be enhanced if they were seen not as free-floating ideas but as instruments that people use critically to define and illuminate the societal, personal, scientific problems they are facing in their time? This was one of John Dewey's basic proposals, but only very partially followed.

The difficulty of pinpointing clear disciplinary boundaries and the contention that there is no clear rationale for either the existing divisions of the disciplines or their methods suggest a measure of arbitrariness, one that can be historically understood, in the institutionalization of learning into departments. Veysey (1965, pp. 317 ff.) has pointed to the economic and territorial interests that have led to the creation of departments of knowledge and their bureaucratization. That the disciplinary divisions owe some of their existence to factors other than the logic of inquiry should make it easier to accept the principle of the reorganization of subject matter for teaching and learning. Such reorganization seems to be particularly desirable in the area of general or liberal education if general or liberal education is to aim at equipping students with the knowledge and skills they will need as people, parents, friends, citizens, participants in the arts (Association of American Colleges, 1988). Especially the introductory course seems ripe for redefinition, and we will turn to it next.

The Students: Redefining Course Content and Mode of Teaching. Only a fraction of students taking any specific course is ever going to be involved in any specialized or continuing way with that subject matter. Often one course is their only exposure to a particular field. Even the major for many people will not be the field on which much of their further lives will center. We need to rethink the introductory course and other courses that are taken by nonmajors. This is made the more urgent by the growing tendency of faculty to offer courses that introduce students not to the discipline but to a specialized area within it. It is tempting to give in an introductory course "capsule" versions of the field or subfield. This usually means emphasis on conclusions rather than the process of inquiry. Even if the course conveys some sense of the methods by which the conclusions were reached, these methods are described in the ways of the finished scholarly or scientific article. But any investigator knows that scholarly articles largely leave out the messy, tortuous concrete details that preceded by many stages the final version of the article accepted by the journal. The *feel* for the real work is missing in the formalized presentation.

In one sense the task of redefining course contents has already been done ad nauseam. There is no dearth of popularized and trivialized textbook renditions of respectable subject matter. But these renditions often rely upon a conception of the student as a passive receiver to be entertained and accommodated by graphs, illustrations, and easy-to-grasp prose. This approach not only assumes that the student is a passive receiver but also assumes that the aim of education is to hand over by way of direct transfer the knowledge "products" generated by a given discipline. Students are expected to be able to make sense of the knowledge contents handed to them and are expected to know how to link up the contents provided with other contents, how to apply and use the knowledge contents, and how to evaluate their worth critically. To those students whose mode of making sense of the world is different from the modes they are expected to assimilate, the contents appear strange, forbidding, uninteresting, and inherently not meaningful. Desperate not to fail the course, they employ every subtle clue in order to use the content in a way which the teacher will approve without really understanding where the knowledge came from or seeing its importance and worth.

Many students do not know how to look for ideas or, indeed, that they *should* look for ideas in what they are learning. Often faculty teach "facts" and do not help students enough to grasp the bases, contexts, and meanings of these facts. One teacher describes his frustration: "I would get up and say what I had read in books and they'd all write it down and give it back as answers on exams, but nothing was happening. I felt as if I were in some sound-proof room" (Adams, 1980, p. 18). In order to move out of the soundproof room, faculty could look for ways to have their students become coinquirers who seek to cope with difficult problems and dilemmas and need to make sense of the world in more effective and satisfying ways. When the student is treated as a coinquirer, the notion of what a course is becomes transformed. It becomes a means for the students to acquire more advanced skills or abilities for questioning the world about them, searching for and attaining understanding, reflection, and self-expression, and imagining, hypothesizing, interpreting, and reality-testing their ideas and those of others.

One could envisage courses as starting with something that is a live problem for the student, and then as the problem becomes more gripping and interesting to the student, the teacher could make increasingly more sophisticated and expanded demands on the cognitive ways the student is dealing with the problem, including having students reflect upon the ways they learn. An approach such as this is likely to involve faculty members to a point at which they will shed some of the conventional talk in the disciplines. We often erect conceptual superstructures that when brought into direct confrontation with a genuine, real-life problem are revealed to have low explanatory power or small heuristic utility. Such confrontation and resulting deflation can provide a healthy spur to the professors' own cognitive abilities and may even help launch them on a more fruitful line of research.

Many real-life problems are relevant: for instance, in psychology, the phenomenon of obedience; in sociology, the bureaucracies surrounding our daily lives or the social structures supportive of racism or male dominance; in linguistics, the patterns of how we communicate and miscommunicate with each other, the often besetting difficulties that students experience and observe in the verbal communications of people with each other. Starting with such problems one can help students to develop flexible and increasingly more powerful ways of thinking about experiences that are a part of their daily lives. We are suggesting both redefinition of content and enhanced attention to students' ways of learning, a deliberate emphasis on the students' gradual acquisition during each semester of cumulative skills and competencies. This means raising of expectations of what students eventually will be capable of; for with changes in direction, attention, and teaching method, a higher quality of student work can be expected.

Such expectations can be realistically entertained only if attention is devoted to the doable steps in the students' progress. Professors require workable maps of the steps students need to go through to make progress in their skills and competencies. To accomplish this task faculty will find it very illuminating to share their work in teaching with their colleagues as they do their work in scholarly inquiry and research activity. As noted by the Group for Human Development in Higher Education (1974, p. 10): "Teaching, unlike research and publishing, remains very much a private professional act, rarely open to collegial scrutiny. Effective teaching remains a stepchild in the hierarchy of academic goals and values." The college teacher's teaching experience, if any, is usually acquired through being a teaching assistant while attending graduate school. This work rarely involves systematic and sophisticated attention to teaching. Beginning college teachers learn to cope with students and the classroom through a long and not necessarily satisfying process of trial and error, or they model their teaching style on the style of their own professors, or some combination of these two. Thus, the isolated classroom focused on the transmission of the contents of a specific discipline to not necessarily very active students, accompanied by a neglect of the *processes* of learning, may be passed off as an acceptable educational experience. Students can exit course after course with nearly the same skills that they had on entry into the course. While enrolled in such courses, students conform as well as they can to the test expectations of their teachers. If the course materials require skills of analysis, interpretation, and synthesis that they do not possess — and few students on entry into college possess these skills to a sufficient degree — they cleverly and intelligently find ways of making cognitively less powerful and sophisticated presentations acceptable. This model allows professors to go on "professing" their topic, insufficiently enlightened by fruitful voyages of discovery into the complexities of teaching.

Student Development. To help students increase their skills, their *present* level of cognitive and emotional development must be taken into consideration. Students are frustrated and feel diminished when demands that are unreachable to them in their current level of development are made upon them. In Piaget's and Perry's theories there are two major transition points that sharply divide students. One is the Piagetian point between concrete and formal operations and the other is the Perry point between multiplistic reasoning, which holds one opinion to be as good as another, and relativistic reasoning, which acknowledges a legitimate variety of views and yet recognizes differing degrees and qualities of evidence that may tilt the balance toward accepting one view or group of views over others. In our approach to development, increased individuation and complexity of development are achieved as the person becomes consciously aware of and experientially acquainted with the different epistemological bases for truth. As individuals learn to accept these diverse modes and become capable of integrating them into a harmonious, creative, reality-testing mode, they become more mature and balanced. Such learning includes becoming aware of and changing the ways in which one learns. Development cannot be forced or commanded. But when teachers understand its processes and progressions, they can better provide the settings and stimulations to encourage growth in their students, and when we ask for this we go beyond the present definitions of teaching and learning. Helping the student to develop requires that those who teach gain more knowledge about students, engage in more experimentation, be more critical and reflective about the classroom, and share their reflections with colleagues more than is now the case.

The student's out-of-classroom experience can be a powerful stimulus to motivated learning. Ever since the growth and acceptance of science as a core disciplinary area, the laboratory has been an accepted addition to the class. The idea of testing ideas in the laboratory was one of the main features that made the scientific approach so engaging and so exciting to earlier teachers and students. Unfortunately, many laboratory experiences are now so conventionalized that they have become mechanical in nature. The excitement of genuine test and discovery is lost as students settle into plodding through "experiments" with well-known conclusions or engaging in steps leading to predictable "discoveries." Along with this loss, the reality of science as a series of very intricate processes that are not linear and well-organized in character is also lost. Revitalizing the laboratory, as for instance practiced by Postlethwait et al. (1972), becomes a desirable task. Beyond the scientific laboratory we can look to other ways of using the student's experience, including observations, service, practice, the continued testing of ideas outside of the classroom, and connecting out-of-classroom learning with the classroom. These will contribute to an education that will not break down when students move beyond the walls of academia.

In recent years the proliferation of audiovisual aids, simulation and other games, computer-assisted instruction, and role-playing testifies to a dawning sense of the need for students to have an enlarged experiential base on which to observe, reflect, and conceptualize. The use of these mechanisms for generating experience can enhance learning. But we must guard against their being contrived or trivialized. The simulation game, for instance, can at times be a not very instructive parlor exercise, and it can diminish the meaning and importance of the subject matter that it is supposed to illuminate. Computer-assisted instruction, if misused, can reinforce an impersonal distancing between students and knowledge, a distancing that is already a major problem in large universities. Ultimately what students can experience and how they relate to their experiences and the experiences of others are the tests of the educational activities and experience. How to generate experience and the proper use of experience in education, a problem that Dewey raised so vividly for the earlier levels of schooling, is still a largely unmet task in higher education. As long as teachers neglect the issue of experience and fail to bring about interactions with students that alert them to how their students experience their lives and learn from their experiences, they will lack one means for aiding their students' development. If students experience what they are asked to learn as boring or meaningless or trivial, then this is what they will have learned. How to get students to experience reading, conversing, writing, thinking, observing, imagining, and feeling as intrinsically rewarding and satisfying experiences is the great challenge to college teachers.

Advising. Most faculty advise their students only about academic matters. They explain to them how the institutional system works. They tell students about "breadth" requirements and electives. They tell them about the prerequisite courses needed for entry into the various disciplinary channels. An approach to education that takes account of the epistemological underpinnings of the disciplines puts a fresh light on advising. It aims at enabling students to move flexibly among the existing divisions of knowledge, each of which is limited and partial in nature, as the students search for an active involvement in questions of worth and meaning to them. We envisage advisors who point students to the partial, unfinished nature of their present interests, challenge them to explore actively areas outside of their present grasp, and convey to them some sense of the interrelation of the disciplines and the quest for knowledge that overrides and extends beyond any one discipline.

The advising activity brings with it the opportunity for personal encounters with students and for sounding the student's experience. Developmental theories, though partial in nature and still evolving, provide some means for examining and interpreting the experiences of students. Advisors who have a grasp of these theories can interact with those students who come to them in ways that are intellectually stimulating; they may seek to make sense of the students' comments and reports of their experiences by using available theories as a basis for reflection along with their own evolving understanding of students. Advisors can learn much that is useful for their teaching practice, classroom design, and out-of-class assignments by picking up clues from students that are suggestive of where the teaching effort is most likely to help the student's learning. As teachers become aware of where individual students are located on a cognitive spectrum, they can design curricular modes, assignments, and examinations that take account of individual differences due to developmental preference and cognitive style. In large educational institutions the faculty are not going to have the opportunity to know every one of their students as individuals. However, if they will use advising opportunities to become acquainted with some of their students, they can develop a knowledge and wisdom about students more generally.

The Art of Teaching. Although we have devoted our attention in this book primarily to faculty, we recognize the degree to which educational institutions make it difficult for faculty to engage in the teaching and learning we are espousing here. Many large universities are designed to promote the generation and dissemination of knowledge. Teaching and students seem to divert energy and time from this endeavor. Hence, professors in these institutions often tend to rely on the lecture mode of teaching, which is efficient, well organized, and can be executed without diverting much additional time or energy once it is developed. In a recent study of a random half of American *universities,* Wagner Thielens (1987) found lecturing to be the mode of instruction of 89 percent of the physical scientists and mathematicians, 81 percent of the social scientists, and 61 percent of the humanities faculty (but 81 percent of the art historians and 90 percent of the philosophers lectured). Faculty—even if they enjoy seeing and talking with students—do not have much spare time to devote to students because they must be productive through what they create, publish, and disseminate. Students are left on their own to listen, to read, to "learn." Most students learn how to get through this system with passing or above average grades. Not enough of them, if given searching interviews, show signs that they have changed, grown, or learned enough that will stay with them in the years beyond college. They may have enjoyed their time in college: the friends they have made, the shared experience of getting through the system, a few engaging and even mind-boggling ideas here and there. But many graduate with insufficient capacity for self-directed learning.

The art of teaching is very different from the arts of research and the design of good lectures. Research and disciplinary scholarship encourage depth and knowing one particular area of knowledge exceedingly well. Teaching encourages breadth and trying to see both how the various strands of knowledge fit together and what knowledge among all that exists is most worth passing on to students, most of whom will not elect to be deeply and systematically interested in the same area of research and study as a given specialist–teacher may be. For teaching to connect with student learning, the teacher must know both the student and the world as it exists, especially the world in which the student has been nurtured and to which the student will return after college. Thus, the teacher must read about and observe areas of the world other than does the researcher–scholar. If students are not to become moles burrowing prematurely into a specialty or memorizer–regurgitators of insufficiently meaningful facts and ideas, they must encounter teachers who enable them to catch a sense of present and past eras and help shape the era in which they will live. Such teachers will, of course, also possess an understanding of where the specialists have been and what they have found.

Implementation. How can the approach and the methods described in this book be translated into the realities of the curriculum and the classroom? There are many procedures and strategies. We would like to list some that are based on successful ventures we have observed or participated in.

1. New educational ventures seem to flourish best when there is a combination of *administrative support* and *faculty leadership.* Initiative can come from either administrators or faculty, but it is essential that faculty who have the respect of their peers have imagination and will that can lead to some basic new departures in teaching. An administrator, such as a dean or vice president for academic affairs, may seek out one or several well-disposed faculty members or one or several faculty may seek out and convince an administrator. Administrative support is very important, not only for funding purposes but for the moral encouragement it lends to faculty who try out new ways of teaching —this is particularly important in the research institutions. The amount of money need not be large. Sometimes events honoring the new effort, retreats, or special dinners provide a boost to morale.

2. It is essential to allow *time* for experiment. Too often new things are tried and declared failures after a trial of one year. In fact, experiments rarely are total failures, and most are at least partial successes. *Ongoing assessment* can isolate the successful from the nonsuccessful aspects and so modify procedures. Some experimental colleges or programs are mislabeled. They *once* developed a new formula but then have stuck with it for years. But the essence of experimentation is *continual revision,* and this is a principle that still largely begs inclusion in our curricular and teaching procedures.

3. Experimentation and trying new approaches to teaching require people who will give their energy, and this raises the specter of *burnout.* The very people who are most useful in infusing vitality into teaching may be particularly subject to burnout. Some anticipate it and never start. Here administrative care and good plans are required. Heavy involvement might be limited to a predetermined number of years. Released time can be judiciously used. Partial or full sabbaticals can

be awarded after a period of heavy service. Sometimes just friendly monitoring and sympathetic advising can keep colleagues from going overboard in the use of their time; many faculty are not very good managers of time and often enough suffer from overgenerosity rather than wastefulness.

4. *Students* should be involved in the planning and evaluation of programs. Students participating can quickly bring lofty faculty ideation down to the realities of the potential and the limits of student responsiveness. No program, however good in the faculty's minds, can be successful without taking into account the student condition. Our experience has consistently shown that students when properly consulted can be very shrewd in critiquing proposals and bringing in fresh ideas of their own. In the wake of vanishing student activism there has often been a reverse institutional tendency to omit students from curricular deliberations. It may not even cross faculty or administrative minds that students might be included. Students themselves have shown a certain lassitude, and their enthusiasms need to be rekindled.

5. Often a new venture focuses on a single plan. But there is value in permitting *a variety of approaches.* For faculty to give their allegiance to new procedures and programs requires that they can find new ways of teaching consonant with their personalities and styles. (We are not speaking about idiosyncrasies, though they too have their uses occasionally.) In the longer run some ideas and practices will fall by the wayside, but we cannot easily determine beforehand what particular approach will stand the test.

6. It is common to attempt to introduce curricular or teaching reforms wholesale. Reform proposals are brought before the entire faculty, and the result of this parliamentary approach can be a regression toward the mean. The "new" plan as eventually adopted is not sufficiently different from what it replaces, though there are some splendid cases of wholesale changes. In many situations, more thorough-going changes may best be tried out first in *experimental patches.* One can test and revise them this way, eliminating "bugs" and major defects. Imitation and contagion may be better means to curricular reform than attempts at imposed uniformity.

    We envisage a progressive application and development of the methods and procedures described in this book. An institution might start with four or five two-person (observer/observed) faculty teams. If each member of the teams, in a second year, works with a fresh faculty member, the number of participating faculty can double in a second year and quadruple in a third.

7. There are few colleges that have in their faculty and administrators the required expertise for new departures in the curriculum or in teach-

ing. Sophistication in these areas is not something that people are trained for in graduate schools. The tendency, therefore, is to invite experts to the campus to help set a program going. The experience can be disappointing. The experts, even if they are good, stay for a little while and not long enough to become effective partners. The expertise continues to reside in them and not become a resource of the campus. A better procedure is to *train* one or several *members of one's own faculty.* Such training might begin with their spending time on one or several campuses on which one or another inventive curricular program is in effect so they can observe it and talk with faculty and students participating in it. Observation should be accompanied by study of the relevant literature. The new local experts can then take on the role of teachers and otherwise affect their colleagues. A good use of experts is to have them come at the beginning of a new venture and then have them return one or several times to have the benefit of their observations and thinking as the project unfolds.

CONCLUSION

The redirection of teaching and learning we have talked about in this book holds the promise of building student excitement about learning and faculty pleasure in teaching. A sense that students and faculty are working together for understanding and mastering the tasks of our increasingly more complex lives could rekindle the almost lost vision of the college or university as a *community of scholars.* Beyond that, education might more fully affect the larger society. In his inaugural address (*New York Times,* September 21, 1986, Section 1, p. 40) Yale's President, Benno Schmidt, made the disturbing point that a literate humanistic culture was no barrier to totalitarianism, that in certain instances, "the citadels of culture and art welcomed the new barbarians." Schmidt then raises the question whether there is "something in the very nature of the intellectual enterprise, in its abstractness, in its neutrality, in its remoteness from the texture and the exigencies of daily life, that diminishes our capacity for moral response" —and, we would add, not for moral response alone. Schmidt implies no derogation of abstractness and impartial scholarship. But they alone are not sufficient. The investigative and emotional dispositions of students must be appropriately engaged if students are to learn and if scholarship, curiosity, moral and social responsiveness are to result. This book has tried to make a contribution toward the educational containment of barbarisms old and new.

References

Adams, J. L. *Conceptual Blockbusting*. San Francisco: Freeman, 1974.

Adams, W. A. *The Experience of Teaching and Learning: A Phenomenology of Education*. Seattle: Psychological Press, 1980.

Association of American Colleges. *Integrity in the College Curriculum*. Washington, D.C., 1985.

Association of American Colleges, *A New Vitality in General Education*. Washington, D.C., 1988.

Ausubel, D. P. *Educational Psychology — A Cognitive View*. New York: Holt, Rinehart and Winston, 1968.

Becker, H. S.; Geer, B.; and Hughes, E. *Making the Grade: The Academic Side of College Life*. New York: Wiley, 1968.

Belenky, M.; Clinchy, B.; Goldberger, N.; and Tarule, J. *Women's Ways of Knowing*. New York: Basic Books, 1986.

Boyer, E. L. *College: The Undergraduate Experience in America*. New York: Harper, 1987.

Brown, R. *Words and Things*. Glencoe, Ill.: Free Press, 1958.

Chickering, A. W. *Education and Identity*. San Francisco: Jossey-Bass, 1969.

Claxton, C. S.; and Murrell, P. H. *Learning Styles: Implications for Educational Practices. ASHE-ERIC Higher Education Reports*. Washington, DC: Association for the Study of Higher Education, 1987.

Cones, J. H.; Noonan, J. F.; and Janha, D., eds. *Teaching Minority Students*. New Directions for Teaching and Learning, no. 16. San Francisco: Jossey-Bass, 1983.

Cross, K. P. "A Proposal to Improve Teaching." *AAHE Bulletin 39,* no. 1 (1986): 9–14.

DeBono, E. *Lateral Thinking*. New York: Harper, 1973.

Deutsch, K. W., and others. "Conditions Favoring Major Advances in Social Science." *Science 171* (1971): 450–459; *172* (1971): 1191–1192.

Dewey, J. *How We Think*. Rev. ed. New York: Heath, 1933.

Elbow, P. *Embracing Contraries: Explorations in Learning and Teaching*. New York: Oxford University Press, 1986.

Feldman, K. A. and Newcomb, T. M. *The Impact of College on Students*. San Francisco: Jossey-Bass, 1969.

Freedman, M. *The College Experience*. San Francisco: Jossey-Bass, 1967.

Gardner, H. *Frames of Mind: The Theory of Multiple Intelligences*. New York: Basic Books, 1983.

Gilligan, C. *In a Different Voice*. Cambridge, Mass.: Harvard University Press, 1982.

Goldberger, N. *Developmental Stage and the OPI.* Great Barrington, Mass.: Simon's Rock of Bard College, 1980.

Group for Human Development in Higher Education. *Faculty Development in a Time of Retrenchment.* New Rochelle, N.Y.: Change Magazine Press, 1974.

Gruber, H. E., and Vonèche, J. J., eds. *The Essential Piaget: An Interpretive Reference and Guide.* New York: Basic Books, 1977.

Heath, D. *Growing Up in College.* San Francisco: Jossey-Bass, 1968.

Heath, R. *The Reasonable Adventurer: A Study of the Development of Thirty-Six Undergraduates at Princeton.* Pittsburgh: University of Pittsburgh Press, 1964.

Heist, P., ed. *The Creative Student: An Unmet Challenge.* San Francisco: Jossey-Bass, 1968.

Heist, P., and Yonge, G. *Omnibus Personality Inventory, Form F.* Manual. New York: The Psychological Corporation, 1968.

Holland, J. *Vocational Choices: Theory of Careers.* Englewood Cliffs, N.J.: Prentice-Hall, 1973.

James, W. *Pragmatism.* Cambridge, Mass.: Harvard University Press, 1979a [1907].

James, W. "Percept and Concept." In *Some Problems of Philosophy.* Cambridge, Mass.: Harvard University Press, 1979b [1911], pp. 31–60.

Jung, C. G. *Memories, Dreams, Reflections.* New York: Vintage Books, 1965.

Kahn, R. L. and Cannell, C. F. *The Dynamics of Interviewing: Theory, Technique, and Cases.* Melbourne, Fla.: Krieger, 1983.

Katz, Jay. *The Silent World of Doctor and Patient.* New York: Free Press, 1984.

Katz, J., ed. *Teaching as though Students Mattered.* New Directions for Teaching and Learning, no. 21. San Francisco: Jossey-Bass, 1985.

Katz, J. "Student Initiative, Self-Help, and Collaborative Learning in the College Classroom." In *Community and Social Support for College Students,* edited by N. Giddan. Springfield, Ill.: Charles C. Thomas, 1988.

Katz, J., and associates. *No Time for Youth: Growth and Constraint in College Students.* San Francisco: Jossey-Bass, 1968.

Kolb, D. A. "Learning Styles and Disciplinary Differences." In *The Modern American College,* edited by A. W. Chickering. San Francisco: Jossey-Bass, 1981, pp. 232–255.

Kuhn, T. S. *The Structure of Scientific Revolutions.* Chicago: University of Chicago Press, 1962.

Loevinger, J. *Ego Development.* San Francisco: Jossey-Bass, 1976.

Milton, O.; Pollio, H.; and Eison, J. *Making Sense of College Grades: Why the Grading System Does Not Work and What Can Be Done about It.* San Francisco: Jossey-Bass, 1986.

Munroe, R. L. *Teaching the Individual.* New York: Columbia University Press, 1942.

Murphy, L., and Ladd, H. *Emotional Factors in Learning.* New York: Columbia University Press, 1944.

Murray, H. A. *Explorations in Personality.* New York: Oxford University Press, 1938.

Myers-Briggs Type Indicator. Palo Alto, Calif.: Consulting Psychologists Press, 1976.

National Institute of Education, Study Group on the Condition of Excellence in American Higher Education. *Involvement in Learning.* Washington, D.C., 1984.

Newcomb, T. M. *Personality and Social Change.* New York: Dryden Press, 1943.

Newman, F. *Higher Education and the American Resurgence.* Princeton, N.J.: The Carnegie Foundation for the Advancement of Teaching, 1985.

Papert, Seymour. *Mindstorms: Children, Computers, and Powerful Ideas.* New York: Basic Books, 1980.

Perry, W. *Forms of Intellectual and Ethical Development in the College Years.* New York: Holt, Rinehart and Winston, 1970.

Polanyi, M. *The Tacit Dimension.* Garden City, N.Y.: Doubleday, 1966.

Postlethwait, Samuel; Novak, J.; and Murray, H. T. *The Audio-Tutorial Approach to Learning, Through Independent Study and Integrated Experiences.* Minneapolis: Burgess, 1972.

Project on the Status and Education of Women. *The Classroom Climate: A Chilly One for Women?* Washington, D.C.: Association of American Colleges, 1982.

Rorschach, E., and Whitney, R. "Relearning to Teach: Peer Observation as a Means of Professional Development for Teachers." *English Education 18* (1986): 159–172.

Sanford, N. *The American College.* New York: Wiley, 1962.

Snow, C. P. *The Two Cultures* and *A Second Look.* Cambridge, Eng.: Cambridge University Press, 1969.

Springer, S., and Deutsch, G. *Left Brain, Right Brain.* New York: Freeman, 1985.

Stewart, C. J., and Cash, W. B. *Interviewing: Principles and Practices.* Dubuque, Iowa: Brown, 1985.

Survey Research Center, Institute for Social Research. *Interviewer's Manual.* Ann Arbor, Mich., 1976.

Thielens, W. "The Disciplines and Undergraduate Lecturing." Paper presented at the annual meeting of the American Educational Research Association, Washington, D.C., April, 1987.

Trow, M. " 'Elite Higher Education': An Endangered Species?" *Minerva 14* (1976): 355–376.

Veysey, L. R. *The Emergence of the American University.* Chicago: University of Chicago Press, 1965.

Vygotsky, L. S. *The Collected Works of L.S. Vygotsky.* Vol. 1, *Problems of General Psychology,* edited by R. W. Reiber and Aaron S. Carton. New York: Plenum, 1987.

Index

K

Kahn, R. L., 113, 166
Katz, Jay, 112, 166
Kohlberg, L., 2
Kolb, D. A., 27, 166

L

Ladd, H., 2, 166
Learning
  active, 6, 16, 32–33, 46, 67, 68, 79,
    82, 85, 89, 94, 129, 131–132,
    142, 159
  collaborative, 7, 17, 29, 36, 90, 95,
    143–144, 157, 164
  experiential, 8–9, 28–29, 32, 42,
    44–47, 64–66, 79, 85, 88, 90,
    159–160
  inquiry-oriented, 7, 18, 53,
    156–158
  obstacles to, 48–51, 79–80, 85,
    88, 111
  outside the classroom, 8–9,
    159–160
  theories and principles, 1, 3–4,
    6–8, 22, 59, 93–95
Lecturing, 16, 67, 73–74, 77, 94,
    111, 138–139, 161
Listening, 113, 121, 122–123
Loevinger, J., 2, 4, 95, 166

M

Mass vs. elite higher education,
    153–154
Metasessions, 6, 13, 57, 58, 61–63
Metateaching, 62, 65, 69–70, 71,
    88–89
Miller, L., x, xi, 16, 52, 81–89
Milton, O., 49, 166
Munroe, R., 2, 166
Murphy, L., 2, 166
Murray, H. A., 2, 166
Murray, J., xi
Murrell, P. H., 12, 27, 165
Myers-Briggs Type Indicator, 27, 166

N

National Institute of Education, x, 166

New College of California, ix
Newcomb, T., 2, 9, 166
Newman, F., xi, 166
Noonan, J., 13, 165
Northwestern University, ix

O

Ohio Wesleyan University, ix
Omnibus Personality Inventory
    (OPI), 11–12, 18–19, 22, 26–
    28, 37–38, 40, 41–46, 50, 52,
    57, 60–61, 66, 69, 74–76, 83,
    96–111, 146, 151
  faculty-student differences,
    18–19, 104, 146, 151
  indicator of individual differences,
    60–61, 66, 69
  interpretation, 96–97, 100–101,
    104
  measure of emotional functioning,
    28, 83, 105–106
  measure of thinking patterns in
    the academic disciplines,
    27–28, 75, 99–103
  tool for discovery, 37, 60–61
  use with faculty and students, 11,
    60–61, 74–76, 151

P

Papert, S., 26, 32, 167
Piaget, J., 2, 4, 20, 22, 25, 27, 40, 94,
    103, 159, 166
Perry, W., 2–4, 19–26, 40, 47, 57,
    91, 94, 108, 121, 159, 167
Personalized System of Instruction
    (PSI), 39
Polanyi, M., 25, 98, 167
Pollio, H., 166
Postlethwait, S., 159, 167

R

Research in relation to teaching,
    130, 133–134, 136–137,
    147–148, 157, 161–162